FOUNDATION PRESS

TORTS:
PROXIMATE CAUSE

by

JOSEPH A. PAGE
Professor of Law
Georgetown University Law Center

TURNING POINT SERIES®

FOUNDATION PRESS
New York, New York
2003

Foundation Press, a division of West Group, has created this publication to provide you with accurate and authoritative information concerning the subject matter covered. However, this publication was not necessarily prepared by persons licensed to practice law in a particular jurisdiction. Foundation Press is not engaged in rendering legal or other professional advice, and this publication is not a substitute for the advice of an attorney. If you require legal or other expert advice, you should seek the services of a competent attorney or other professional.

Turning Point Series is a registered trademark
used herein under license.

COPYRIGHT © 2003 By FOUNDATION PRESS
395 Hudson Street
New York, NY 10014
Phone Toll Free 1-877-888-1330
Fax (212) 367-6799
fdpress.com

All rights reserved
Printed in the United States of America

ISBN 1-56662-978-0

TEXT IS PRINTED ON 10% POST
CONSUMER RECYCLED PAPER

TURNING POINT SERIES

CIVIL PROCEDURE

Civil Procedure: Class Actions by Linda S. Mullenix, University of Texas (Available 2003)

Civil Procedure: Economics of Civil Procedure by Robert G. Bone, Boston University (Available 2003)

Civil Procedure: Preclusion in Civil Actions by David L. Shapiro, Harvard University (2001)

Civil Procedure: Jury Process by Nancy S. Marder, Illinois Institute of Technology (Available 2003)

Civil Procedure: Territorial Jurisdiction and Venue by Kevin M. Clermont, Cornell (1999)

CONSTITUTIONAL LAW

Constitutional Law: Equal Protection by Louis M. Seidman, Georgetown University (2002)

Constitutional Law: Religion Clause by Daniel O. Conkle, Indiana University, Bloomington (Available 2003)

CRIMINAL LAW

Criminal Law: Model Penal Code by Markus D. Dubber, State University of New York, Buffalo (2002)

Criminal Law: Habeas Corpus by Larry W. Yackle, Boston University (Available 2003)

INTERNATIONAL LAW

International Law: United States Foreign Relations Law by Phillip R. Trimble, UCLA (2002)

LEGISLATION

Legislation: Statutory Interpretation: Twenty Questions by Kent R. Greenawalt, Columbia University (1999)

PROPERTY

Property: Takings by David Dana, Northwestern University and Thomas Merrill, Northwestern University (2002)

CORPORATE/SECURITIES

Securities Law: Insider Trading by Stephen Bainbridge, UCLA (1999)

TORTS

Torts: Proximate Cause by Joseph A. Page, Georgetown University (2002)

Dedicated to the memory of

Elena Maria Margherita Santosuosso

(1903–1985)

*

Preface

Any author embarking on a project dealing with proximate cause must first address the issue of terminology. The phrase "proximate cause" has generated near universal distaste because of the confusions associated with it ever since courts first coined the expression, but efforts over the years to replace it with more accurate terms such as scope of liability or extent of liability have had only modest success, as courts seem unwilling to relinquish an expression to which they have become accustomed.

Therefore, I have opted to go with the familiar and use the phrase in my title, but will frequently invoke scope of liability or extent of liability as synonyms for proximate cause, for the purpose of making a modest contribution to a hopefully inevitable universal shift in terminology.[1]

Another problem arising from a project such as this relates to choice of approach. Because I see my main audience as first-year students, my paramount goal is to address the difficulties they have with understanding how to define the scope of a tortfeasor's

1. The new Restatement of Torts has tentatively adopted the heading "Scope of Liability (Proximate Cause)" in an effort to speed the process of change. *See* AMERICAN LAW INSTITUTE, RESTATEMENT, THIRD, TORTS: LIABILITY FOR PHYSICAL HARM (BASIC PRINCIPLES) Ch. 6 (Tentative Draft No. 2, March 25, 2002).

liability. After nearly four decades of teaching torts, I have reached the conclusion that what vexes students most about the concept of proximate cause is how to recognize, in the context of a particular fact pattern, when it presents an issue worth raising. Although courts often list proximate cause as part of plaintiff's *prima facie case* in negligence, it will seldom amount to a matter worth disputing. But when will it? Students might grasp in the abstract the theoretical and practical differences among various approaches to limiting a tortfeasor's liability, but when to apply these approaches may remain a mystery. For this reason, I have framed my presentation of the subject around the sorts of factual scenarios that might provoke disputes about extent of liability. One lesson this approach teaches finds encapsulation in the maxim *ex facto ius oritur*, or the law arises out of fact, referring to how the process of law-making under the common law is absolutely dependent on factual predicates supplied by actual cases.

I have applied to my scenarios three basic approaches to extent of liability: what I call the hindsight test, which in fact is a catch-all category containing a number of variants that share the view that determining of extent of liability requires a look backward, from the harm inflicted to the conduct inflicting it, in order to determine in retrospect whether it is appropriate to hold defendant liable; what I call the risk-foreseeability test, which asks what a reasonable person in defendant's position should have anticipated, in order to limit liability to harm caused by those risks that made defendant's action (or inaction) unreasonable; and what I call the duty-risk test, which contains elements of both by expressly permitting judges to apply policy, moral and practical considerations when they determine how far a defendant's liability ought to reach.

My goal here is to convey a sense of the methodologies by which courts can deal with proximate cause. The notion that there are no easy or automatic answers to the scope-of-liability conundrum is an important one to stress. Therefore, students should seek to understand the different ways of deciding whether and how to limit liability, and to appreciate their strengths and weaknesses. The ultimate purpose of this book is to encourage and enable readers to engage in critical reflection, a central part of the enterprise of legal education.

There are many individuals to whom I owe a debt of appreciation for helping me in this undertaking. My torts teacher, Professor (now Judge) Robert E. Keeton introduced me to proximate cause and his insights have continued to stimulate my thinking on the subject. I should like to acknowledge the assistance provided by Dean Judith C. Areen of the Georgetown University Law Center, in the form of summer writer's grants that helped make this book possible. I found invaluable the detailed, insightful and unsparing comments I received from my sister- and brothers-in-torts, Doriane Lambelet Coleman of the Duke Law School, Patrick J. Kelley of the Southern Illinois University School of Law and Robert Rabin of the Stanford Law School. I also wish to thank my colleagues at Georgetown for suggestions on the occasion of a Faculty Workshop presentation, and to credit the research assistance of Carolyn Bannon, Janice Johnson and Vanessa Walts, and the encouraging feedback I received from Georgetown torts students to whom I exposed earlier drafts. Finally, I must convey immeasurable gratitude for inspiration and support provided by Martha Gil-Montero, *minha musa maga*.

About the Author

Joseph A. Page is a Professor at the Georgetown University Law Center. A graduate of Harvard College and Harvard Law School, he served as Assistant Editor-in-Chief of the NACCA Law Journal from 1960 to 1963. After earning an LL.M. from Harvard Law School in 1964, he taught for four years at the University of Denver College of Law, and then moved to Georgetown. The courses he has given include torts, damages, insurance, unfair trade practices, products liability, legislation, food and drug law, legal process and workplace health and safety. Professor Page has authored BITTER WAGES: THE NADER REPORT ON DISEASE AND INJURY ON THE JOB (with M. O'Brien), THE LAW OF PREMISES LIABILITY and numerous articles on torts, products liability, worker's compensation, occupational safety and health and food and drug law. He is a member of the Members Consultative Group for the American Law Institute's RESTATEMENT OF TORTS: LIABILITY FOR PHYSICAL HARM (BASIC PRINCIPLES), and a director of both Public Citizen, Inc. and the American Museum of Tort Law. In a parallel life, he has written THE REVOLUTION THAT NEVER WAS: NORTHEAST BRAZIL, 1955-1964; PERON: A BIOGRAPHY; and THE BRAZILIANS.

*

TABLE OF CONTENTS

Preface	VII
About the Author	XI
Chapter 1 An Introduction to The Mysteries of Proximate Cause	1
Chapter 2 From Casablanca to the Buffalo River, via East New York and Sydney Harbor	29
Smith: An Early Fumble	33
The Direct–Consequences Rule: Herein *Polemis*	39
The Risk Rule: Herein *Palsgraf*	43
The Risk Rule, British–Style: Herein the *Wagon Mound*	66
Chaos on the Buffalo River	71
Vox Clamantis in Deserto	74
Chapter 3 Into the Crucible—Part I	82
The Unexpectedly–Serious–Harm Scenario	82
The Manner-of-Occurrence Scenario	93
The Different–Risk Scenario	99
The Persons-at-Risk Scenario	111
The Accidental–Self–Injury Scenario	130
The Risk-or-Injury-to-Another Scenario	137
Chapter 4 Into the Crucible—Part II	140
Non-Human Interventions	146
Human Interventions	157

TABLE OF CONTENTS

CHAPTER 5 BEYOND NEGLIGENCE 212
Proximate Cause and Intentional Torts 212
Proximate Cause and Strict Liability 228

CHAPTER 6 WHITHER PROXIMATE CAUSE (SCOPE OF LIABILITY)? 251

TABLE OF CASES 261
INDEX 265

TORTS:
PROXIMATE CAUSE

*

Chapter 1

An Introduction to The Mysteries of Proximate Cause

If novice students of tort law had to pick a subject area they found most memorable and at the same time most bothersome, the odds-on favorite would have to be proximate cause, a doctrine courts use to place boundaries on the scope of a tortfeasor's liability.

What makes proximate cause difficult to forget is its association with cases whose facts beggar the imagination. The chain of consequences set off by the dropping of a paper bag containing explosives in a Long Island Railroad station, and the havoc wreaked by two unmanned ships as they careened down the ice-clogged Buffalo River, come most readily to mind, although a host of other stranger-than-fiction scenarios trail closely behind.

What makes proximate cause baffling is first of all the practical question how to recognize when fact patterns give rise to plausible questions about scope of liability; secondly, once the issue has been properly raised, how to choose from among various competing doctrinal approaches courts and commentators have constructed in efforts to put just and sensible limits on how far liability should extend; and lastly, once an approach has been chosen, where and how to apply it rationally and effectively within the elements of the cause of action.

The very term "proximate cause" strikes an off-key note, since courts and commentators often (but not always) use it in senses far removed from the precincts of proximity and causation. Blameworthy conduct that occurred long before or at a considerable distance from the accident it caused might still render an actor liable for harm the activity produced, and determinations of proximate cause may require the weighing of factors that go far beyond simple cause and effect.

How to limit the scope of a tortfeasor's liability has generated considerable interest among jurists and scholars.[1] To put it gently, there is a notable lack of consensus. A perceptive observer has wryly noted that "Judges not only disagree with judges; and professors with professors and judges; it is a field where a professor may disagree with himself."[2]

---

1. The literature on the subject is oceanic. For a representative sampling, *see* VICTOR E. SCHWARTZ ET AL., PROSSER, WADE AND SCHWARTZ'S TORTS 289 (10th ed. 2000). For a neglected and underappreciated overview of the doctrine, *see* D.E. Bickner, *Comment Note—Foreseeability As an Element of Negligence and Proximate Cause*, 100 A.L.R.2d 942 (1965).

Useful recent contributions include Jane Stapleton, *Legal Cause: Cause-in-Fact and the Scope of Liability for Consequences*, 54 VAND. L. REV. 941 (2001); Patrick J. Kelley, *Restating Duty, Breach, and Proximate Cause in Negligence Law: Descriptive Theory and Rule of Law*, *id.* at 1039.

2. DAVID MELLINKOFF, THE LANGUAGE OF THE LAW 382 (1963) (citing changes of positions taken by one eminent torts scholar to illustrate his last point).

One matter of contention is whether proximate cause deserves even to exist. Some have argued that the label merits consignment to history's dustbin, to be replaced by terms such as scope of liability, extent of liability or legal cause. However, the phrase has demonstrated a remarkable staying power, perhaps because of force of habit on the part of judges and attorneys. In selecting a title for this literary endeavor, I have yielded to tradition, but in so doing I reserve the right to reiterate my own disapproval of the term.

Proximate cause can have various meanings, which is one of the reasons for the confusion the term generates. First of all, in its broadest sense the proposition that an actor's conduct is the proximate cause of plaintiff's harm can signify a legal conclusion that harm causally related to a defendant's action or inaction falls within the proper scope of that defendant's liability. What this means is that if a court decides that defendant's conduct was not a proximate cause of the harm plaintiff incurred, defendant will not be liable for it. Another way of stating this conclusion is that defendant's conduct, even though harm-producing, was outside the scope of defendant's liability, or that defendant's liability does not extend to the particular harm suffered by the particular plaintiff. This is the meaning conveyed by the title of this book, which will examine how courts do and should reach this conclusion, both in the substantive or doctrinal sense, and in the context of the process by which courts apply the approach they have selected.

As we shall see, courts use (and commentators urge the use of) various substantive or doctrinal approaches to decide how far to extend a defendant's liability, or at what point to limit it. Moreover, as a matter of process, some courts have given the name proximate cause to a discrete, liability-limiting element of a plaintiff's cause of action in tort, while others have performed the liability-limiting function through the mechanism of either the duty or breach-of-duty element of the *prima facie* case. The procedural choice here may have at least one important consequence, since it will determine the respective roles of judge and jury.

Notice that I have introduced here a second and more limited meaning of proximate cause. The term can also signify the element of plaintiff's *prima facie* case that requires plaintiffs to establish and courts to decide how far the scope of a defendant's liability should sweep. Thus, enumerations of the elements of a cause of action in negligence often include duty, breach of duty, cause-in-fact, proximate cause and actual loss.[3]

What complicates matters here is that, as has been noted, courts may also place functionally equivalent limits on a defendant's liability by the way they determine duty or breach of duty. If so, the need to consider proximate cause as a separate element of the tort of negligence evaporates. This

3. *See, e.g.*, Thomas C. Galligan, Jr., *A Primer on the Patterns of Negligence*, 53 LA. L. REV. 1509, 1510 (1993); RICHARD A. EPSTEIN, TORTS 109–10 (1999) (treating cause-in-fact and proximate cause as two components of a single element).

has suggested a need to resort to another term for the substance of what the courts are doing, since it would be awkward to say that they are determining proximate cause within the framework of the duty or breach-of-duty elements. A more sensible way of putting it would be to use the expression scope of liability, or extent of liability. Thus, a court might limit the scope or extent of a defendant's liability by concluding either that defendant's duty did not include protecting plaintiff from the risk that actually caused the harm, or that defendant did not breach a duty to protect plaintiff from the injury-producing risk.

There is a second, distinct problem of terminology associated with proximate cause. Judges and scholars have used it (or the definitionally equivalent expression "legal cause") as an umbrella term covering the element of causation-in-fact, which dictates that there be a but-for or substantial causal relationship linking tortious conduct and the harm it has inflicted, as well as the separate requirement that there be a reasonably close nexus between wrongful activity and the loss it has produced. Notice the potential for overlap between the two concepts, because conduct that amounts to an "insubstantial" cause of harm might also be found to lack a "reasonably close nexus" to that harm. Proximate cause also can convey the second connotation only, which gives it a meaning apart from, rather than incorporating, cause-in-fact. I have limited myself to the latter—proximate cause as a mechanism for limiting the scope of liability for harm-producing conduct—itself a sufficiently challenging subject, and I shall let others wrestle with the conceptually distinct issue of cause-in-fact.

To illustrate the difference between proximate cause, as I shall employ the term throughout this book, and cause-in-fact, we can summon forth from the storehouse of tort lore a familiar fact pattern. If railroad employees had not pushed a man carrying a package as he was about to board a train and had not caused him to drop it in a way that made it explode with such force that a scale at the end of the platform toppled, the unfortunate passenger struck by the falling scale would not have suffered harm. Such a finding would satisfy the cause-in-fact requirement. However, before awarding damages, a court would also have to find that there was a sufficiently close link between the ill-considered push and the passenger's injury so as to justify the imposition of tort liability on the railroad. This would raise the issue of proximate cause (or extent of liability, or scope of liability).

Hence, proximate cause in this sense of the term is really a cryptic expression that hides the reluctance of courts to impose legal liability for tortious conduct as far as the ripples of cause-in-fact might radiate in a particular case. Mrs. O'Leary might have carelessly permitted her cow Daisy to kick over the lantern that ignited the fire that burned Chicago to the ground in 1871,[4] but we might not

4. Mrs. O'Leary's responsibility has been a matter of some historical debate. In 1997 a Chicago insurance-company employee with access to 1871 property records argued that the culprit

want to hold her liable, even theoretically, for the full sweep of the disastrous consequences that befell the city. Thus, the requirement that there be in some sense a reasonably close connection between faulty conduct and the harm it occasions permits courts to make what is in essence an evaluative judgment that a defendant should or should not pay for the entire loss she has occasioned. However, judges often drape the notion of proximate cause in verbal formulations that obscure not only what they are really doing, but also the values that animate their decisions.

The reasons for limiting liability have roots in the basic theories undergirding tort law. One of them, corrective justice, seeks to restore the moral balance between the wrongdoer and his victim.[5] Grounded in considerations of philosophy and ethics, corrective justice focuses on the need to determine the rights enjoyed by individual victims and the responsibilities owed by individual injurers.[6] Thus, in cal-

might have been a one-legged horse-cart driver suspected of smoking in Mrs. O'Leary's barn. *See* Pam Belluck, "Barn Door Reopened on Fire After Legend Has Escaped," N.Y. Times, Aug. 17, 1997, Sec. 1, p. 20. The Chicago City Council susequently passed a resolution exonerating her. *See* Jennifer Harper, "Mrs. O'Leary's Cow Not Guilty of Arson," Wash. Times, Oct. 9, 1997, p. A9.

5. *See* Kenneth S. Abraham, The Forms and Functions of Tort Law 14 (2d ed. 2002).

6. On corrective justice generally, *see* Dan B. Dobbs, The Law of Torts § 9 (2000); Philosophical Foundations of Tort Law (David G. Owen ed., 1995); Symposium, *Corrective Justice and Formalism: The Care One Owes One's Neighbors*, 77 Iowa L. Rev. 403 (1992).

culating how far the liability of an injurer should extend, a court animated by principles of corrective justice might find that it violated the community's sense of fundamental fairness to hold a defendant responsible for harmful results on the remote reaches of series of consequences emanating from his carelessness.

A second theory derives from efficiency concerns, and assigns to tort law the function of creating and applying rules that will deter potential defendants from engaging in conduct that might foreseeably produce accidents that would be more costly to society than the measures potential defendants might have taken to prevent them.[7] Thus, a rule relieving a defendant of liability for remote consequences might underdeter careless conduct, if defendant could or should have taken them into account in deciding how much to invest in accident avoidance, and a relatively modest investment would have prevented the infliction of harm; by the same token, a rule extending defendant's liability to remote consequences might overdeter if it discourages actors from engaging in socially useful conduct that might lead to harmful results no one might reasonably have anticipated.

Moreover, once courts decide to terminate a defendant's responsibility somewhere short of the end point on the causal chain, they need to consider how to do it and whether the tort-litigation process

7. For a concise descriptions of deterrence as a goal of tort law, *see* KENNETH S. ABRAHAM, *supra* note 5, at 15–16; DAN B. DOBBS, *supra* note 6, at § 11.

can effectively administer the liability-limiting approach they propose to take. In other words, even though a particular conception of scope of liability might make theoretical sense, in practice we might not be able to fashion it into a workable mechanism that will produce consistently just and efficient results. For example, if the jury is to perform the liability-limiting function, one important consideration is whether judges can frame instructions in language that lay persons can comprehend and apply sensibly in their deliberations in order to reach fair verdicts.

Although the most common context that gives rise to extent-of-liability concerns involves the need to determine how far to stretch the liability of a negligent defendant, the issue may also surface when courts grapple with whether to attach legal consequences to a plaintiff's careless conduct that contributed to the harm she suffered at the hands of a tortfeasor. In the latter instance, a plaintiff may raise lack of proximate cause to counter defendant's invocation of contributory (or comparative) negligence as an affirmative defense. Thus, a driver may have extended her left arm outside the window of her car in a way that created an unreasonable risk that she might be struck by a passing vehicle, but the harm she in fact suffered materialized when a box carelessly stacked on the bed of defendant's pick-up truck fell on her arm.[8] Her argument would be that even though she might have acted carelessly

8. *See* Schilling v. Stockel, 26 Wis.2d 525, 133 N.W.2d 335 (1965).

in a way that put her in danger of certain kinds of harm, there was an insufficiently close connection between her own unreasonable conduct and the harm she in fact incurred as a result of it. Proximate-cause doctrines applicable to contributory fault do not differ from those employed to place bounds on a defendant's liability.

In rare cases, courts will have to consider how far to extend liability where plaintiff is seeking recovery under other legal theories, such as strict liability or intentional tort. For example, defendants might market a defective drug that causes harmful abnormalities not only in the children of pregnant women who consumed the medication, but also in the children of the children of the original consumers, and in a suit by the latter seeking recovery in strict tort, the manufacturers might argue that the courts should not impose liability beyond the first generation of victims.[9] Or a logging company engaged in dynamite blasting might frighten mother minks on a nearby farm, to such an extent that they kill their offspring; and might contend, in a suit seeking recovery in strict tort for the loss of the kittens, that the response of the mothers should not fall within the scope of any strict liability that might be imposed for harm caused by an abnormally dangerous activity.[10] Or a defendant might knowingly cause water to enter and accumulate on a

9. *See* Enright v. Eli Lilly & Co., 77 N.Y.2d 377, 568 N.Y.S.2d 550, 570 N.E.2d 198, *cert. den.*, 502 U.S. 868 (1991).

10. *See* Foster v. Preston Mill Co., 44 Wash.2d 440, 268 P.2d 645 (1954).

neighbor's property and form a stagnant pond in which mosquitos breed; one of the insects bites plaintiff's child and transmits a serious disease; in a suit based on trespass to land, the defendant might ask the court not to hold him liable for an unanticipated and remote harm caused by the trespassory invasion.[11] Or a plaintiff intentionally confined by defendant might suffer burn injuries caused when lightning struck the shed in which defendant had locked him, and defendant might argue that plaintiff's harm fell outside the scope of any liability that a court might impose for false imprisonment.[12] Because the liability-limiting issue in these cases involves conduct that might be either more or less blameworthy than the kinds of carelessness giving rise to liability in negligence, it may make sense to take these differences in fault into account when we fix the extent of a defendant's responsibility.

Finally, the concept of proximate cause casts its shadow beyond the boundary of torts. A basic premise of criminal law posits that where conduct amounts to a crime only if it produces some particular result, the conduct must be a "proximate cause" of that result in order to justify conviction.[13] Where a policy of insurance protects against a certain risk, in order to recover under the policy the loss in-

11. *See* Gallick v. Baltimore & Ohio R. Co., 372 U.S. 108, 83 S.Ct. 659 (1963).

12. This fact pattern has not yet occurred, but as every law professor knows, if you wait long enough, all your hypotheticals will come true.

13. *See* WAYNE R. LaFAVE & AUSTIN W. SCOTT, SUBSTANTIVE CRIMINAL LAW § 3.1 (1986).

curred by the insured must have been proximately caused by that risk.[14] The United States Supreme Court has utilized proximate cause to determine the scope of liability under federal antitrust law[15] and the Racketeer Influenced and Corrupt Organizations (RICO) Act.[16] Lower courts have followed the Supreme Court's proximate-cause jurisprudence in disposing of antitrust and RICO claims brought by union health and welfare funds seeking reimbursement from the tobacco industry for the costs of treating their participants' smoking-related illnesses.[17] And finally, courts limit breach-of-contract damages to consequences reasonably foreseeable at the time the binding agreement was entered into,[18] an approach quite similar to one of the tests used to limit the scope of tort liability.

Proximate cause seldom rises to the level of a disputed matter. In the great majority of tort cases, there clearly exists a reasonably close connection between a defendant's tortious conduct and the harm incurred by the plaintiff, so that the courts have no need to concern themselves with proximate

14. *See* LEE R. RUSS & THOMAS F. SEGALLA, 7 COUCH ON INSURANCE § 101:44 (3d ed. 1997).

15. *See* Blue Shield v. McCready, 457 U.S. 465 (1982).

16. *See* Holmes v. Securities Investor Prot. Corp., 503 U.S. 258 (1992); *see also* Stephen Scallan, *Proximate Cause Under RICO*, 20 So. ILL. U. L. J. 455 (1996).

17. *See, e.g.,* Steamfitters Local 420 v. Philip Morris, Inc., 171 F.3d 912 (3d Cir.1999) (denying liability because of lack of proximate cause).

18. *See* CHARLES T. MCCORMICK, HANDBOOK ON THE LAW OF DAMAGES § 138 (1935).

cause. There are occasions, however, when defendants seek to convince the court or the jury that their conduct, even though it might have been in some sense blameworthy, fell outside an appropriate ambit of liability. Hence, proximate cause often takes on the look and flavor of a defensive weapon. Yet once the issue has been raised and joined, the courts have not explicitly shifted to defendant the burden of proving that the harm suffered by plaintiff fell outside the scope of liability.

As has been suggested, the problem of how to spot when a legitimate proximate-cause or extent-of-liability issue may arise in a particular fact pattern seems especially troublesome for students. To address this difficulty, let us consider a set of illustrative scenarios that have raised questions about scope of liability, or that are reasonably analogous to cases that have produced judicial opinions dealing with proximate cause. This early focus can also serve as a reminder of the importance of factual context to the development of legal rules and principles.

Let us assume that in each of these cases, plaintiff seeks recovery under a theory of negligence, and defendant tries to avoid liability on the ground that her allegedly unreasonable conduct was not the proximate cause of plaintiff's harm, or that the harm fell outside the scope of defendant's liability.

Example 1: Defendant can foresee some harm to plaintiff, but because of a pre-existing weakness of which defendant was unaware, the harm turns out to be much more extensive than it would have been if plaintiff had been a sound person (the unexpectedly-serious-harm scenario).

> *Unaware that plaintiff is a hemophiliac, defendant carelessly inflicts a superficial cut on her arm. She nearly bleeds to death and is hospitalized for a month.*

Example 2: Defendant can foresee some harm to plaintiff, but not the exact way it occurs (the manner-of-occurrence scenario).

> *Defendant carelessly navigates his tugboat toward a row of wooden pilings despite the obvious presence of workers performing repairs on them. One of the worker attempts to jump off the pilings just as the tug strikes the first of them. One piling hits another, which hits another. The worker's leg is caught when he slips between two collapsing pilings and serious harm results.*

Example 3: Defendant creates a risk of harm to plaintiff or a third party, but his conduct also brings into being a different risk to plaintiff, and the latter risk not only materializes but causes harm (different-risk scenario).

> *Defendant brings into a restaurant kitchen an unmarked package he knows contains rat poison, but he does not know it might blow up if left too close to an open flame. He places it on a counter near a stove, and it explodes, harming plaintiff.*

Example 4: Defendant creates an unreasonable risk of harm to a specific person or class of persons, but causes harm to plaintiff, who is not that person nor within the class, and who is unexpectedly within the ambit of risk (the person-at-risk scenario).

Defendant carelessly places someone in a position of peril. Plaintiff, whose presence defendant could not possibly have anticipated, comes to the aid of the threatened person's rescue and is injured in the process of helping him.

Example 5: Defendant creates an unreasonable risk of harm that

(a) causes plaintiff to take action that results in injury to himself (the self-injury scenario);

Defendant carelessly creates the threat of an explosion. Plaintiff, in an attempt to flee, trips over a chair and is injured. or

(b) inflicts on a third party injuries or a risk of injury that cause him in turn to injure plaintiff (the risk-or-injury-to-another scenario);

Defendant drives his car into a young boy, who sustains serious head injuries. Seven years later, having been deprived, as a result of the accident, of his capacity to control himself, the boy shoots plaintiff.

Example 6: In the following intervention scenarios, defendant subjects plaintiff to an unreasonable risk of harm, and defendant's conduct subsequently causes harm to plaintiff when it combines with

(a) natural forces;

16   INTRO TO MYSTERIES OF PROXIMATE CAUSE

> *Defendant carelessly causes gasoline to spill. A bird picks up a lighted cigarette butt and drops it into the pool of gasoline. Plaintiff is injured by the resulting explosion.* or

(b) the innocent act of a third party;

> *Defendant carelessly causes gasoline to spill. A, unaware of the presence of an inflammable liquid, drops a cigarette butt into the pool of gasoline. Plaintiff is injured by the resulting explosion.* or

(c) the negligent act of a third party;

> *Defendant carelessly causes gasoline to spill. A, who should have been aware of the presence of gasoline, carelessly drops a cigarette butt into the pool of gasoline. Plaintiff is injured by the resulting explosion.* or

(d) the intentionally tortious or criminal act of a third party.

> *Defendant carelessly causes gasoline to spill. A, aware of the spillage and its flammability, intentionally drops a cigarette butt into the pool of gasoline. Plaintiff is injured by the resulting explosion.*

Example 7: Defendant subjects plaintiff to a risk of harm, a third party assumes responsibility to protect plaintiff from the risk but fails to do so and the risk causes harm to plaintiff (the termination-of-responsibility-for-the risk scenario).

> *Defendant carelessly sells a gun to a 12-year-old child. The child's mother takes the gun from him and hides it in what she believes to be a*

INTRO TO MYSTERIES OF PROXIMATE CAUSE 17

secure place. Some time later the boy manages to find the gun, accidentally discharges it and wounds a playmate.

Keep in mind that these scenarios may also provoke what we might call mirror-image issues. In the usual case, plaintiff argues that defendant had the requisite foresight, and therefore should be liable for a particular harmful result, while defendant might maintain that he could not reasonably have anticipated some aspect of what happened, and therefore should not be liable. However, in some situations, defendant may argue that even if he had the necessary foresight, he should not be responsible for the damage suffered by plaintiff. For example, he might urge that even though his conduct might have created foreseeable risks of both physical harm and emotional distress, he should not be liable if plaintiff suffers only emotional distress.

In addition, it is important to remember that the list above does not purport to exhaust the field of possibilities. Defendant's careless conduct might set off a chain of events that implicate more than one of our illustrative situations. Thus, the carelessness of a shipowner's employees might allow a vessel to break loose from its mooring on an ice-clogged river and collide with and unmoor a nearby vessel, with the result that both ships float downstream, smash into a drawbridge whose span was not raised in time because of the negligence of bridge workers, and eventually come to rest in a way that forms a dam and causes water to back up and flood farmland several miles away. Or a fact pattern might fall in a "gray area" not fitting neatly into a scenario, such as when a railroad's employees carelessly push a man with a package as he was boarding a train and thereby create an unreasonable risk that he might fall and hurt himself or drop the package and destroy its contents; the package, which the employees had no reason to know contained fireworks, falls and detonates, causing a scale to fall on a passenger some distance away—a case straddling the different-risk and persons-at-risk scenarios. An understanding of possible approaches to the fact patterns on our list should provide a useful starting point and basis for analyzing more complex or "gray area" extent-of-liability issues.

Although courts will find that the fact patterns in all the categories listed above raise what they consider to be extent-of-liability issues, it is crucial to consider carefully whether any single rule can resolve all of these issues in ways that would yield consistently acceptable results. There may well not be a universal solvent that will produce appropriate outcomes in all the various kinds of cases in which extent of liability is disputed. As one perceptive Canadian commentator has argued, efforts to limit the scope of liability are doomed to failure "as long as we persist in our quest for one magic formula to solve all the varied problems raised by the proximate cause question."[19] Certain approaches may work better in one kind of typical fact situation than in others, a hypothesis that suggests the need

19. Allen M. Linden, *Down with Foreseeability! Of Thin Skulls and Rescuers*, 57 Can. Bar Rev. 545, 547–48 (1969).

for a flexible approach to the issue. Indeed, some courts already recognize this when they apply different tests to different scope-of-liability issues that arise within a single jurisdiction.[20]

Once a court (or a student confronting a fact pattern) concludes that the extent-of-liability issue has been appropriately raised and needs to be resolved, the next step is to determine what approach to use, and how to apply it procedurally. I have identified three basic substantive tests, two of which have multiple variations, that are available to limit liability, and courts have employed them procedurally in the context of the duty, the breach-of-duty and the proximate-cause elements of the negligence formula.

The Hindsight Tests. Under one approach, courts determine proximate cause or scope of liability from the perspective of hindsight. This requires a look backward from the harm sustained by the plaintiff to the defendant's careless conduct, in order to determine whether the link between the two was sufficiently close, or, to put it negatively, was not too attenuated. There are a number of versions of the hindsight test. One of them asks whether in retrospect plaintiff's harm was a "natural and probable consequence" of defendant's carelessness, with some courts adding the requirement that the latter be an "efficient cause," in the sense that it produced an unbroken sequence of events that culminated in harm to plaintiff, or that it was a "cause"

20. *See* Osborne M. Reynolds, *Proximate Cause—What If the Scales Fell in Oklahoma?*, 28 OKLA. L. REV. 722 (1975).

of the harm rather than a mere "condition" serving as a background to the infliction of damage. Another considers whether the plaintiff's injury was a direct consequence of defendant's unreasonably risky conduct. Remoteness in time or space might be a factor that helps persuade a court to limit liability. Some judges and scholars have suggested that what is really happening when courts purport to use these verbal formulations is the rendering of commonsense judgments whether under all the factual circumstances of the cases, defendants should fairly be held responsible for the actual consequences of their carelessness.

It is crucial to keep in mind that the tests are not necessarily mutually exclusive. For example, a court might use the direct-consequences to impose liability when the harm *directly* results from defendant's negligence, but might use a different test to deal with cases where the careless conduct *indirectly* causes injury to plaintiff.

As a matter of process, the courts employ these various hindsight approaches when they determine whether or not plaintiff has satisfied the proximate-cause element of her *prima facie* claim in negligence. Normally the question of proximate cause is for the jury, but judges do not shy away from deciding the issue if they feel the factors they are weighing push the scale overwhelmingly in favor of one side or the other. One of the most persistent problems for courts is the drafting of hindsight-test instructions that juries can both comprehend and apply.

The Risk–Foreseeability Test. The hindsight test early on faced a spirited challenge from what eventually came to be known as the risk-foreseeability test (or the risk rule, as a version of it is called). The first courts to use this approach limited liability when defendant could not have anticipated the harm produced by his conduct. They did this in the context of the proximate-cause element of negligence. They would ask at the outset whether defendant's conduct fell below a standard of reasonable care, and if so, whether plaintiff's harm was a "natural and probable consequence" of defendant's carelessness. In so doing, they made it obvious that if a consequence was natural and probable, defendant should have anticipated it. Thus, proximate cause here was in reality based on the foresight a reasonable person in defendant's position should have exercised.

An alternative procedural approach used in conjunction with the foresight test in effect folds together the elements of breach of duty and proximate cause. If defendant could not have anticipated creating a risk of harm that threatened plaintiff's interest, he could not have breached his duty of due care to plaintiff. A court might reach this conclusion by applying the famous "Hand formula," derived from the holding in *United States v. Carroll Towing Company*,[21] which postulated that if the cost of avoiding an accident exceeds the foreseeable costs of the accident, defendant's failure to prevent the acci-

21. 159 F.2d 169 (2d Cir.1947).

dent from happening would not be unreasonable. Here, a finding that the foreseeable probability of harm was zero would justify exonerating a defendant who made no effort to avoid such harm. This in effect would eliminate proximate cause as a separate element of negligence and use breach of duty to determine the extent of liability. A variation on this approach may be found in the most famous proximate-cause opinion in American torts jurisprudence, where the majority limited liability by using a foresight test not to determine whether defendant violated a duty of reasonable care, but rather whether defendant owed a duty to the injured plaintiff to use due care to protect her from the particular risk that caused her injury, and eliminated any consideration of proximate cause.[22]

A subsequent refinement of the risk-foreseeability test asks whether plaintiff's harm was within the scope of the risks that made defendant's conduct unreasonable toward plaintiff.[23] This approach directs attention to the risks created by defendant, rather than to their consequences. This is the default approach taken by the new *Restatement of Torts* in dealing with the scope of a tortfeasor's responsibility.[24] The *Restatement* prefers to call this

22. Palsgraf v. Long Island R.R., 248 N.Y. 339, 162 N.E. 99 (1928).

23. For an elaboration of this approach, *see* ROBERT E. KEETON, LEGAL CAUSE IN THE LAW OF TORTS 10 (1963). Judge Keeton preferred to call it the "risk rule."

24. *See* AMERICAN LAW INSTITUTE, RESTATEMENT THIRD, TORTS: LIABILITY FOR PHYSICAL HARM (BASIC PRINCIPLES) § 29 (Tentative Draft No. 2, March 25, 2002).

a risk standard, rather than a foreseeability test, although it concedes that the risks that render a defendant negligent are limited to those that defendant could reasonably have foreseen. As a Comment notes, "The risk standard focuses on the appropriate context, although a foreseeability standard, properly explained, could do this as well."[25] (I have opted to straddle the point by using the term risk-foreseeability.) Thus, under this test, if defendant's duty is a general one that obliges him to exercise due care to prevent foreseeable plaintiffs from foreseeable risks of harm, extent of liability will turn on what a reasonable person in defendant's position should have foreseen before engaging in the conduct that caused the harm, a question for the jury unless reasonable people could reach but one conclusion. Unforeseeable risks will thus fall outside the scope of liability.

However, it is crucial to keep in mind that just because a risk is foreseeable does not in and of itself mean that defendant will be liable for harm resulting from it, because if a foreseeable risk is very small and the cost of avoiding it is substantial, a court might find that defendant's conduct in failing to avoid this risk was not unreasonable and therefore did not satisfy the breach-of-duty element of plaintiff's *prima facie* case.

A number of policy factors arguably militate in favor of this polished version of the risk-foreseeability test or the risk standard. It is more consistent with fault-based liability, in that the same consider-

25. *Id.* cmt. k, at 212.

ations determining whether an actor has breached a duty of due care will also limit the scope of her liability. It makes extent of liability commensurate with fault, so that there will be some proportionality between defendant's culpability and the extent of the damages for which he will be held liable. It is not complicated, but rather straight-forward, a quality that promotes ease of administration in the course of the litigation process.

The Duty–Risk Test. A third way one might deal with extent of liability is to focus on the scope of the legal obligation owed by defendant to plaintiff, an approach I refer to as the duty-risk test. Unlike the hindsight and risk-foreseeability tests, which have roots in a long series of judicial decisions, the duty-risk formulation is associated with the advocacy of one extraordinary scholar, the late Dean Leon Green,[26] and has lived on through the efforts of a devoted band of his disciples.[27] It insists that the fundamental scope-of-liability issue to be resolved is whether under all the circumstances a defendant should or should not be held responsible for the extended consequences of her risky conduct. The test places upon the trial judge, rather than the

26. For a collection of articles paying homage to Green and assessing his influence on tort law, *see* 56 TEX. L. REV. 381–578 (1978).

27. *See, e.g.,* Timothy J. McNamara, *The Duties and Risks of the Duty–Risk Analysis*, 44 LA. L. REV. 1227 (1984); E. Wayne Thode, *Tort Analysis: Duty–Risk Versus Proximate Cause and the Rational Allocation of Functions Between Judge and Jury*, 1977 UTAH L. REV. 1; *see also* Dewey v. A.F. Klaveness & Co., 233 Or. 515, 519, 379 P.2d 560, 562 (1963) (concurring opinion of Justice O'Connell).

jury, the burden of determining whether the scope of the legal duty owed by defendant to the plaintiff encompassed the particular risk that caused the particular harm to the particular plaintiff. In so doing, he may take into account considerations such as the deterrence of future harm, moral blame, and any practical (administrative or otherwise) difficulties recognition of a duty might create. Foreseeability of harm would be relevant but not the alpha and omega of the inquiry. If the judge finds that the harm-producing risk fell within the scope of a legal duty owed by defendant to plaintiff, the jury would then decide whether defendant had breached it on the facts of the specific case, by determining whether a reasonable person in the position of the defendant should have foreseen the risk generated by his conduct and the endangering of persons like the plaintiff, and should have taken precautions to eliminate the danger.

Thus, as suggested above, the duty-risk test differs from the risk-foreseeability test in one key specific—it does not make extent of liability turn exclusively on a finding of foreseeability, but instead insists that a range of considerations carefully articulated and weighed by trial and appellate judges can provide a more desirable basis for deciding how far to extend a defendant's legal obligation. The duty-risk approach has found slight support in the case law, but has yet to produce a polestar judicial opinion that embraces and applies it in a validating way.

As has been noted, there is widespread, and at times heated, disagreement within courts, among courts of different jurisdictions and within the academic community about which test best solves the riddle of proximate cause. Supporters of the hindsight test have criticized the concept of reasonable anticipation as *the* determinant factor for delineating the scope of liability, on the ground that it is too easy to manipulate, in part because how broadly or narrowly a court defines the relevant risk can in effect dictate the result to be reached in a particular case. Risk-foreseeability fans, on the other hand, have found little substantive meaning and the seeds of considerable confusion in words or terms such as "direct," "natural and probable," "remote," "condition" and "efficient," and have spurned as unprincipled the use of vague notions of fairness and common sense to determine on a case-by-case basis the extent of a careless defendant's liability. The duty-risk people fault both the hindsight and the risk-foreseeability approaches for hiding the fact that what courts are really doing, under the rubric of proximate cause, is making value judgments about whether it is just or socially desirable to hold particular defendants liable for the extended consequences of their negligent conduct. Those in the hindsight and the risk-foreseeability camps find that the duty-risk test is excessively *ad hoc*, asks too much of the duty element of the negligence formula, and places too much authority in the hands of judges.

Dean William L. Prosser once referred to proximate cause as "a tangle and a jungle, a palace of mirrors and a maze."[28] Is there any way to impose order on this unkempt cranny of tort law, the source of headaches for generations of students? One approach would be to invent a new, simple formula that would solve, once and for all, the scope-of-liability dilemma in tort law, and that would gain broad acceptance both by the courts and within the precincts of academia. No one has yet succeeded in doing this. A less ambitious alternative, for which I have opted, is modestly analgesic rather than miraculously curative, and will seek to guide novices through the maze, in the hope that they will be able to appreciate the efforts that have been made to place rational and equitable limits on the scope of tort liability, recognize the obstacles that have frustrated these attempts, and form their own conclusions about how best to limit the scope of tort liability.

In Chapter Two I shall analyze in detail the **hindsight, risk-foreseeability** and **duty-risk** tests. Since the first and second of these tests developed in large part in reaction to each other, they defy unitary treatment; it is best to lay them out side by side and examine how they emerged and developed, through the prism of the leading cases that fashioned and applied them. I shall then conclude the Chapter with a careful look at how the

28. William L. Prosser, *Proximate Cause in California*, 38 CALIF. L. REV. 369 (1950).

duty-risk approach emerged as an alternative to hindsight and risk-foreseeability.

In Chapters Three and Four I shall subject the hindsight, risk-foreseeability and duty-risk approaches to closer scrutiny, by applying them to our illustrative scenarios, and by testing their efficacy as determinants of extent of liability.

Chapter Five will consider proximate cause in the context of two areas of tort law other than negligence—intentional wrongdoing and strict liability—and Chapter Six will offer some suggestions for dealing with the scope-of-liability issue.

Chapter 2

From Casablanca to the Buffalo River, via East New York and Sydney Harbor

The term "proximate cause" originated in a postulate authored by the philosopher Francis Bacon and published posthumously in 1630, when he famously declared in his volume of legal maxims that *"In jure non remota causa, sed proxima, spectatur"*[1] ("In the law, one looks not at remote cause, but proximate cause"). The bare axiom gave no clue how to calculate at what point in a sequence a cause becomes "remote." Therefore, the noted philosopher and Lord Chancellor of England saw fit to elaborate by noting that: "[The law] contenteth itself with the immediate cause; and judgeth of acts by that, without looking to any further degree."[2]

When Bacon issued his maxim, it had no specific relevance to tort law, which in the seventeenth century gestated quietly in the writs of trespass and trespass on the case. He derived it not from jurisprudence, but rather from inductive logic, which posited that to achieve true knowledge one must

1. Francis Bacon, Collection of Some Principal Rules and Maximes of the Common Lawes of England 1 (1630).
2. *Id.*

understand why things happen. This in turn required the identification of proximate causes, which were defined as causes that plainly and necessarily produced effects. All other causes were considered remote. Thus, these notions of proximate and remote cause concerned themselves with neither time nor space. They were concepts meant to promote comprehension of why natural phenomena occurred as they did, and hence would provide crucial keys to all the sciences. Inasmuch as Bacon considered law to be a science, it was natural for him to incorporate proximate cause into jurisprudence.[3]

More than two centuries passed before the courts began to develop the concept of negligence as a basis of tort liability, and the notion of proximate cause soon emerged as a mechanism courts used to limit the extent of a defendant's responsibility for harm caused by careless conduct.[4] Although judges adopting the doctrine occasionally referred to Bacon's maxim, they never really explicated and developed the doctrine in a systematic and thoughtful way.

Some have argued that the hidden agenda behind this newly minted tort doctrine was to protect entrepreneurs in an industrializing society, since the imposition of unlimited tort liability upon actors for

3. The first legal scholar to interpret Bacon's view of proximate cause in this manner was Nicholas St. John Green, in *Proximate and Remote Causes*, 4 AM. L. REV. 201 (1870), reprinted in 9 RUTGERS L. REV. 452 (1954).

4. *See* Patrick J. Kelley, *Proximate Cause in Negligence Law: History, Theory, and the Present Darkness*, 69 WASH. U. L. Q. 49 (1991).

every consequence of their failures to exercise due care might result in awards of mega-sized damages that could stifle economic growth.[5] In point of fact, however, not every formulation of proximate-cause doctrine relieved enterprises from responsibility for all the harm they caused. Indeed, one scholar has pointed out that most of the courts that first applied the concept of proximate cause (including in cases that involved railroads) did not limit defendants' liability and ruled in plaintiffs' favor.[6] Moreover, it is plausible that rules developed for the purpose of limiting liability might have reflected a conclusion, driven by considerations of corrective justice, that at some point damage may be so far removed from careless conduct that holding the perpetrator liable would run counter to basic ideas of fairness prevalent in the community, or that without some way of limiting a defendant's responsibility for loss causally related to his unreasonably risky conduct, liability might reach dimensions vastly out of proportion to the defendant's culpability.

Some courts utilized Bacon's notion of "immediate" causes in fashioning a test that restricted liability to the "direct consequences" of a defendant's carelessness. However, more often than not, judges minting the new doctrine on both sides of the Atlantic rejected the Baconian conception of proximate cause. Some extended liability only to

[5]. *See* Morton J. Horwitz, The transformation of American Law, 1780–1860 ch. 17 (1977).

[6]. *See* Peter Karsten, Heart versus Head: Judge-Made Law in Nineteenth-Century America 103 (1997).

consequences that a defendant could or should have anticipated. Other courts fashioned tests that looked backward in time from the occurrence of harm to the careless conduct of defendant and focused on the sequence of events linking conduct to harm. However, putting together a coherent and workable version of the latter approach proved challenging, as judges and scholars failed to reach a consensus about the appropriate elements of what might be termed hindsight tests, and to distinguish them in a meaningful way from a test based on foreseeability. They ended up sounding several variations on the theme, and in so doing, often resorted to imprecise terminology that shrouded proximate cause in the graying mists of confusion and uncertainty—an unhappy situation that has persisted to the present day.

This Chapter will seek to find a way out of the confusion and uncertainty first by looking at an early English case that not only demonstrates the basic difference between the foresight and hindsight approaches to extent of liability, but also typifies the difficulties that have beset attempts to articulate the latter in logical, practical terms. It will then crisscross the Atlantic, and consider first the leading English decision adopting a hindsight rule; then an American classic featuring a majority opinion that has become the touchstone of the foreseeability test, and a dissent that managed to invoke virtually all the variants of the hindsight approach; then an opinion by England's House of Lords rejecting hindsight and embracing foresight; and finally an admiralty decision handed down by a United States Court of Appeals and demonstrating the vitality of retrospection as a method of limiting liability. The Chapter will conclude by placing the duty-risk approach on the table, and by examining how it came into being, how it purports to solve the extent-of-liability riddle, and how it differs from its competitors in the proximate-cause sweepstakes.

Smith: **An Early Fumble**

The first English decision to demonstrate vividly the conflicts (and confusions) over where to draw the liability line in negligence was *Smith v. London and South Western Railway*.[7] There the employees of a railroad trimmed grass and hedges, and then heaped the trimmings in piles alongside the hedges, which skirted the tracks. They permitted the piles to remain in place for a fortnight in mid-August during a hot, dry spell, until a spark from a passing train ignited them. The resulting fire spread to the hedges, crossed an adjacent stubble field and a public road, and ended up destroying plaintiff's cottage, some 200 yards from the tracks.

Plaintiff claimed that the workers had been negligent in leaving the piles next to the hedges and near the tracks under existing weather conditions, because of the foreseeable risk of fire. The issue addressed by the appellate courts was whether there was sufficient evidence of negligence to justify submitting the case to a jury. Two of the three justices on the Court of Common Pleas, the first

7. L.R. 5 C.P. 98 (Common Pleas), *aff'd*, L.R. 6 C.P. 14 (Ex.1870).

appellate tribunal to hear the case, and all seven justices of the Court of Exchequer answered in the affirmative. However, the opinions they filed served to blur rather than to clarify the issue before them.

The basic point of disagreement was over whether liability should attach only if defendant's servants could have foreseen the ultimate consequences of their negligence (here the loss of plaintiff's cottage), or only if plaintiff could make out a good case for recovery by proving that the risk of some immediate harmful result (here the ignition of the hedges) fell within the range of reasonable anticipation. In the Court of Common Pleas, one of the justices took the former position, and stated forthrightly that the test should be whether defendants might have foreseen that sparks would spread to plaintiff's cottage, language that seemed to position him squarely in what we would call today the risk-foreseeability camp. One of his colleagues thought that the question to be decided by the jury was whether the destruction of the cottage was a "natural consequence" or a "probable consequence" of the servants' negligence, but he failed to clarify whether he was using a foresight or a hindsight test. Since the servants could easily have been charged with anticipation of the burning of plaintiff's cottage as a natural and probable result that would follow from a carelessly set fire, the justice may well also have been taking, in a functional sense, what amounted to a risk-foreseeability approach.

On appeal to the Court of the Exchequer one justice posited that even though the defendants could not have anticipated a risk of damage to plaintiff's cottage when they left the pilings, if they knew the hedges might ignite, they "were responsible for all the natural consequences of [their actions]."[8] This language seems to be equivalent to a hindsight test, since it would hold defendant liable even for creating an unforeseeable hazard (danger to the cottage), but at the same time it is difficult to image why reasonable men in the position of defendant's employees would not have anticipated the "natural" results of their heedlessness. Another opinion stated that "when it has been determined that there is evidence of negligence, the person guilty of it is equally liable for its consequences, whether he could have foreseen them or not,"[9] which suggests the absence of any limiting test at all, since it would apparently hold a negligent defendant responsible for all the harm causally linked to his faulty conduct. Yet another justice declared that "if the negligence were once established, it would be no answer to say that it did more damage than expected,"[10] which seems to conflate situations in which a defendant's negligence did more harm to the plaintiff than could reasonably been expected (as illustrated in Example 1, the unexpectedly-serious-harm scenario), with cases like *Smith*, where a defendant's negligence might have done harm to

8. L.R. 6 C.P. at 20.
9. *Id.* at 21.
10. *Id.* at 22.

persons other than those within the ambit of foreseeable risk. Thus, one can survey the array of opinions *Smith* and find support for both a foresight and a hindsight approach to extent of liability.

Under the *de facto* foresight approach, the court would first determine whether defendant's employees had acted negligently by breaching a duty of due care, and then whether the damage sustained by plaintiff was a consequence that the employees might have expected (because it was "natural and probable"), in which case their carelessness was a proximate cause of the harm. But whether defendant's conduct fails to meet the standard of due care will depend in part on foreseeability, that is, whether a reasonable person in defendant's position should have anticipated that his conduct might create an unreasonable risk of harm to plaintiff or someone in plaintiff's position. Thus, unless the foresight prerequisite to a finding of breach of duty somehow differs from the foresight necessary to establish proximate cause under this test, the courts seem to be requiring plaintiffs to prove foreseeability to establish both breach and proximate cause. Such a redundant enterprise hardly seems logical.

One way to avoid this duplication would be to demand, as part of the proximate-cause element, proof that defendant should have foreseen that harm would *probably* result from his conduct, a plausible prerequisite in light of the "natural-and-probable-consequences" formulation. But under the breach-of-duty element, proof that defendant should have anticipated the mere *possibility* of harm might in some cases justify the imposition of liability, if the harm threatened was substantial, and might have been averted at modest cost or effort. Hence, the strong suspicion arises that what judges would be really saying, if they find no proximate cause because there was a possibility rather than a probability of harm, is that as a matter of law defendant did not breach his duty of ordinary care because the cost of avoiding the harm far exceeded the potential gain, a conclusion reached because of the very small amount of foreseeable risk threatened.[11]

The problem with trying to extract a hindsight test from the *Smith* is that none of the justices seemed concerned about fashioning a general principle that could readily be used in other cases to limit the scope of liability. They were willing to hold the railroad responsible for the loss of plaintiff's cottage, whether or not such damage could have been anticipated, but specified neither whether they would place any bounds on responsibility for a carelessly lit fire that spreads from one property to another, nor how they would draw any bounds, other than by using the term "natural consequence" as a limiting factor. The latter is singularly unhelpful, since it is difficult to imagine what the unnatural consequences of burning bushes might be. (Perhaps if a bird had snatched up a glowing

11. For a similar interpretation of the meaning of the word "probable" in the proximate-cause context, *see* Jeremiah Smith, *Legal Cause in Actions of Tort*, 25 HARV. L. REV. 103, 116–18 (1911), reprinted in HARVARD LAW REVIEW ASSOCIATION, SELECTED ESSAYS ON THE LAW OF TORTS 649, 662–63 (1924).

twig, had flown away with it and had dropped it on a haystack a mile away, the resulting fire might be considered "unnatural;" it would also be totally unforeseeable.)

A second problem is that in order to hold the railroad liable for the loss of plaintiff's cottage under a hindsight test, plaintiff would have to establish some negligence on defendant's part. If a reasonable person would have foreseen only that the piles of trimmings near the railroad tracks might ignite and burn the hedges, without more this would not seem to establish actionable negligence, because the railroad owned the hedges, and to make out a *prima facie* case, plaintiff should have to show that defendant breached a duty to someone other than itself. The owner of any property lying between the hedges and the cottage might have qualified, but the opinions do not indicate who owned the stubble field. Hence, it would seem that under the facts of *Smith*, in order to find the railroad negligent (or in breach of its duty to use due care), the court would have to conclude that defendant violated a legal obligation it owed to plaintiff, the only other party who might have been adversely affected by the spreading fire. The duty might derive from a finding that the careless setting of a fire on its own land might foreseeably create a risk that the fire would spread to land owned by an adjacent property-holder. But such a conclusion would then have obviated the need even to consider the issue of proximate cause, since the finding that the railroad owed a duty of due care to plaintiff would also determine the extent of defendant's liability.

Smith exemplified the difficulty of formulating a meaningful and usable hindsight test based on the phrase "natural and probable consequences." A number of years would pass before an English court would seize an opportunity to articulate in an authoritative way a different and more workable version of the hindsight approach.

The Direct–Consequences Rule: Herein *Polemis*

Although a number of courts had previously used the touchstone of "direct consequences" to limit liability, it was a landmark English decision in 1921 that explicitly found the test to be preferable to a rule that would limit liability to those risks whose foreseeability made defendant's conduct negligent in the first place. In a factual context that fits within Example 3, the different-risk scenario, the court chose a hindsight test echoing Bacon's conception of proximate cause.

On July 20, 1917, as World War I continued to ravage Europe, some Moroccan stevedores dropped a plank into the hold of a vessel called the *Thrasyvoulos* as it lay by a dock in the harbor of Casablanca (perhaps not far from the future location of Rick's Café Americain of cinematic legend). Its Greek owners had chartered (an admiralty term for "leased") the *Thrasyvoulos* to defendants, and the ship was transporting containers of benzine and petroleum. The containers began to leak as the vessel made its way to the Moroccan port of Casablanca. Shortly after it docked, stevedores employed by the defendants shifted the cargo in the hold and put some heavy planks across the forward end of the hatchway. One of the planks fell into the hold. There was a spark, which ignited some petroleum vapors, and the ensuing fire destroyed the *Thrasyvoulos*.

The disaster led to litigation in a court of admiralty. The owners sued for the value of the ship, and the terms of the lease agreement between the parties referred the dispute to a board of arbitration, which decided in favor of the petitioners. Their claim sounded both in contract, under the terms of the lease, and in tort. The owners dropped their contract claim after the decision by the arbitrators, so the subsequent appeal raised only the claim in tort.[12]

The arbitrators based their decision on a provision in the contract exempting the defendant from liability for loss caused by fire. They concluded that the exemption did not apply to fire losses occasioned by defendant's negligence, that the falling of the board was due to the carelessness of the stevedores (for whose negligence defendant would be vicariously responsible), and that although defendant might have foreseen some damage might result from the dropping of the board, the generation of a spark in the hold fell beyond the bounds of reasonable anticipation. However, despite the latter finding of fact,

12. *See* Arnold D. McNair, *This* Polemis *Business*, 4 Cambridge L.J. 125 (1931).

they concluded that the exemption would not apply, and defendant would be liable for the loss of the ship.

The charterer appealed to the King's Bench, which had jurisdiction to review only questions of law, and therefore the reviewing court could not disturb the fact findings made by the arbitrators—including what some have found to be the dubious conclusion that defendant could not possibly have anticipated that a plank falling into a hold known to contain explosive vapors and inflammable petrol would create a risk of fire. (As Leon Green once noted, "No person with his senses about him would dare hurl a heavy timber into a storage area of inflammables filled with petrol vapor."[13])

The court unanimously upheld the arbitration board's ruling.[14] The three opinions in the case, unlike those in *Smith*, understood clearly that the issue in *Polemis* required a choice between on the one hand a risk-foreseeability approach, which would condition recovery on a finding that while laying the planks defendant's employees should have anticipated the risk of the harmful consequences (here the explosion and fire), and on the other hand a test that would ask first whether defendant might have foreseen subjecting plaintiff to some risk of harm (here damage to the cargo or the ship from the impact of the falling plank), in

13. Leon Green, *Foreseeability in Negligence Law*, 61 COLUM. L. REV. 1401, 1411 (1961), reprinted in LEON GREEN, THE LITIGATION PROCESS IN TORT LAW 283, 293 (1977).

14. *In re* Polemis & Furness Withy & Co., [1921] 3 K.B. 560.

which case defendant would have breached a duty of due care, and secondly whether defendant's conduct proximately caused the harm that actually resulted (the explosion). All the justices opted for the latter. As one of them put it, "if the act would or might probably cause damage, the fact that the damage it in fact causes is not the exact kind of damage one would expect is immaterial, so long as the damage is in fact directly traceable to the negligent act ..."[15] Thus, the rule in *Polemis* imposed liability for the direct consequences of a defendant's negligence, even if defendant could not have reasonably foreseen them.

Polemis clearly qualifies as a hindsight test for extent of liability. If by "direct" the court meant "immediate," it approximates Bacon's gloss. But suppose the consequences of defendant's careless conduct were interrupted by intervening acts or forces. One of the justices in *Polemis* indicated that when a "series of physical phenomena" intervened between defendant's conduct and plaintiff's harm, proximate cause might be determined by means of a foresight test, under which a court might deem as remote results, and hence outside the ambit of liability, consequences that ordinarily do not occur or might not reasonably be expected to occur.[16] What this suggests is that while *Polemis* held that a defendant might be liable for the direct consequences of a careless act or omission even though they might not have been foreseeable, it does not

15.   3 K.B. at 577.
16.   3 K.B at 570–71.

necessarily exclude the possibility of imposing liability for indirect consequences under a different test for extent of liability.

The Risk Rule: Herein *Palsgraf*

While the British courts were favoring a hindsight approach to extent of liability, their American counterparts were displaying the same kind of ambivalence found in *Smith*, as they waffled between a rule that would limit a defendant's responsibility to harm caused by the same risks that made her conduct unreasonable in the first place, and a rule that would enlarge the scope of a defendant's liability to include harm from hazards beyond those that justified concluding that her conduct had been unduly risky. Yet it was not until the New York Court of Appeals handed down its landmark decision in *Palsgraf v. Long Island Railroad Company*[17] that a panel of judges fully and eloquently debated the issue and resolved it, albeit narrowly, in favor of using foreseeability as the measure of extent of liability.

Commentators have spilled barrels of ink over *Palsgraf*,[18] and their lucubrations have gone beyond the legal questions raised by the case. Scholars have convincingly demonstrated the likelihood that what really transpired that fateful day on the platform at the Long Island Railway station in East New York could not possibly have been as described in the

17. 248 N.Y. 339, 162 N.E. 99 (1928).

18. For the most original gloss, *see* David Gray Carlson, *"Tales of the Unforeseen,"* 27 Hastings L. J. 776 (1976) (cartoon).

opinions,[19] and have convincingly debunked the charge that the author of the majority opinion, Judge Benjamin N. Cardozo, discussed the case at an American Law Institute meeting before the court decided it.[20]

The operative facts of the case, as set out succinctly in the opinions, indicate that employees of the defendant pushed a man with a package as he attempted to board a crowded train; he dropped the package, and to the surprise of everyone except possibly the package-bearer, it turned out to contain fireworks; they exploded, dislodging some scales at the far end of the station platform (although exactly how far away was never made explicit), and the scales fell on Mrs. Palsgraf, a passenger standing next to them. (Neither the majority nor the dissent saw fit to mention that the injury for which Mrs. Palsgraf claimed damages was mere-

19. *See* VERNON X. MILLER, WHAT SOME PEOPLE OUGHT TO KNOW ABOUT PERSONAL INJURY LAW 19–21 (1978); RICHARD A. POSNER, CARDOZO, A STUDY IN REPUTATION 33–35 (1990); *see also* ANDREW L. KAUFMAN, CARDOZO 286 (1998) (quoting from New York Times report).

20. *See* ANDREW L. KAUFMAN, *supra* note 19, at 294–95, disproving the allegation made by Prosser in William L. Prosser, Palsgraf *Revisited*, 52 MICH. L. REV. 1, 4–5 (1953), reprinted in WILLIAM L. PROSSER, SELECTED ESSAYS IN THE LAW OF TORTS 195–97 (1953). This was not the first time that Prosser misstated critical facts in accounts of the history of tort doctrine. *See* James H. Barron, *Warren and Brandeis,* The Right to Privacy, *4 Harv. L. Rev. 193 (1890): Demystifying a Landmark Citation*, 13 SUFFOLK L. REV. 875, 891–94 (1979) (demonstrating the inaccuracy of Prosser's account of what he claimed motivated Warren to coauthor the article credited with inspiring the judicial creation of the tort of invasion of privacy).

ly a traumatic neurosis that caused her to stutter.[21]) The trial court sent the case to the jury, which found for plaintiff, and the Appellate Division affirmed by a three-to-two vote. The New York Court of Appeals then reversed, four to three, and ordered the entry of judgment for defendant.

The majority and dissenting opinions mooted whether the proper test for determining the railroad's liability for Mrs. Palsgraf's injuries should be based on foresight or hindsight. Cardozo presented the case for limiting the scope of a defendant's liability to risks that a reasonable person in defendant's position might have anticipated at the point in time when the ill-advised push occurred, while Judge William S. Andrews argued that if the employees foreseeably created an unreasonable risk of some harm to somebody, the railroad might be held liable for resulting harm even though it could not reasonably have been foreseen.

Cardozo framed the issue in terms of the scope of the duty owed by the railroad to Mrs. Palsgraf, and limited the railroad's obligation to risks of harm its employees might reasonably have expected to endanger plaintiff at the point in time that they decided to push the man with the package. To use his exact words, "the orbit of the danger as disclosed to the eyes of reasonable vigilance would be the orbit of the duty."[22] Andrews framed the issue in terms of proximate cause, and would have per-

21. On Mrs. Palsgraf's injuries, *see* JOHN T. NOONAN, PERSONS AND MASKS OF THE LAW 127 (1976).

22. 248 N.Y. at 343, 162 N.E. at 100.

mitted a jury to find that the liability of the railroad for the carelessness of its employees might extend to a plaintiff who was not foreseeably within the ambit of unreasonable risk created by its employees.

The Majority Opinion. According to Cardozo's biographer, the majority opinion made *Palsgraf* one of the "best known American common law cases of all time."[23] Indeed, it has challenged generations of law students and has served as a favorite tool for Socratically-inclined law professors. Let us now take a closer look at what gives *Palsgraf* its lasting appeal.

Cardozo somewhat reluctantly agreed with Andrews that the actions of the railroad employees might have been careless toward the mysterious man with the package, so that if he had suffered the kind of loss one might expect to have resulted from the dropping of a package, he might have been able to hold the railroad liable. In Cardozo's view, the reasonably expected loss would have been damage to the package. But he left specifically open the question whether the stranger might have recovered for a personal injury—such as harm from an explosive—that might not have been foreseeable.[24]

Cardozo's refusal to take a stand on this point is perhaps the major puzzle of *Palsgraf*. Consider, for

23. A. KAUFMAN, *supra* note 19, at 287. The linkage between Judge Cardozo and Mrs. Palsgraf has endured. "On August 10, 1991, in Hamburg, New York, Lisa Newell, who is the first cousin four times removed of Benjamin Cardozo, married J. Scott Garvey. Mr. Garvey is the great-grandson of Helen Palsgraf." *Id.* at 303.

24. 248 N.Y. at 346–47, 162 N.E. at 101.

a moment, *Polemis*. Cardozo might presumably have permitted the owner of the ship to recover for any damage from impact to the hull as a result of the dropping of the plank, since it could have been foreseeable that such damage might occur. But how would he have ruled on the actual facts of the case? The damage from the explosion was a direct result of the careless handling of the plank, just as the hypothetical firework-related injury to the man with the package would have been a direct consequence of the careless push by the railroad employees. Cardozo was able to avoid answering this question by giving dispositive weight to the fact that the injured plaintiff was not the package-bearer, but rather the unfortunate Mrs. Palsgraf, standing on the platform at some distance away. He seemed reluctant to suggest that the unidentified passenger might have been able to recover for injuries from the unforeseeable explosion, because it then would have been difficult to justify denying recovery to a victim standing next to the package-holder, or by extension to Mrs. Palsgraf.[25] Yet the majority opinion would have the clarity it lacks if it had held simply that there could be no liability to anyone for physical harm resulting from unforeseeable risks, and since no one could have anticipated that the package contained fireworks that might detonate on impact, the railroad's liability would not extend to

[25]. For an elaboration of this point, *see* William L. Prosser, *Palsgraf Revisited*, 52 MICH. L. REV. 1 (1953), reprinted in WILLIAM L. PROSSER, SELECTED TOPICS ON THE LAW OF TORTS 191, 226 (1953).

this kind of harm, whoever happened to be the victim.

Note that Cardozo could not have been classifying Mrs. Palsgraf as a plaintiff whose presence the railroad could not have anticipated, so as to put the fact pattern within Example 4, the person-at-risk scenario. She was a paying passenger, waiting on defendant's platform, and clearly entitled to protection. If the railroad employees had reason to know that the man was carrying a package of explosives that might detonate on impact and they carelessly caused him to drop it, there can be no doubt that Cardozo would have permitted Mrs. Palsgraf to recover, no matter where in the station she was standing.

A singular feature of Cardozo's opinion is that he used the substance of the risk-foreseeability test to hold that the railroad owed no duty to protect Mrs. Palsgraf against the particular risk that caused her injury. As a matter of process he might found that even if the railroad employees had been negligent in pushing the man with the package, their negligence was not a proximate cause of Mrs. Palsgraf's injuries because the risk that caused injury to her could not have been foreseen by the guards. Instead, he stated bluntly that "the law of causation, remote or proximate, is ... foreign to the case before us."[26] Since the risk of an explosion was unexpected, and foreseeability of risk is an accepted element of breach of duty, he might also have concluded that as a matter of law, the railroad did not breach the

26. 248 N.Y. at 346, 162 N.E. at 101.

obligation of duty care they owed to passenger Palsgraf when the employees carelessly shoved the man with the package. However, he chose to work within the parameters of the duty element of the negligence formula.

Since determination of the existence and scope of a duty is an issue of law within the exclusive purview of the trial judge, under Cardozo's *modus operandi* the latter would have exclusive responsibility for defining the ambit of liability. If this function were for the jury to perform, within the elements of either breach of duty or proximate cause, the trial judge could intervene only upon a finding that there was no way a reasonable person could conclude that defendant should have foreseen the risk that caused harm to plaintiff (a determination that the court might easily have made in *Palsgraf*). Thus, Cardozo's approach assigned exclusively to trial judges and appellate courts the liability-limiting function.

The Dissenting Opinion. Andrews, on the other hand, saw the issue as one of proximate cause, and was willing to conclude that the conduct of the railroad employees was negligent, in that it fell below the duty of due care that the railroad owed to society at large. For him the issue was whether the railroad's negligence proximately caused Mrs. Palsgraf's injuries.

In order to decide this issue, Andrews opted for an approach that combined pragmatism and flexibility. He enumerated most of the tests courts had previously developed to limit a negligent defendant's liability, and characterized them not as fixed rules but rather as "hints" that could point judges in the direction of a solution. However, in a bow toward the virtue of flexibility, he refrained from indicating a method by which courts might determine which of these tests to apply in which type of fact situation, nor did he even make explicit which test he would use in *Palsgraf* to uphold a finding of liability on the part of the railroad.

All but one of Andrews' "hints" amounted to hindsight approaches to proximate cause. Buried in his list was the suggestion that courts might consider whether a particular result might reasonably have been anticipated—a concession that in some unspecified circumstance a court would be justified in resorting to foreseeability as the measuring rod for extent of liability. In this respect he seemed to be following the lead of the justice who declared, in one of the *Polemis* opinions, that a court might use a foresight test under certain conditions. However, unlike the *Polemis* judge, Andrews did not point out when this might be appropriate.

The hindsight "hints" offered by Andrews included an examinations of whether there was a direct link between cause and effect, without too many intervening causes. This incorporated the "direct-consequences" test applied in *Polemis*. He also listed four other hindsight variants: (1) does a "natural and continuous sequence" tie cause to effect? (2) was the cause a substantial factor in bringing about the result, or was the connection between the two "too attenuated"? (3) was there sufficient "remoteness in time or space" to justify exonerating defendant from liability? and (4) was it fair to hold the railroad liable, a test suggested by his declarations that "proximate cause" required considerations of "convenience," "public policy" and "a rough sense of justice," and that "This is not logic. It is practical politics ... It is all a question of expediency."[27]

I have already discussed "directness" in the context of *Polemis*. At this point I shall interrupt my chronological account with some elaboration of the remaining four approaches, as well as three other hindsight tests not mentioned by Andrews. One of the latter would use arbitrary line-drawing as a method of limiting liability. Another, occasionally cropping up in cases involving interventions (Example 6), distinguishes between causes, for which a responsible defendant might be liable, and conditions, the creation of which would not lead to liability. A third, adopted by the first and second editions of the *Restatement of Torts*—would find proximate cause when a defendant's careless conduct produced a result that was "not so highly extraordinary" that it would be inappropriate to extend liability.[28]

The "Natural-Continuous-Sequence" Test.

In our discussion of *Smith*, I suggested the difficul-

27. 248 N.Y. at 352, 354, 162 N.E. at 103–04.

28. *See* 2 AMERICAN LAW INSTITUTE, RESTATEMENT, TORTS § 433 (b) (1934); *see also* 2 AMERICAN LAW INSTITUTE, RESTATEMENT, SECOND, TORTS § 435 (2) (1965) (conduct not a legal cause if actor's negligence "appears to the court highly extraordinary that it should have brought about the harm").

ties that have bedeviled efforts to fashion a hindsight test based upon a finding that plaintiff's injury was a "natural and probable consequence" of defendant's carelessness. It is difficult to conceptualize this as a genuine hindsight test, since something that is generally recognized as "natural and probable," such as the spreading of a fire, would surely have been foreseeable to a reasonably prudent person. The phrase has a lilt to recommend it, but little more. The concept of unnatural consequences resists comprehension, since "all the consequences of one's negligence are natural in a physically scientific sense."[29] "Probable consequences" suggest results that are more likely than not to occur, which would make them highly foreseeable, and would make the term rather out of place in a hindsight test. What additional meaning might derive from using the terms "natural" and "probable" in tandem rather than separately puts further strain on efforts to comprehend them.

Therefore, in an attempt to make the "natural-and-probable-consequences" test workable as a hindsight approach to extent of liability, some courts have added a requirement that the events proceeding from defendant's carelessness and culminating in plaintiff's injury follow in a continuous or unbroken sequence, uninterrupted by any new and independent agency.[30] This brings into play conceptions of causation that purport not only to

29. ROBERT E. KEETON, LEGAL CAUSE IN THE LAW OF TORTS 27 (1963).

30. *See* Milwaukee & St. P. R. Co. v. Kellogg, 94 U.S. 469 (1876).

separate efficient causes from mere conditions, but also to identify the kinds of factors whose intervention will relieve a defendant from liability.[31] In the context of a spreading fire, for example, one might reasonably conclude that the normal progress of a fire qualifies as a continuous or unbroken sequence, and the necessary elements (combustibility, wind direction, etc.) are conditions, so that any landowner whose property sustained damage in the natural course of a carelessly set fire might be able to recover. Thus, unusual circumstances causing a fire to spread in an abnormal way (for example, as in my hypothetical of the bird and the glowing cigarette butt) might constitute grounds for finding in defendant's favor.

Note that this version of the hindsight test, at least in spreading-fire cases, will probably produce results identical to those reached with the use of a foresight test, since a defendant should certainly expect that the course of a blaze might follow the dictates of the laws of physics and respond to the influence of the state of the physical environment. Hence, if an unusually and unexpectedly high wind causes a fire to spread beyond the point it might have reached under normal conditions, both the unbroken-sequences hindsight test and the foresight test might exonerate defendant.

How would the "unbroken-sequence" rule apply in a *Polemis*-type situation? *Christianson v. Chica-*

31. *See* Atchison, T. & S.F. Ry. Co. v. Stanford, 12 Kan. 354 (1874).

go, St. P., M. & O. Ry. Co.[32] involved a railroad worker who was riding in a hand car that was followed by a second hand car, operated by careless co-workers. The latter closed the distance between the two vehicles, in violation of railroad rules that required hand cars to remain apart by a distance equivalent to three telephone poles laid out horizontally. As plaintiff saw the second car approach to within 60 feet, he became dizzy, fell from his car and suffered traumatic injuries.

Defendant's argument was that the negligent operation of the second vehicle was not the proximate cause of plaintiff's injuries, since the only foreseeable risk created by the co-worker's conduct was that the vehicles would collide; plaintiff's dizziness and tumble could not have reasonably been anticipated; hence it was not a natural and probable consequence of defendant's negligence.

The Supreme Court of Minnesota placed itself squarely in the hindsight camp by stating that "What a man may reasonably anticipate is important, and may be decisive in determining whether an act is negligent, but it is not at all decisive in determining whether that act is the proximate cause of an injury which ensues."[33] The opinion first defined the test for proximate cause as whether the injury was a "natural and probable consequence" of a negligent act, and then elaborated on it in the following language: "Consequences which follow in unbroken sequence, without an interven-

32. 67 Minn. 94, 69 N.W. 640 (1896).
33. 67 Minn. at 97, 69 N.W. at 641.

ing efficient cause, from the original negligent act, are natural and proximate; and for such consequences the original wrongdoer is responsible, even though he could not have foreseen the particular results which did follow."[34]

The court emphasized that it was adopting a hindsight test for extent of liability, and that foresight would be relevant only to the issue of defendant's breach of duty. Thus, it would not matter that the risk of plaintiff falling from his hand car before the second vehicle collided with it could not have been foreseen, so long as defendant's employees might have anticipated the risk of collision. However, the court also pointed out that "The only possible difference [between the risk of falling and the risk of collision] is that it might be anticipated that the sudden stoppage of the car was more likely to happen than the falling of one of its occupants upon the track."[35] This represents an obvious retrenchment, since it suggests that there might indeed have been a foreseeable risk, albeit to a lesser degree, that plaintiff would fall from dizziness related to the emergency created by defendant's carelessness.

Christianson adopted an "unbroken-sequences" standard that required a look backward from the accident to defendant's careless conduct. It differed from *Polemis* in that the court indicated it might impose liability for the indirect consequences that followed in an unbroken sequence from the negli-

34. *Id.*
35. 67 Minn. at 98, 69 N.W. at 643.

gence of the defendant, so long as no "intervening efficient cause" broke the causal chain. However, this dictum bore the seeds of circularity, since the adjective "efficient" expressed not a criterion but rather a legal conclusion, in that a cause that broke the linkage between defendant's negligence and plaintiff's harm would be efficient, and an efficient cause was one that broke that linkage.

The "Substantial–Factor" or "Not–Too–Attenuated" Test. Andrews' invocation of a "substantial-factor" or "not-too-attenuated" test for proximate cause gives no hint as to what objective criteria a court should use in determining "substantialness" or unduly excessive attenuation, and as to whether the trial judge or the jury should resolve the issue. Moreover, the test is problematic, because it injects considerations of cause-in-fact into the scope-of-liability element of the negligence formula.

Another way of looking at this would be to ask whether a situation might arise in which harm would not have occurred but for defendant's careless conduct, but one still might conclude that such conduct was not a substantial factor in bringing about the harm, or the link between the conduct and the harm was too attenuated to justify the imposition of liability. Since it is difficult to imagine that this question could be answered in the affirmative, it seems to make no sense to view the substantial-factor test as a device to cut off responsibility that might otherwise fall on a defendant whose carelessness was a cause-in-fact of the harm.

The "Remoteness" Test. The use of remoteness as a justification for limiting the liability of a careless defendant has roots that extend back to an early Massachusetts decision exonerating a defendant who had assaulted a town pauper and thereby increased the expenses incurred by plaintiff, who had contractually agreed with the town to support its financially challenged residents. The court held that plaintiff could not recover because "[t]he damage is too remote and indirect."[36] The court did not explain what it meant by "remote," or what made the harm suffered by plaintiff "too" remote. The accident did not seem to have happened at a great distance from the town, and the recitation of the facts does not suggest any temporal remoteness. Admittedly, the damage suffered by plaintiff as a result of the assault was "indirect," as compared to the direct harm sustained by the pauper, but there was no explanation as to what made the harm "too" indirect.

A number of decisions have subsequently utilized the concept of remoteness to justify exonerating a careless defendant. The term seems to be used in two distinct contexts,[37] but the underlying if often unarticulated justifications lurking behind judicial incantation of the term "remote" may be identical.

First, courts have denied liability when, as in the case of the assaulted pauper, the plaintiff suffered

36. Anthony v. Slaid, 52 Mass. (11 Met.) 290 (1846).

37. *See generally,*Victor E. Schwartz, *The Remoteness Doctrine: A Rational Limit on Tort Law*, 8 CORNELL J. OF L. & PUB. POL'Y 421 (1999).

some kind of derivative harm as a consequence of defendant's breach of a duty owed to the primary victim of its tortious conduct. Thus, in a decision arising out of a freak accident in mid-winter on the Buffalo River, the owner of grain elevators sought to recover the costs of securing replacement wheat for wheat it could not unload from its elevators on account of fluvial obstructions caused when a ship broke loose, drifted downstream and made a stretch of the river impassable for several months, all as a result of defendants' negligence. The court denied recovery on the ground that the link between the defendants' carelessness and claimants' damages was "too tenuous and remote to permit recovery."[38] Recent cases denying liability for financial harm indirectly incurred by plaintiffs as a result of defendants' allegedly tortious infliction of lung damage on smokers similarly invoke remoteness as a reason for refusing to allow recovery.[39]

A more convincing rationalization for dismissing a plaintiff's claim in these kinds of cases might rest on a policy-driven analysis of efficient loss distribution, with perhaps some consideration of corrective justice shedding light on who should bear the loss in question. (Indeed, in the grain elevator case, the court cited language from Andrews' dissent in *Pals-*

38. Petitions of Kinsman Transit Co., 388 F.2d 821, 825 (2d Cir.1968). A prior decision involving the same mishap will be discussed later in this Chapter.

39. *See, e.g.*, Laborers Local 17 Health & Benefit Fund v. Philip Morris, Inc., 191 F.3d 229 (2d Cir.1999); United Food and Commercial Unions v. Philip Morris, 223 F.3d 1271 (11th Cir. 2000).

graf, in the effect that limiting liability was a matter of expediency and fair judgment—considerations having nothing to do with remoteness.[40])

A second kind of case in which courts have resorted to the standard of remoteness involves the intervention of a considerable amount of space or time between defendant's careless act and the harm incurred by plaintiff. Deciding cases on the basis of remoteness seemed to cloak a judicial determinations that it simply would not be fair to hold defendant liable for something so far removed, in time or space, from defendant's tortious conduct that it could not possibly have entered into defendant's mind when she engaged in the act or omission that ultimately caused the harm

The "Fairness" Test. An approach that has won the support of some commentators and is occasionally suggested in judicial dicta posits that extent of liability is in essence an issue of fairness, and therefore it should be left to the jury to decide, on a case-by-case basis, whether holding a particular defendant responsible would constitute a just result. As one court noted early on, "The question of proximate cause is often obscured by technical learning, but in its last analysis it is ordinarily a fact for the jury, to be solved in the exercise of common sense in the consideration of the evidence in each particular case."[41]

40. 388 F.2d at 825.

41. Healy v. Hoy, 115 Minn. 321, 323, 132 N.W. 208, 209 (1911).

A more recent opinion elaborated on this point as follows:

> When an issue of proximate cause arises in a borderline case, as not infrequently happens, we leave it to the jury with appropriate instructions. We do this because it is deemed wise to obtain the judgment of the jury, reflecting as it does the earthy viewpoint of the common man—the prevalent sense of the community—as to whether the causal relation between the negligent act and the plaintiff's harm which was in fact a consequence of the tortious act is sufficiently close to make it just and expedient to hold the defendant answerable in damages.[42]

In practice, if this is what juries are supposed to be doing, they have certainly been left in the dark about it, since the "appropriate" instructions given to them customarily focus their attention upon "natural and probable consequences," or "unbroken sequences," without letting them in on the secret that they should bring their "earthy viewpoint" to bear in reaching a "just or expedient result."

However, there *is* a strong case to be made for allowing juries to apply their common sense and their notions of fundamental fairness in chain-reaction cases that involve freakish concatenations of circumstances not likely to recur. A defendant's negligence may set in motion a sequence of events

42. Marshall v. Nugent, 222 F.2d 604, 611 (1st Cir.1955).

that might suggest a Rube Goldberg cartoon[43]—bizarre causes and effects following one after another in ways that defy the imagination. Professor Jane Stapleton decribes these cases as involving what she calls "*compounded* bad luck," and gives as a hypothetical example the farmer who carelessly leaves an insecticide near his front gate, where his neighbor's dog eats it; the owner first thinks his dog is acting listlessly because of a lack of exercise, and then asks a friend to take the dog to a veterinarian; the friend gets lost and has to try again a week later; the veterinarian correctly diagnoses what is wrong with the dog and orders a serum, but a labor dispute and the negligence of the delivery service delay its arrival; by the time the vet administers the serum, it is barely too late, and the dog dies.[44]

Generally worded tests for extent of liability are not likely to work well in a case such as this. Whether the scope of liability should extend to what happened here ought to be determined by resort of considerations of fairness. As Professor Stapleton has noted, "There comes a point ... in relation to extremes of bad luck where the law refuses to intervene to shift losses."[45]

A further question needs to be addressed. Who should strike the balance between the unfortunate farmer and his unfortunate neighbor? I would argue

43. These were cartoons "designating any very complicated invention, machine, scheme, etc. laboriously contrived to perform a seemingly simple operation." WEBSTER'S NEW WORLD COLLEGE DICTIONARY 1172 (3d ed. 1997).

44. *See* Jane Stapleton, *Legal Cause: Cause-in-Fact and the Scope of Liability for Consequences*, 54 VAND. L. REV. 942, 1001–02 (2001).

45. *Id.*

that jurors drawn from a cross-section of the community would be better suited than an individual trial judge to resolve such issues. Moreover, since these cases involve non-recurring scenarios that could not possibly be anticipated by even the most imaginative tortfeasor, the risk of being held liable by *ad hoc* jury decisions would not affect anyone's behavior or frustrate anyone's expectations. But if courts want jurors to make these kinds of judgments, they should forthrightly instruct the factfinders about what is being asked of them.

Some advocates of a hindsight test based on fairness suggest that the trial judge rather than the jury should apply it to decide the extent-of-liability issue. This approach recognizes that fairness is but one of several factors that should come into play in fixing the extent of liability. But one may question why the test should be applied as a determinant of the proximate-cause element, which has traditionally been the province of the jury, rather than to delineate the scope of the duty, traditionally reserved for the trial judge to decide. One way around this would be for the trial judge to determine preliminarily whether the case at bar involves only considerations of "rough justice." If so, twelve people representing the community might be better able to reach a just solution than a single judge. However, if other policy considerations should be weighed—and this might be so in cases involving fact patterns that are likely to recur—then the judge should take it upon herself to fix the extent of liability.

The Arbitrary Line. In sharp contrast to a fairness-based approach that permits the jury to draw liability lines on a case-by-case basis would be the fixing of an arbitrary limit that would apply in all similar cases. It would be the function of the court to set this outer boundary. The rationale for this approach would be ease of administration and the need for a fixed, consistent rule on which persons subject to it might rely.

The only example of this approach emerged from nineteenth-century New York and Pennsylvania decisions limiting liability for the spreading of negligently set fires.[46] The courts in those jurisdictions held that only adjacent owners who suffered fire damage could recover from the party originally responsible for the fire. Thus, if A carelessly ignited a fire on his property and it caused damage to the property of B, his immediate neighbor, B might be able to recover. But if the blaze spread from B's land to C's, C would not be able to recover. The Pennsylvania Supreme Court backed off from arbitrary line-drawing only seven years after it had adopted the approach.[47]

The problem with asking courts to set arbitrary limits on extent of liability would be that judges would have to exercise discretion, rather than reason from principle, in drawing the line. This is a task appropriate to the legislative function, in the exercise of which elected lawmakers might limit

46. *See* 4 Fowler V. Harper, Fleming James, Jr. & Oscar S. Gray, The Law of Torts § 20.6, at 170 (2d ed. 1986).

47. *See* Pennsylvania R. Co. v. Hope, 80 Pa. 373 (1876).

liability by, for example, setting maximum monetary limits on recovery.

Causes versus Conditions. Some courts have sought to use a distinction between causes and conditions as a way to limit liability. If defendant's carelessness was an "efficient" or "producing" cause of the harm, she might be liable for it. But if her substandard conduct merely gave rise to a "passive" condition, liability would not follow.

This approach occasionally complements the remoteness test. Thus, where a worker in a chemical plant slipped off an above-ground pipe rack wet with water or fire-fighting foam when she was sent to turn off a valve two hours after the extinction of a fire caused by a defective pump manufactured by defendant, the Texas Supreme Court denied the worker's claim for tort damages because defendant's alleged negligence was too remote from plaintiff's injuries, and was not a producing cause of them, but rather a condition that made defendant's tumble possible.[48]

But if plaintiff would not have suffered any injuries in the absence of defendant's careless conduct, it is difficult to understand how the court could conclude that they were not caused by defendant. I shall have more to say about the distinction between causes and conditions in Chapter Three.

The "Not–So–Highly–Extraordinary–Result" Test. In an effort to construct a hindsight test for

[48]. Union Pump Co. v. Allbritton, 898 S.W.2d 773 (Tex. 1995).

limiting liability, the drafters of the original *Restatement of Torts* first placed the proximate-cause function under the general rubric of "legal cause," which required that negligent conduct be a "substantial factor" in bringing about harm, and then added that courts should consider "whether after the event and looking back from the harm to the actor's negligent conduct it appears highly extraordinary that it should have brought about the harm."[49] A comment explained that even though the result of an actor's negligence might be totally different from what a reasonable person in the actor's position should have foreseen, "after the event, such a result may not appear to the court or the jury to be so highly extraordinary" as to preclude liability.[50]

One interpretation of the Restatement approach is that it amounts to a foreseeability test in disguise. A conclusion that a consequence was not highly extraordinary could mean that a defendant should have expected it. At the same time, the Restatement's emphasis on looking backward from the harm to the carelessness that produced it could convey a sense that with the benefit of hindsight, nothing is extraordinary.[51] This could extend a defendant's liability indefinitely, because as the song says, "On a clear day/ You can see forever."

49. 2 Restatement, Torts §§ 430, 431(a), 433(b) (1934).

50. 2 *id.* § 433 cmt. e.

51. *See* 4 F. Harper, F. James & O. Gray, The Law of Torts § 20.5, at 168 (2d ed. 1986).

The "not-so-highly-extraordinary" test might also be interpreted as a disguised fairness- or common-sense-based approach to extent of liability. A trial judge or a jury might comfortably conclude that to hold a defendant responsible for highly extraordinary consequences of her carelessness would be grossly inequitable. If liability is to be cut off for this reason, it would perhaps make more sense for the court to be "up front" about what it is doing.

The Risk Rule, British–Style: Herein the *Wagon Mound*

Although *Palsgraf* attracted widespread notice, both in academic writings and in judicial opinions struggling with the extent-of liability issue, its actual influence was somewhat limited, in part because it was extremely difficult to extract a workable rule from the holding. Hence, a lack of consensus continued to hold sway.

While American courts had the opportunity to choose among a smorgasbord of approaches to proximate cause, the British courts were encountering difficulties in applying the *Polemis* rule to the extent-of-liability issues they had to confront. In addition, the "direct-consequences" test had generated a sustained outpouring of critical academic commentary.[52] It was not until 1961, however, that *Polemis* received what would turn out to be a fatal blow.

The incident that led to the demise of *Polemis* had occurred a decade earlier in the harbor of

52. *See, e.g.*, Arthur L. Goodhart, *The Imaginary Necktie and the Rule in* Re Polemis, 68 L.Q. REV. 514 (1952).

Sydney, Australia, where an oil-burning vessel called the *Wagon Mound* moored at a dock for repairs. Before commencement of the work, seamen aboard the ship carelessly discharged a large quantity of bunkering oil, which oozed over an extensive area of the harbor. The captain of the ship made no effort to do anything about the spill, and headed out to sea soon thereafter. Some time later, having been assured that there was no danger that they might ignite the now-ubiquitous oil, welders at a wharf six hundred feet away from where the *Wagon Mound* had berthed caused some debris under the wharf to catch fire, and suddenly the reassuring words on which they had relied proved to ring like a lead dollar on the bar. The burning debris set the oil aflame, and the resulting conflagration caused substantial property damage throughout the harbor.

Bringing suit in admiralty, the owners of the wharf charged the owners of the *Wagon Mound* with negligence and the creation of a nuisance. The trial judge found for plaintiffs, and the Supreme Court of New South Wales dismissed defendants' appeal. The shipowners then sought review before the Judicial Committee of the Privy Council, which was the only avenue of appeal available from decisions of the highest courts in the British colonies. The Committee reversed the decision, upheld defendant's appeal on the negligence claim, and ordered that it be dismissed.[53] Although decisions of the

53. Overseas Tankship (U.K.) Ltd. v. Morts Dock & Engineering Co., [1961] A.C. 388 (Privy Council).

Judicial Committee of the Privy Council did not constitute precedent such as would bind English courts, the opinion in the case turned out to have such persuasive force that it in effect excised *Polemis* from the body of the British common law.

The rule in *Polemis* might have supported recovery for the wharf owner, because prior to the fire, the oil from the *Wagon Mound* fouled the plaintiff's slipways (platforms descending into the water from the dock) and made them impossible to use. Thus, one might argue, as the trial judge in fact pointed out, that the vessel's crew created an unreasonable risk of some foreseeable harm—the type of property damage likely to occur as a result of an oil spill—and the fire was a direct, albeit unforeseeable, consequence of this risky behavior. However, the Judicial Committee rejected this analysis and postulated that defendant would be liable only for results (such as the fouling of the slipways) that might have been anticipated.

The holding in what became known as *Wagon Mound I* (to distinguish it from a subsequent opinion dealing with another cases arising out of the same fire) made foreseeability the touchstone of extent of liability. It provided that a defendant would be liable for the consequences of his acts not because such consequences were direct, or natural and probable, but because a reasonable person would have foreseen them. "If ... [defendant's] liability (culpability) depends on the reasonable foreseeability of the consequent damage, how is that to be determined except by the foreseeability of the damage which in fact happened ...?"[54] Thus, the defendant would not be culpable if the seamen who let the oil spill could not have reasonably anticipated the damage for which plaintiff sought recovery—destruction of the wharf by fire.

The Judicial Committee's opinion is notable because it nowhere mentions the term "proximate cause," nor does it specify where in the negligence formula the liability-limiting function should be performed. This sets the case apart from Cardozo's opinion in *Palsgraf*, which specified that extent of liability should be determined as part of the duty element. A sensible interpretation of *Wagon Mound* might posit that the defendant did not breach the duty owed to plaintiffs, since the danger of setting the wharf ablaze was could not have been anticipated by defendant, and therefore there was no foreseeable risk of fire damage to the wharf. Thus, the seamen could not be found to have created an unreasonable risk of harm by doing what they did. (In the familiar language of the famous Hand formula,[55] since the probability of harm, or "P" equaled zero, "P" x "L" would equal zero, and hence could not exceed "B".)

The holding and opinion in a later case involving a claim against the same vessel and known as *Wagon Mound II*[56] buttresses the interpretation of

54. *Id.* at 425.

55. *See* U.S. v. Carroll Towing Co., 159 F.2d 169 (2d Cir. 1947).

56. Overseas Tankship (U.K.) Ltd. v. Miller Steamship Co., [1967] A.C. 617 (Privy Council).

Wagon Mound I as a case deciding scope of liability within the breach element of negligence. Here the owners of two ships damaged in the same fire sought recovery on grounds of both negligence and nuisance. The trial court, in dismissing the negligence count, made a finding of fact that the engineer on the *Wagon Mound* could and should have known that there was a slight possibility that the discharged oil might ignite. The Judicial Committee reversed the judgment below and held that because the foreseeable loss that might result from a fire was extensive, foreseeability of even a small risk of ignition would lead a reasonable person to take the inexpensive preventive measures that might prevent it. This is standard Hand-formula analysis performed to determine the breach-of-duty element of the negligence calculus and at the same time placing the damage suffered by plaintiffs within the bounds of the outer limits of liability to be imposed on defendants. It is worth noting, *en passant*, that the Committee also found that liability would extend to the damage sustained by the vessels even though the risk of such harm was not probable, but merely possible.

Palsgraf and *Wagon Mound I* invigorated risk-foreseeability as a determinant of extent of liability on both sides of the Atlantic. However, they did not sweep away the competition. The Minnesota Supreme Court, for example, in 1961 reiterated its adherence to a hindsight test that imposed liability for the natural and probable consequences of a negligent act.[57] And several years later, the United Stated Court of Appeals for the Second Circuit relied on an *ex post* approach in deciding a case presenting a fact pattern that took real life far beyond the fevered imagination of any torts professor.

Chaos on the Buffalo River

On a dark and stormy night in late January of 1959, swift currents carried broken chunks of ice down the Buffalo River in upstate New York, and began to form an ominous accumulation between the river bank and the bow of the *Shiras,* a large vessel owned by the Kinsman Transit Company,[58] loaded with grain and moored without power at a dock next to a grain elevator operated by the Continental Grain Company. The lines of the ship began to part, as a result of what was later found to have been carelessness by employees of Kinsman Transit and Continental in securing her to the dock. In addition, as the situation became increasingly precarious, the shipkeeper aboard the *Shiras* neglected to prepare the release of the ship's anchors, in the event of need. The lines finally gave way, and the *Shiras,* stern first, set out on its fateful journey.

57. Dellwo v. Pearson, 259 Minn. 452, 107 N.W.2d 859 (1961).

58. For trivia buffs, the Steinbrenners owned Kinsman Transit. At the time of the accident George Steinbrenner was the company's treasurer and moving force. He subsequently left the family business and put together a group of investors purchased the New York Yankees. *See* John Cassidy, "Yankee Imperialists," THE NEW YORKER, July 8, 2002, at 40, 43, col. 3.

An initial and momentary interruption in the *Shiras'* odyssey occurred as a result of brief contact with the bow of a second ship, the *Tewkesbury*, moored in a relatively protected area and devoid of its crew, the shipkeeper having gone off to watch television at the home of his girlfriend. The impact caused the lines of the *Tewkesbury* to snap, and suddenly not one but two unmanned vessels were careening downstream.

Meanwhile, workers at the Michigan Avenue drawbridge, which stood in the way of the approaching ships, received a warning call from the Coast Guard. Acting with glacial speed, the bridge workers were just beginning to raise the span, a full half hour after the notification had reached them, when both errant vessels crashed into the bridge and its towers, with two immediate consequences. One of the towers fell, causing injuries to two members of the bridge crew; and the *Shiras* and the *Tewkesbury* spun about and grounded, which created a damming effect and caused flooding and other consequential losses nearly three miles upstream. As if this were not enough, a second tower on the ill-fated drawbridge subsequently collapsed, damaging adjacent property.

This aggregation of mishaps led to various lawsuits from which extent-of-liability issues gushed like steam from an overheated radiator. The proceedings initiated in the United States District Court and subject to review in the Second Circuit were in admiralty. A 1932 decision by the Second Circuit had adopted *Palsgraf* as furnishing the criterion that should be used in resolving the extent-of-liability issue in maritime law.[59] However, the opinions in the case styled as *Petition of Kinsman Transit Company*[60] leaned more toward Andrews' dissent in *Palsgraf* than Cardozo's majority opinion.

Writing for the majority, Judge Henry Friendly began by acknowledging the authority of *Palsgraf*. However, he then misconstrued the decision as denying recovery because the risk of explosion was unforeseeable. This would mean that even the man with the package could not have recovered for injury from the discharged fireworks, a proposition, as we have seen, that Cardozo himself specifically refrained from endorsing. This made it easy for Friendly to distinguish *Palsgraf*, since *Kinsman Transit* in his view involved the careless creation of a bundle of risks to anyone "within the reach of the ship's known destructive power,"[61] which would include persons and property downstream and in harm's way. Moreover, he observed that one whose carelessness foreseeably created a substantial risk of small damage and a small risk of substantial damage of the same general sort should not be permitted to escape liability if the latter materialized.

But the court still had to face the question where, if anywhere, to draw the outer limit of liability when the forces unleashed by defendants' unreason-

59. Sinram v. Pennsylvania R.R. Co., 61 F.2d 767 (2d Cir. 1932).

60. 338 F.2d 708 (2d Cir.1964).

61. 338 F.2d at 722.

able conduct caused an attentuated series of harmful consequences—which is exactly what occurred in *Kinsman Transit*. Friendly resolved this by citing Andrews' recognition in *Palsgraf* that "expediency" and "fair judgment" were the most effective mechanisms for reaching results consistent with "the general understanding of mankind" in cases involving bizarre fact patterns. Therefore, the court affirmed the trial court's decision imposing liability on Kinsman.

Thus far, I have suggested how the head-on conflict between hindsight and risk-foreseeability has produced what seems to be a standoff. But the story would not be complete without reference to an approach that marches to a different drummer—the so-called duty-risk test for determining how far courts should hold defendants responsible for the results of their careless conduct.

Vox Clamantis in Deserto

William L. Prosser once referred to Leon Green as a "voice crying in the wilderness,"[62] a tribute to the persistent efforts of Green to clear the murky waters immersing judicial efforts to define the scope of a defendant's liability in tort. Beginning with one of his first law-review articles in 1923,[63] Green

62. William L. Prosser, *Palsgraf Revisited*, 52 MICH. L. REV. 1 (1953), REPRINTED IN in WILLIAM L. PROSSER, SELECTED TOPICS IN THE LAW OF TORTS 241 (1954).

63. Leon Green, *Are Negligence and "Proximate" Cause Determinable by the Same Test?—Texas Decisions Analyzed* (Pts 1 & 2), 1 TEX. L. REV. 243, 423 (1923). Four years later he published a critique that analyzed cases from every jurisdiction. LEON GREEN, RATIONALE OF PROXIMATE CAUSE (1927).

attacked the way courts used the concept of "proximate cause" as a mechanism for setting limits on responsibility for careless conduct. Indeed, as one commentator has observed, "he must have expended considerable energy just thinking up new ways to insult it."[64]

Green found the term "proximate cause" to be vague and illusive, a talismanic phrase invoked to mask what courts were really doing, which had nothing to do with causation and everything to do with deciding to what extent a defendant *should* be held liable for the attenuated consequences of his carelessness. He argued throughout his long career that limiting liability was a proper function of the duty element, under which the courts had responsibility for determining first whether plaintiff's interest was protected by law, and if so, whether the rule of law protecting that interest covered the particular hazard that caused the harm for which the particular plaintiff was seeking recovery. If these questions produced answers in the affirmative, he maintained that the court should assign to the jury the task of deciding whether defendant had violated the rule that protected plaintiff's interest, whether the violation of the rule caused the harm, and what damages plaintiff should recover.

Green insisted that the duty element should determine of scope of liability. Recall that under the negligence formula, it is the function of the judge to decide whether defendant owed any duty of care to

[64]. David W. Robertson, *The Legal Philosophy of Leon Green*, 56 TEX. L. REV. 393, 403 (1978).

the class of persons to which plaintiff belonged, and what the parameters of that duty might have been. Normally, she renders this judgment by invoking a legal rule in general terms. Thus, courts have held that defendants have no duty to exercise any care to help a stranger in peril; or that participants in recreational sports owe a duty merely to refrain from recklessness or wanton misconduct for the protection of other participants.

In formulating these rules (as opposed to applying them in accord with the dictates of binding precedent), judges may take into account a variety of considerations, such as public policy (for example, the desirability of deterring unreasonably harmful conduct and its flip-side, the undesirability of discouraging socially useful conduct), moral blame (based on standards prevalent in the community), and any practical or administrative problems recognition or non-recognition of a duty might create (such as the encouragement of trivial claims or the difficulty of proving cause-in-fact). Green himself wrote extensively on these constituent elements,[65] and most courts recognize them.[66] Foreseeability would be relevant only in a general sense here. Courts considering whether to impose a duty for

65. *See, e.g.,* Leon Green, *The Duty Problem in Negligence Cases*, 28 COLUM. L. REV. 1014, 1034–43 (1928); *The Duty Problem in Negligence Cases: II*, 29 *id.* 255 (1929). These articles have been reprinted in reprinted in LEON GREEN, *supra* note 13, at 153, 185.

66. *See* W. PAGE KEETON ET AL., PROSSER AND KEETON ON THE LAW OF TORTS § 53, at 359 (5th ed. 1984). Professor Stapleton calls these factors "legal concerns." Jane Stapleton, *supra* note 44, at 985–96.

purposes of deterrence would evaluate the likelihood that the recognition of the duty would reduce levels of unduly risky conduct or eliminate it entirely.

Green's contribution was his insistence that judges also determine extent of liability through the mechanism provided by the duty element. But how would they accomplish this task, if duty is an issue of law and takes shape through the formulation of legal rules?

The answer lies in Green's concept of legal rules. He recognized that rules might derive from statutes or common-law precedent. However, statutes defining or creating tort duties, either explicitly or by implication, are relatively rare. (They are more likely to set standards of conduct, which courts might use to determine breach of duty under the doctrine of negligence *per se*.) Moreover, precedents culled from prior holdings, while potentially a fertile source for rules of law, would be easy to distinguish for those sharing Green's view that legal rules embodied in precedent were reflections of their factual predicates and the social and economic environments within which they arose.

At heart an adherent of the school of legal realism, Green looked with great skepticism on the practice of applying rules derived from prior holdings. In his view, judges purporting to do this often were in reality manipulating precedent and doctrine to reach desired results. He argued that courts should face up to the fact that in performing the judicial function in tort cases they were much more often than not making rather than following rules of law, and hence they should do so openly. As he once observed, the best one can hope for is that "rules will carry [judges] into the neighborhood of a problem and then [they] must get off and walk."[67]

What this meant was that judges sharing Green's outlook, when they had to decide cases raising legitimate issues about extent of liability, should seize the occasion as an opportunity to develop new rules applicable to the specific disputes before them. The facts of a case would heavily influence the holdings and would produce rules narrow in their application. Moreover, when judges engaged in this creative task, they would invoke policy considerations (such as deterrence of social wasteful conduct), moral values and the practical necessities of the litigation process.[68]

One critic has argued that Green's theory amounts to an "invitation to theoretical nihilism and judicial autonomy."[69] Indeed, if each issue could be found to embody a uniqueness based on the peculiar facts and the environment in which it arose, the holding of the case could hardly be said to

67. LEON GREEN, JUDGE AND JURY 214 (1930).

68. *See generally* Leon Green, *The Duty Problem in Negligence Cases*, 28 COLUM. L. REV. 1014 (1928); *The Duty Problem in Negligence Cases: II*, 29 COLUM. L. REV. 255 (1929), reprinted in LEON GREEN, *supra* note 13, at 153.

69. Patrick J. Kelley, *Proximate Cause in Negligence Law: History, Theory, and the Present Darkness*, 69 WASH. U. L. Q. 49, 100 (1991).

qualify as a rule, since the essence of rules is their general applicability.[70]

Green's use of such rules to define extent of liability in negligence cases closely tracked the way courts had traditionally utilized statutory provisions as standards of care. Recall that under the doctrine of negligence *per se*, courts preliminarily inquire, in deciding whether to adopt a statutory standard in the cases before them, whether plaintiff was within the class of persons the statute meant to protect, and whether the injury suffered by plaintiff was within the class of harms the statute meant to prevent.[71] Under Green's approach, the trial judge would ask these same questions about the legal rule that she was creating as the basis of the obligation owed by defendant to plaintiff.

Therefore, in Green's world, "proximate cause" had no place in the negligence formula. The court would determine extent of liability when it considered whether any rule of law safeguarded plaintiff from the risk created by defendant and inflicting harm on the plaintiff. This approach has come to known as the duty-risk test.

Green's theory might be viewed as a hybrid combining elements of both the risk-foreseeability and hindsight approaches. It permits the trial judge to take into account a range of factors that include foreseeability in a very general sense, but leaves open the possibility of imposing liability for risks

70. *See* LARRY ALEXANDER & EMILY SHERMAN, THE RULE OF RULES: MORALITY, RULES, AND THE DILEMMAS OF LAW 26–27 (2001).

71. *See* DAN B. DOBBS, THE LAW OF TORTS § 137 (2000).

that defendant might not have anticipated. It also allows the judge to extend or limit liability because of policy considerations applicable through the lens of hindsight. As Green once pointed out, "Here [in the exercise of the law-making function of the courts] it is always *hindsight* that must be relied on for judgment—hindsight that may call into play far-flung considerations affecting the welfare of persons not parties to the litigation ..."[72]

Another way of looking at Green's test is to consider it a variant of Cardozo's approach in *Palsgraf*. The crucial difference between the two is that Cardozo would make foreseeability the critical and sole determinant of duty, whereas Green would allow judges to be more flexible and consider policy, moral and practical factors that might justify the imposition of liability even for harm caused by unforeseeable risks, or, conversely, the denial of liability for harm caused by foreseeable risks.

Although the duty-risk test has elicited enthusiastic responses from commentators,[73] it has had much less impact on the courts. One jurisdiction it seems to have penetrated is Louisiana. An illustrative decision, *Hill v. Lundin & Associates, Inc.*[74] involved a

72. Leon Green, *Foreseeability in Negligence Law*, 61 COLUM. L. REV. 1401, 1418 (1961), reprinted in LEON GREEN, *supra* note 13, at 283.

73. *See, e.g.*, E. Wayne Thode, *Tort Analysis: Duty–Risk v. Proximate Cause and the Rational Allocation of Functions Between Judge and Jury*, 1977 UTAH L. REV. 1.

74. 260 La. 542, 256 So.2d 620 (1972). For an imaginative analysis of the case, *see* David W. Robertson, *Reason Versus Rule*

suit against company whose employees left a ladder leaning against a house they were repairing. A third party not connected with the company lowered the ladder to the ground. Plaintiff saw a child running toward it and tried to prevent him from injuring himself, but in her effort she tripped on it and suffered harm. In holding that plaintiff should not recover as a matter of law because defendant had no duty to protect her from the risk that caused her injury, the Supreme Court of Louisiana concluded there was no evidence that defendant might reasonably have foreseen a third party might put the ladder in a position where it created the risk that someone might trip over it.

Although the holding in *Hill* seemed to derive from the application of the risk-foreseeability test, the Court took pains to stress that it was actually using the duty-risk approach, under which risks are not automatically excludable from the scope of a defendant's duty merely because they could not have been foreseen, and that courts must take policy factors into account when they determine scope of duty. However, no such considerations seemed to have affected the outcome of the case.

This Chapter has laid out the various ways courts have limited the extent of a defendant's liability. It is now time to test these methods against fact patterns that call upon court to decide at what point if any responsibility for carelessness should terminate.

in Louisiana Tort Law: Dialogues on Hill v. Lundin & Associates, Inc., 34 LA. L. REV. 1 (1973).

Chapter 3

Into the Crucible—Part I

Courts may confront the extent-of-liability issue in an array of discrete factual contexts, which Chapter One enumerates. Chapter Two describes the evolution of the three basic approaches (risk-foreseeability, hindsight and duty-risk) courts and commentators have taken to resolve the issue, and in so doing demonstrates the lack of any general consensus in proximate-cause doctrine. At the nub of the disarray that rumples the jurisprudence of proximate cause lurks the suspicion that none of the methodologies set out in Chapter Two produces satisfactory resolutions for all the illustrative fact patterns listed in Chapter One. Chapters Three and Four will explore this supposition further by applying the risk-foreseeability, duty-risk and hindsight tests to each scenario. The multiplicity of hindsight approaches necessitates a certain degree of selectivity, and therefore I have limited myself to the subsets based on directness, remoteness and fairness, which might offer supportable results in some of the scenarios.

The Unexpectedly–Serious–Harm Scenario

Let us begin with the plaintiff with hemophilia or a metal plate in his skull or an infection in his leg, just below the knee; the familiar legal maxim that a defendant takes her plaintiff as she finds him; and the quip that it is no defense, when you carelessly smash into the rear of a truck that happens to be carrying eggs and destroy its cargo, that the vehicle might have been transporting golf balls.

This scenario brings to center stage a defendant who had no knowledge that the particular individual she put at risk with her careless conduct had a pre-existing physical weakness, and who even in the exercise of due care could not have discovered the condition of the person she was about to endanger. Because of plaintiff's infirmity, defendant's careless act or omission causes harm greatly in excess of what a person without such a condition would have suffered under circumstances identical in every other significant respect. Although courts have consistently held in these kinds of cases that plaintiffs will recover for the full extent of the damages sustained, a close look at the reasons supporting this consensus may help us deal with more problematic scenarios.

What are the arguments for and against awarding damages for the full extent of the harm? A reasonably intelligent actor with time to reflect on the deleterious effects his conduct might trigger should realize that the pool of persons potentially put at risk by such conduct might contain individuals with unusual susceptibilities (as well as unusual tolerances), even though the odds of actually encountering one of them in any given instance might be minuscule. Thus, defendant could not have known ahead of time that the group of persons endangered by her conduct *would* include an unusually susceptible person, but she should have appreciated the very slight risk that such an individual *might* be put at risk by her conduct. To relieve defendants of responsibility for the entire amount of actual harm inflicted on such victims would reduce the deterrent effect of tort liability to a less than optimal level, since it would eliminate from the "PL" side of the Hand formula the tiny but real and foreseeable risk of injuring an unusually susceptible victim, and would thereby proportionately reduce the quantum of care a defendant would have to expend in order to avoid liability.[1] This mode of analysis, based on an efficiency or utilitarian approach to tort law, in effect posits that there is really no such thing as a personal injury the extent of which is totally unforeseeable.

In addition, given the high costs unwary plaintiffs might have to incur in order to discover their own unusual susceptibilities, and the high costs plaintiffs aware of their susceptibilities might have to incur in order to protect themselves, defendants as a class might well be the cheaper cost-avoiders, which would justify putting on them the burden of taking reasonable precautions to avoid the infliction of susceptibility-aggravated harm. If in an individual case it would have been less expensive for plaintiffs to protect themselves (for example by wearing protective devices), defendants should be able to

1. *See* RICHARD A. POSNER, CASES AND ECONOMIC ANALYSIS 26–27 (1982).

assert this as an affirmative defense, in the form of contributory or comparative negligence. In a normative sense, the optimum solution for cases where plaintiff is the cheaper cost-avoider might be to leave the entire risk of aggravated harm on plaintiff so as to create a proper incentive for self-protection.

The perspective of corrective justice, when applied to cases where defendants had time to choose their course of conduct as well as to situations in which they acted instinctively or under other circumstances not permitting considered thought, might inquire whether an innocent victim or a wrongdoer whose carelessness caused the victim's injury ought to bear the aggravated loss. (Putting the issue in these terms would seem to resolve it.) One might counter-argue here that there should be some proportionality between the degree of a defendant's culpability and the amount of damages for which he should be liable as a result, and it would therefore be unjust to burden defendants with massive tort liability for inadvertence that might have inflicted a simple scratch or bump on a normally healthy person. But as the late Dean Prosser once noted in this regard, "If the loss is all out of proportion to the defendant's fault, it can be no less out of proportion to the plaintiff's innocence."[2]

Another argument in favor of allowing full recovery derives by analogy from the law of damages, which does not limit recovery to the monetary loss-

2. William L. Prosser, *Palsgraf Revisited*, 52 MICH. L. REV. 1 (1953), reprinted in WILLIAM L. PROSSER, SELECTED TOPICS IN THE LAW OF TORTS 191, 217 (1953).

es defendant might reasonably have expected plaintiff to incur if defendant acted carelessly and plaintiff suffered harm, but instead permits plaintiffs to recover for the full amount of their medical expenses, impairment of earning capacity and pain and suffering. Thus, if an inattentive driver hits someone who looks like a derelict but in fact turns out to be a high-salaried actor trying to learn a role, the driver must pay damages based on the diminution in plaintiff's expected future wages, in order to restore plaintiff to his pre-accident earning capacity—a principal goal of the law of tort damages. The alternative, limiting recovery to the lost future wages of the homeless person defendant reasonably believed plaintiff to be, would hardly seem to be fair to an innocent non-homeless victim of defendant's careless driving.

Here, defendant could not have foreseen the amount of pecuniary loss that he might cause if he acted carelessly, while in the scenario under discussion, the extent of the physical harm that a particular victim might suffer fell outside the range of reasonable anticipation. However, under both circumstances, a contrary rule would seem to be unworkable on a case-by-case basis, since it would permit plaintiff to recover only for the monetary damages, or the type of physical injury, defendant might reasonably have foreseen—a fact that would be extremely difficult for plaintiff to prove (especially in cases where defendant had no opportunity to have a close look at his victims ahead of time), and for a jury to calculate.

Of course, the measure of damages in a case involving a plaintiff with a pre-existing vulnerability would necessarily take into account the plaintiff's condition if it affected such elements of recovery as the victim's pre-accident work-life expectancy or his ability to earn. Thus, if defendant carelessly causes an accident that triggers a psychotic condition in a plaintiff who was carrying within her the seeds of mental disorder, the calculation of damages in the case would take into account the fact that plaintiff was not a "whole person" before the accident.[3] This would serve to mitigate the defendant's liability burden.

The reasons discussed above have justified the adoption of a rule that would permit any plaintiff with an unusual susceptibility to recover for harm aggravated by her condition even when a defendant did not know, nor in the exercise of due care could have known, of his victim's particular weakness. Extent of liability here would not depend on case-by-case determinations by a judge or a jury, but rather on the application of the principle that "you take your plaintiff as you find her" (also known as the "thin-skull" or "egg-shell-skull" rule). Would the various approaches to proximate cause justify the same result?

Unexpectedly Serious Harm and Risk–Foreseeability. In a jurisdiction utilizing the risk-foreseeability approach, defendant might contend that he owed no duty to protect plaintiff against the

---

3. *See* Steinhauser v. Hertz Corp., 421 F.2d 1169 (2d Cir. 1970).

extra harm attributable to the pre-existing condition; or that even if he breached his duty of care to the extent that he might have avoided the infliction of some harm on plaintiff, he did not violate his obligation with respect to the extra harm caused by the pre-existing condition; or that his allegedly careless conduct was not a proximate cause of the additional harm. Each of these contentions would rest upon the claim that he could not have foreseen a plaintiff put at risk by his conduct would have a pre-existing weakness that would exacerbate any injuries inflicted.

A court wishing to impose liability for unexpectedly serious harm under risk-foreseeability might do so by defining the test in such a way as to require that defendant foresee only that her conduct might cause some actual physical harm, but not necessarily the full extent of the injury actually sustained.[4] This tweaking of risk-foreseeability necessitates a rationalization that implicates the considerations discussed above, and demonstrates how policy concerns may shape the contours of the test.

Unexpectedly Serious Harm and Duty–Risk. Under the duty-risk approach, on balance the policy reasons supporting full liability—the need for a rule

4. *See* ROBERT E. KEETON, LEGAL CAUSE IN THE LAW OF TORTS 66–73 (1963). The latest version of the new *Restatement of Torts*, which adopts what amounts to the risk-foreseeability test as its default rule for scope of liability (proximate cause), contains a separate black-letter provision incorporating the so-called "thin-skull rule." AMERICAN LAW INSTITUTE, RESTATEMENT OF TORTS: LIABILITY FOR PHYSICAL HARM (BASIC PRINCIPLES) § 30 (Tentative Draft 2, March 25, 2002).

that can achieve optimal deterrence, considerations of justice and the foreseeability of the presence of people with pre-existing weaknesses in the general population—would seem to outweigh the reasons against it. Hence, a court using this test might define the duty owed by defendant as incorporating a rule that where defendant injures a plaintiff with a pre-existing weakness, no matter how unforeseeable it might have been in the particular instance, and as a result plaintiff's injuries were much more extensive than they would have been if the victim had been a person without a pre-existing condition, defendant will be liable for the full amount of damages incurred.

Inasmuch as this rule is general in scope and would apply to every case involving the aggravation of a pre-existing weakness, would it not run counter to the distaste for, and distrust of, general rules characteristic of the duty-risk approach? Perhaps yes, unless courts eschewed the general rule and instead examined the facts of each case carefully to determine whether the burden of furnishing safeguards against the serious harm to which a pre-existing vulnerability might contribute should fall on the plaintiff, because of her knowledge and ability to protect herself at a cost less than the injury-prevention costs defendant would have to have incurred. In such a case, a court using duty-risk could conclude that under certain circumstances defendant owed no duty to this particular plaintiff to protect her against unexpectedly serious injury.

Thus far, I have applied the risk-foreseeability and duty-risk test to the aggravated-harm scenario. It would not be unreasonable to suggest that both are in fact using hindsight when they permit full recovery for damages aggravated by a plaintiff's pre-existing weakness. Let us now consider how full-bore hindsight tests might determine extent of liability in these cases.

Unexpectedly Serious Harm and Hindsight. Under the hindsight approaches, defendant would argue that his conduct was not a proximate cause of the aggravated harm. But the injury suffered by a hypersensitive plaintiff would seem to be a direct and immediate consequence of the defendant's carelessness. Moreover, hindsight approaches do not concern themselves with the need for any proportionality between the degree of fault on the part of a defendant and the amount of harm it produces; the fact that the conduct led immediately and directly to the harm would be sufficient. Hence, a plaintiff with a pre-existing susceptibility could always recover against a tortfeasor if these standards come into play. Outcomes would be consistent, although courts might still permit defendants to argue that in a particular circumstance plaintiff was contributorily or comparatively negligent in not taking reasonable protective measures against a foreseeable risk of damage.

A "rough-justice" or fairness test might require always putting the question to the jury. However, this issue is apt to recur, and it would be unsatisfactory for results to vary from case to case. Whether a hypersensitive plaintiff may recover full damages should depend on a consistently applied rule, rather than the "earthy viewpoint of the common man," rendered afresh each time the issue arises. The same criticism would apply to case-by-case exercises of common sense by trial judges confronting this problem.

Unexpectedly Serious Property Damage. An intriguing related question is whether this full-responsibility rule should apply to property damage. Here one confronts the hoary hypothetical of the 1623 folio containing Shakespeare's original text of Hamlet stored in the cottage next to the railroad tracks and destroyed in a fire caused by the carelessness of railroad employees in the operation of a locomotive.[5] If the railroad would have to pay full loss-of-earning-capacity damages in the event several high-salaried professional athletes were unforeseeably in the cottage and perished in the fire, why shouldn't the company have to pay for the full market value of the rare and precious folio? Under a literal application of the risk-foreseeability test as refined above, if defendant might have anticipated its careless conduct might create a risk of some personal injury or some property damage, liability should extend to the full value of the losses that eventually result, unless a court decided to create a separate rule to apply only to property-damage cases. But note that it is much easier and cleaner to

5. *See* Leon Green, *Foreseeability in Negligence Law*, 61 COLUM. L. REV. 1401, 1405–07 (1961), reprinted in LEON GREEN, THE LITIGATION PROCESS IN TORT LAW 283 (1977).

accomplish either result through the duty element, rather by refining and re-refining the risk-foreseeability test.

Using duty-risk, a court would consider whether sound policy considerations would dictate a conclusion that where property damage rather than personal injury results, defendant should not be liable for the extraordinary value of what was destroyed. Leon Green has argued that defendant's liability should not extend to the extraordinary value even if defendant actually knew that its negligent conduct might put at risk the Hamlet folio or any other item of incalculable worth.[6] This conclusion might derive from a desire, as a matter of appropriate loss allocation, to place on the owner of highly valuable items the responsibility for insuring them against damage or loss caused by the negligence of others or as a result of an unavoidable accident.[7]

The suggested rule in these kinds of cases is that when defendant's carelessness damages property of extraordinary worth, defendant will not be liable (at least for the surplus value). This would require case-by-case determinations whether the goods in question have such worth as to justify restricting defendant's liability by the application of what would amount to a limited-duty rule, and hence would not give owners of valuable property much

6. *Id.* at 1406.

7. *See* Guido Calabresi, *Concerning Cause and the Law of Torts: An Essay for Harry Kalven, Jr.*, 43 U. CHI. L. REV. 69, 97 (1975) (hypothesizing presence of a vase from the ancient Ming dynasty in China in the paper bag in *Palsgraf*).

guidance about when they should insure it, or how much insurance coverage they should purchase. There also remains the practical problem of how judges should go about the task of fixing the boundary between extraordinary value and ordinary value, so as to trigger a limited-duty rule only for the former. This may be an area where it would be best to leave line-drawing to the common sense of the trial judge, an approach that would still create uncertainties about how courts might decide these cases. Yet they arise so infrequently that a pragmatic indeterminacy might not be intolerable.

The Manner-of-Occurrence Scenario

Where defendant's carelessness creates an unreasonable risk of a certain kind of harm, and in fact that harm materializes, but in a way that no one might have anticipated, are there any compelling reasons to relieve the defendant of liability? In other words, should defendant escape responsibility because she could not have foreseen the precise sequence of events or mechanisms her careless conduct triggered? I shall limit this scenario to cases in which the forces set in motion by defendant's act or omission play themselves out in a freakish way, and save until later a discussion of situations where the manner of occurrence implicates forces generated by natural phenomena or human interventions that defendant may or may not have been able to anticipate.

Just as the minute possibility that a plaintiff put at risk by a defendant's negligence might have a pre-existing vulnerability that makes the resulting harm much more serious than what an ordinary person might sustain, so also is there omnipresent, whenever a defendant acts negligently, the faintest of chances that resulting harm to plaintiffs to whom defendant owes a duty of care might come about in a freakish, totally unexpected way. To exclude the latter kinds of accidents from the ambit of liability would reduce defendant's incentives to take reasonable precautionary measures for the benefit of persons to whom he owes an obligation of ordinary care. If the courts adopted a rule permitting recovery in these cases, just as in the aggravated-harm scenario, they would be positing that in effect the manner in which harm occurs has no legal significance.

Alternatively, as a matter of corrective justice, it might seem unfair to relieve from responsibility a negligent defendant who has caused injury to an innocent plaintiff to whom he owed a duty of reasonable care not to inflict such harm, just because that harm happened to come about in a bizarre manner that no one could have anticipated. This would seem especially true where no intervening natural forces or human actions interrupted the effects unleashed by defendant's carelessness.

Thus, it would seem logical for courts to disregard manner of occurrence, and by and large this is what they do. However, it is worth examining how they might reach this result under each of our approaches to scope of liability.

Manner of Occurrence and Risk–Foreseeability. Under the risk-foreseeability test, one may adopt the same solution applicable to the aggravated-harm scenario, and define the application as postulating that defendant need not have foreseen the exact details connecting the creation of the risk with the harm that the risk threatened in order to justify the imposition of liability. Thus, when the master of a tugboat navigates it in such a way that the vessel heads straight for a group of pilings on which men are working, one foreseeable risk is that the tug's collision with the pilings might cause some kind of physical injury to workers unable to escape in time. The risk comes to fruition in a highly unusual way, as one of the fleeing workers slips, the tug strikes one piling, which strikes another in a falling-domino effect, and the pilings catch and crush the worker's leg as they topple.[8] It would seem to make little sense to hold that the owner of the vessel would not be liable to a worker suffering traumatic injury in such a freakish chain of circumstances, but might be liable if the tug had directly struck one of the latter's co-employees as he stood on the pilings. Risk-foreseeability would support a finding for plaintiff if the question put to the finder of fact was whether defendant might reasonably have anticipated that the careless operation of the tug might put waterfront workers in danger of physical injury if the vessel should strike the pilings.

8. These facts come from Hill v. Winsor, 118 Mass. 251 (1875).

Note the importance of the way the court phrases the issue, which suggests how skillful lawyering can affect the outcome of a case. A famous Texas decision aptly demonstrates this. Defendant carelessly allowed a mud hole to develop in a right of way he owned beneath a railroad trestle, and an automobile became stuck in it. The owner of the car summoned a truck from a nearby garage. Plaintiff, who had a wooden leg, was an employee at the garage, and he accompanied the truck driver. In the process of towing the automobile out of the hole, the rope became coiled, caught plaintiff around his good leg and inflicted a severe injury that resulted in amputation. The appellate court adopted the formulation of the facts offered by plaintiff's attorney: "[Plaintiff] was on the highway, using it in a lawful manner, and slipped into this hole, created by [defendant's] negligence, and was injured in undertaking to extricate himself."[9] The court also accepted plaintiff's argument that in order for liability to attach, defendant need not have foreseen the exact happening, but merely that the mud hole might endanger travelers on the roadway.

Manner of Occurrence and Hindsight. How would the hindsight tests handle manner-of-occurrence cases? An instructive example is *Bunting v. Hogsett*,[10] a proximate-cause classic involving a "dinkey," or small locomotive used to haul supplies

9. Hines v. Morrow, 236 S.W. 183, 187–88 (Tex.Civ.App. 1921); *see also* CLARENCE MORRIS & C. ROBERT MORRIS, JR., MORRIS ON TORTS 164–65 (2d ed. 1980).

10. 139 Pa. 363, 21 A. 31 (1891).

to and from a furnace. The "dinkey" ran on a track that described an arc crossing railroad tracks at two points. As it pushed a car loaded with coke, its engineer carelessly caused a collision with a passenger train at one of these intersections, as a result of which the train came to a halt, and in so doing managed to block both intersections. The engineer of the "dinkey," in an unsuccessful effort to avoid hitting the train, threw his engine into reverse, turned off the steam and, in fear for his own safety, jumped to the ground. The car being pushed by the doughty "dinkey" hit the train, and the impact jarred open the throttle. Still in reverse and now unmanned, the "little engine that could" set out backwards on the curving tracks and slammed into one of the train's coaches, which was now obstructing the second intersection. A passenger on the coach suffered injuries and sued the owner of the "dinkey."

Applying a hindsight approach based on the "natural-and-probable-consequences" test, the court held that since no intermediate forces intervened between the original negligence that produced the first collision and the second collision injuring plaintiff, the careless operation of the "dinkey" was a "natural, primary, and proximate cause of the entire occurrence." Another justification for the result reached by the court would derive by reasoning from the hypothesis that someone on the train suffered harm in the first collision. Would it not be difficult to square holding defendant liable to the victim of the first collision but not the second? In both collisions the victims might be found to have been identically situated within the scope of the risks created by the engineer's initial negligence in operating his locomotive, and to treat them differently, even though the first accident was "normal" and the second was bizarre, might strain one's sense of justice, as well as the basic principle that courts should decide like cases alike. Thus, a hindsight test based on fundamental fairness would also support a finding of liability.

The harm in the tug-boat case was a direct and immediate consequence of defendant's sloppy navigation, so that a hindsight test based on these factors could produce a judgment for plaintiff. There is an element of indirectness and a lack of immediacy in the mudhole case, but it is not clear whether this might justify a judgment for defendant. The difficulty in knowing what constitutes an "unbroken sequence," or when a consequence becomes "remote," other than arbitrarily or on the basis of gut feeling, suggests a problem with the workability of these hindsight criteria.

Manner of Occurrence and Duty–Risk. The duty-risk approach would ask whether the harm fell within the scope of the duty owed plaintiff by defendant. A court using this test might rely on the principle of deciding like cases alike to conclude that defendant's obligation extends to foreseeable harm caused in an unanticipated way—an approach that might require case-by-case judicial determinations whether plaintiff and a person injured in a way that could have been foreseen were so similarly situated that as a matter of fairness they both should be permitted to recover.

The Different-Risk Scenario

We have seen that when a defendant creates a foreseeable risk of harm and the risk comes to fruition in an unexpected way, liability may nonetheless attach. A more challenging issue arises in the *Polemis*-like context, when defendant's carelessness subjects plaintiff to one kind of risk, and a different risk materializes. Should plaintiff be permitted to recover for harm inflicted by this second risk?

A classic fact pattern illustrates the issue here. Defendant inadvertently leaves an unmarked packet he knows contains rat poison on a counter in the kitchen of a restaurant. If someone inadvertently uses its contents in preparing food, clearly defendant would be liable for a resultant accidental poisoning, since the reason why it is highly dangerous to leave unmarked rodenticide on a kitchen restaurant counter is because someone might mistake it for an ingredient that was suitable for human consumption. But suppose defendant, with no reason to suspect that the poison might explode if left in the immediate vicinity of an open flame, puts the container near a stove. Should he be held liable for harm caused by an explosion?

Different Risks and Risk-Foreseeability. Under the risk-foreseeability test, the danger of an explosion was not within the ambit of foreseeable risks that made defendant's placement of the poison on the counter a negligent act. If defendant had thought about taking precautionary measures with respect to the placement of the poison, he would not have factored into his decision the possibility that the substance might explode, since he could not have known this. Therefore, a court might conclude that defendant should not be held responsible for explosion-related injuries. The risk that materialized was different in nature from the foreseeable risk created by defendant.

Note the similarity between this analysis and the way a court would address the same issue if plaintiff asserted a statutory violation rather than common-law negligence as the basis for liability. Indeed, in *Larrimore v. American National Insurance Company*,[11] the actual case involving the explosion of rat poison in a restaurant kitchen, plaintiff's claim of breach of duty rested on allegations that defendant had violated a statute making it a crime to lay out rat poison anywhere but in a safe place. One of the requirements for finding that such a violation might be negligence *per se* is that the danger created be the type of risk the statute or regulation meant to prevent.[12] In *Larrimore*, by concluding that the statute or regulation aimed only to prevent inadvertent poisonings, the court reached the identical result it might have arrived at in a common-law-based negligence action. In a similar classic applica-

11. 184 Okla. 614, 89 P.2d 340 (1939).

12. *See* DAN B. DOBBS, THE LAW OF TORTS § 138, at 326–28 (2000).

tion of this rule, a British court ruled that a defendant who violated an administrative order requiring that cattle shipped on vessels be confined to pens would not be liable for the loss of cattle that rough seas washed overboard, because the statute authorizing the order was intended only to prevent the spread of communicable diseases.[13]

Different Risks and Duty–Risk. Duty-risk might produce the same result, if the court concluded that the rule of law providing protection against the careless handling of unmarked containers of poison in a restaurant did not protect the interests of persons in the vicinity from the risk of unforeseeable explosions. Note that this approach would at least make it possible for plaintiff to argue there were policy reasons that supported protecting people from *any* risks attributable to misplaced poison. For example, a court might find the hazards of using rat poison in a restaurant kitchen were so serious as to justify, as a matter of deterrence, imposing liability even for unforeseeable risks generated by the substance, as a matter of deterrence. Indeed, reference to the imposition of strict liability for harm caused by foods containing harmful substances might provide analogical support for such a position.

Different Risks and Hindsight. Under the hindsight test formulated in *Polemis*, the explosion was a direct result of defendant's careless act in placing the unmarked container of rat poison on a kitchen counter, and therefore defendant might be

13. Gorris v. Scott, L.R. 9 Ex. 125 (1874).

liable for any harm immediately linked to the poison, whether or not defendant could have anticipated the risk of the accident that actually occurred. The simplicity of this mode of analysis is both a plus and a minus, in that it makes the test easy to administer but provides no clue why a liability line should be drawn between directly and indirectly inflicted injuries.

Rationales for No Recovery in Different–Risk Cases. What arguments support the results dictated by risk-foreseeability, and reachable under duty-risk? The same approach used to test outcomes in the aggravated-harm and the unforeseeable-manner-of-occurrence scenarios might be helpful here. Suppose, after the owner of the restaurant placed the packet on the counter, with knowledge that it contained rat poison but unaware of its explosive properties, a kitchen worker inadvertently put some of the poison into a stew and a customer consumed it, to her eventual and substantial detriment; shortly thereafter someone else moved the unlabeled container close to an open flame, and it exploded. Would it strain one's sense of fairness to grant recovery to the poisoned customer, but not to a victim of the blast? Would such results amount to disparate treatment of similarly situated plaintiffs? The differences between the two distinct risks created by defendant, and between the types of harm sustained by the two plaintiffs, suggest that perhaps the cases are not so similar that reaching different results would necessarily violate the principle of deciding like cases alike.

Another argument is that subjecting defendant to liability for creating the unforeseeable risk of explosion might not add any additional deterrence, since the threat of liability for any accidental poisoning that might result from the sloppy placement of the packet should be sufficient to deter that type of carelessness. Indeed, hanging over defendants' heads the specter of liability for harm from risks they cannot anticipate might conceivably produce socially unwarranted overdeterrence.

A good recent example of risk-foreseeability analysis in this type of case is the opinion in *Di Ponzio v. Riordan*,[14] where defendant left his vehicle unattended, and with its engine running, at a gas pump; the parking gear unexpectedly failed to remain in place, and the automobile lurched forward, striking another patron of the station. Invoking *Palsgraf*, the court held that defendant did not have a duty to protect plaintiff from the risk that actually materialized and caused the injury; the hazard that might have made defendant's conduct actionable negligence was the foreseeable possibility of fire or explosion resulting from the ignition of highly flammable gasoline; hence, what occurred was not a foreseeable consequence of defendant's failure to turn off his engine.

Different-Risk vs. Manner-of-Occurrence. The line between the different-risk and the manner-of-occurrence scenarios may at times be a fine one. At the margin, distinguishing manner of occurrence from essential nature of risk may involve the exer-

14. 89 N.Y.2d 578, 657 N.Y.S.2d 377, 679 N.E.2d 616 (1997).

cise of judgment in close cases, which in turn leaves the door open for the criticism that judges may manipulate the distinction in order to justify the result they want to reach. A broad characterization of the case as involving manner or mechanism of occurrence will extend the ambit of liability, while characterizing the case as involving nature of risk will have a constrictive effect. A pair of English decisions applying the risk-foreseeability test as formulated in *Wagon Mound* illustrate this danger.

In *Hughes v. Lord Advocate*,[15] defendant's employees left an open manhole uncovered and surrounded by kerosene lanterns. Two boys discovered the site and climbed into the manhole. Having sated their juvenile curiosity, they clambered out, and on their way they caused a lantern to fall into the hole. Some of the kerosene from the lantern turned to vapor, an unforeseeable phenomenon, according to the court. It came into contact with the flame of the lantern and exploded. One of the boys was thrown into the manhole as a result of the blast, and sustained serious burns on contact with the rungs of a metal ladder he had to grasp in escaping from the hole. Defendant argued that since what caused plaintiff's harm—the explosion—had been unforeseeable, liability should not attach. Under this analysis, defendant might have created a foreseeable, unreasonable risk of a fire caused by the lanterns, but what caused plaintiff's injury was an unforeseeable explosion. The court rejected this characterization, and in effect treated the case as presenting an

15. [1963] A.C. 837 (House of Lords).

manner-of-occurrence scenario; the harm suffered by plaintiff arose from a foreseeable burning accident that came about in an unanticipated way.

Yet one year later, in *Doughty v. Turner Manufacturing Company, Ltd.*[16] a worker knocked a cover made of asbestos and cement into a vat of 800–degree-C. molten liquid; instead of causing a splash, the cover slid gently beneath the surface; but several minutes later it underwent an unexpected chemical change that produced an eruption, spewing liquid on a bystander. Ruling in defendant's favor, the court found that although scalding by liquid ejected in a splash was foreseeable, scalding by liquid ejected in a volcanic-like eruption could not have been anticipated by defendant. *Hughes* was distinguished on the ground that there plaintiff's burn injuries were of the same kind as defendant might reasonably have anticipated (only the manner of occurrence was unforeseeable), but in the case at bar, the accident was different in kind. This seems a bit of a "stretch," since a splash is a splash is a splash, whether it occurs because of displacement or because of some unforeseeable chemical process.

The criticism that applies here is that judges can manipulate the risk-foreseeability test by delineating risks broadly or narrowly, depending on the result they desire to reach. Under risk-foreseeability, if the court defines hazard broadly, as implicating burn injuries generally in *Hughes* and *Doughty*, plaintiffs' harm in those cases would fall within the scope of liability. On the other hand, if the court

16. [1964] 1 Q.B. 518 (C.A.1963).

defines the risk narrowly as encompassing only burn injuries from explosion or eruption, the harm would fall inside the ambit of liability. To the extent that the risk-foreseeability approach leaves to the discretion of the trial judge whether to adopt a cramped or expansive delineation of the danger created by a defendant, the argument of the critics gains force.

Would the other approaches to proximate cause work any better here? An advantage of duty-risk would be the frank recognition that courts should look carefully at possible policy justifications for defining risks broadly or narrowly in a particular factual context. Requiring courts to articulate policy justifications for their approach to risk characterization would seem clearly superior to an approach that permitted courts to define risks according to unspoken outcome preferences. Hindsight tests based on direct consequences or remoteness would permit plaintiffs to recover in these kinds of factual contexts, but in a mechanical way that ignores the complexities of the issues posed.

Mirror-Image Cases. The scenario under discussion might also include cases where courts have denied recovery for harms caused by certain additional risks even though defendant's careless conduct foreseeably generated them. Suppose that a plaintiff suffers purely emotional or financial harm as a result of negligence on the part of a defendant whose carelessness threatened the plaintiff with physical injury. Under some circumstances a defendant might have foreseen causing mental distress to the person such conduct directly put at risk, even though no bodily harm resulted; or careless conduct that threatens to destroy business premises might foreseeably cause the owners to suffer a loss of future business opportunities. Might a judgment for defendant in these kinds of suits properly rest on a determination that the emotional distress or monetary loss was not within the scope of liability to be imposed as a result of his substandard conduct?

The risk-foreseeability test would not always support a denial of liability, since under the circumstances a defendant might reasonably have foreseen a risk of purely emotional or purely economic harm. The various hindsight tests would similarly produce outcomes that varied, depending on case-specific findings of directness, proximity in place or time, unbroken sequences or fundamental fairness.

In order to achieve consistent, principled results, courts would need to decide these cases not by asking whether defendant might have foreseen the harm, or whether defendant's conduct was a proximate cause of the harm, but rather whether the duty of reasonable care actors owe to persons who might foreseeably suffer harm if the obligation is breached extends to purely emotional or purely financial harm. General considerations of policy would furnish bases for the formulation of general rules applicable to all defendants and framed in either absolute or conditional terms.

A complicating factor would be the infliction of emotional distress or financial loss on someone other than the direct victim of defendant's careless conduct. For example, plaintiff may be a bystander who suffers shock as a result of witnessing an accident in which the negligence of defendant causes severe injury to plaintiff's spouse or child. Or defendant's carelessness causes the destruction of harbor facilities that inflict financial detriment on business that ship their goods through the port. I shall discuss these variations in the context of the persons-at-risk scenario later in this Chapter.

The Multiple–Foreseeable–Risk Variation. A defendant's conduct might create several distinct types of foreseeable risk. One or more might be unreasonable, while the other or others might be reasonable. The favorite hypothetical here involves a defendant who hands a loaded gun to a child.[17] This clearly creates an unreasonable risk that the child might accidentally discharge the weapon and injure himself or another. But suppose instead the child drops the gun and it breaks his toe. If a heavy gun was placed in the hands of a child of tender years, the risk of harm from dropping the object might also make it unreasonable to give it to the child. But what about the sturdy child who receives a handgun from defendant and drops it on his foot? To complicate matters and raise once again the issue of consistency of results, add the fact that the gun not only fractures the child's toe but it also goes off on impact with the floor and injures a bystander.

17. This hypothetical dates back at least to 2 AMERICAN LAW INSTITUTE, RESTATEMENT, TORTS § 281 cmt. e (1934).

Under a risk-foreseeability analysis, it could be argued that the chance of injury to the child's toe was not within the scope of the risks that would make it unreasonable to give a loaded gun to a child, but the danger of some kind of accidental discharge was; therefore, the child could not recover for the toe injury, but the bystander could recover for the bullet wound. This result could be justified in efficiency terms by positing that the threat of liability for concussive injuries from the dropping of the gun would provide no additional deterrence in this scenario, because the risk of being held responsible for a shooting injury should be enough to make defendant refrain from presenting a loaded weapon to a child. A logical corollary here would be that if a defendant's unitary conduct created several distinct risks that might cause distinctive harms, and none of these risks when considered individually might be found unreasonable but when weighed collectively the cost of the accidents they might cause exceeds the cost of avoidance, the scope of liability should include harm sustained as a result of any one of those risks, in order to create the proper level of deterrence.

Moreover, the child and the bystander do not seem so similarly situated, with respect to the risks involved, that to award damages to the one but not the other might create the impression of unequal treatment before the law. In other words, tort law might justifiably protect the interests of the bystander in not being shot by guns carelessly entrusted to children, but might justifiably not want to protect the interests of young children in not being hurt by dropping on their toes objects that one might reasonably expect they could carry.

Interestingly, in a debate of the advisors to the Reporter of the first Restatement of Torts, Judge Cardozo argued that the defendant in this very hypothetical should be liable for the foot injury. He urged that children and loaded weapons are a dangerous mix, and that once a defendant has been careless enough to let a child have a loaded gun, he should be liable for "any injury caused thereby."[18] Is is possible to square Cardozo's position here with his opinion in *Palsgraf*? He seems to be not only embracing the *Polemis* rule but even going beyond it, by suggesting that defendants who hand children loaded weapons should be liable for all harm that results, whether or not directly inflicted!

One factual distinction that separates the hypothetical and *Polemis* is that in the latter the risk of an explosion was deemed to have been totally unforeseeable. In the gun case the risk of harm from impact with the weapon was foreseeable but not unreasonable (so that where defendant has given the unloaded gun to a sturdy child, he might not be liable if she dropped it on her toe).

Another distinctive feature of the hypothetical is the extreme danger created by handing a loaded gun to a child, and the probable lack of any social utility in such conduct. This could have been what motivated Cardozo's comment. If so, he might have

18. *See* ANDREW L. KAUFMAN, CARDOZO 289 (1998).

been implicitly classifying defendant's action as gross negligence or recklessness, in which case the normal rules limiting liability might not apply. Or he might have meant that in light of the extreme danger involved in this situation and the because of imperfections of the Hand formula in providing appropriate levels of deterrence, even reasonable risks should fall within the scope of risks for which a defendant might be held liable. Note that it would be easier to justify this conclusion by using the duty-risk test, in that a court could rely on policy factors (such as deterrence) for extending the scope of liability to include low-level risks.

How would the hindsight tests apply to the gun scenario? As has been noted, the injury to the child was a direct result of defendant's ill-considered action, which would therefore be a proximate cause of the harm under the *Polemis* test. No remoteness in either time or space separates the gift of the gun from the harm. Arguably as a matter of fairness, "rough justice" and "practical politics," a defendant who commits such a careless act should be held liable for all harm closely connected to the act, or at least the court should let the jury make this determination.

The Persons-at-Risk Scenario

Suppose defendant injures someone of whose presence he was unaware and whom he could not have discovered in the exercise of due care. The notion that liability should attach here would seem to smack of unreason. Courts might deny recovery in such cases by one of two routes. First, they might rule that defendants owe no duty to unknown and unknowable plaintiffs. Secondly, they might find as a matter of law that defendant did not breach any duty of due care, if defendant could not have foreseen harm to anyone.

The key point here is that defendants would have no way to calculate ahead of time what precautions would constitute reasonably sufficient care for the protection of unknown persons, inasmuch as the quantum of preventive action varies in accordance with the quantum of risk of which defendant was or should have been aware. If defendant has no knowledge that his conduct might put anyone at risk, imposing liability would not serve as an effective deterrent, since defendant would not know how much precaution to exercise.

Note that defendant might not be aware of a victim's identity, but might still know that someone might face hazards generated by his conduct, as in the case of defendants whose actions or omissions in manufacturing products might put a range of future consumers, users and bystanders at risk. Indeed, some potential victims might not even be alive at the time of the careless conduct, but they still might fall within the range of foreseeable risk.[19]

19. *See* Jorgensen v. Meade Johnson Labs., Inc., 483 F.2d 237 (10th Cir.1973); Renslow v. Mennonite Hosp., 67 Ill.2d 348, 10 Ill.Dec. 484, 367 N.E.2d 1250 (1977); *contra*, Albala v. City of New York, 54 N.Y.2d 269, 445 N.Y.S.2d 108, 429 N.E.2d 786 (1981).

Moreover, courts might easily embrace as virtually omnipresent the chance that somebody might always turn up within the ambit of risk created by defendant's allegedly risky conduct—which would in effect eliminate foreseeability as a liability-limiting factor. One finds an example of this expansive view in *Fuentes v. Consolidated Rail Corporation*,[20] in which railroad employees failed to exercise due care in operating a train at night in a litter-strewn area of the South Bronx, and it struck against a stack of radiators behind which a homeless person was sleeping. Utilizing what amounted to a risk-foreseeability approach, the court held that whether the victim's injuries were a foreseeable consequence of the crew's negligence was for the jury; the finders of fact might conclude that the employees should have anticipated the risk that unless they took reasonable precautions, they might injure someone, since this was an area known to be frequented by the homeless and other passers-by. Thus, if defendant could have anticipated the presence of homeless persons who might be put at risk if the train hit some large objects, the fact that the actual victim happened to be sleeping behind objects hit by the train would be at worst an unforeseeable manner of occurrence, which would not relieve defendant of liability.

The Unknown–Other–Person Variant. A variation of the unforeseeably-present-plaintiff scenario involves cases in which a defendant carelessly puts one person at risk, but in fact injures someone else,

20. 789 F.Supp. 638 (S.D.N.Y.1992) (applying New York law).

or carelessly injures one person and in addition injures someone else, and the presence of the second person in both instances was unknown and unknowable to him. The rule of transferred intent applicable in intentional-tort cases holds that if a defendant intends to inflict harm on Alpha but instead injures Bravo, Bravo will be able to recover even though defendant could not have known of his presence.[21] The degree of defendant's culpability serves as a rationale for imposing liability on an intentional tortfeasor in this context. Where a defendant, without any excuse, tries to inflict physical harm on another, to hold him liable for injuries to unforeseeably present persons would not seem to place an unjust and disproportionate burden on him, especially when the victims are innocent bystanders.[22] But where defendant is merely careless toward foreseeable victims, should courts permit the unforeseeable victim to recover?

One argument against imposing liability here would be that to do so would not necessarily make potential defendants more careful, since they already have a duty to use reasonable care to protect the potential victims of whom they are or should be aware. In addition, they would not know how much additional care they should exercise for the benefit of unknown persons.

On the other hand, plaintiffs could make a strong fairness argument, to the effect that to award dam-

21. *See* W. PAGE KEETON ET AL., PROSSER AND KEETON ON THE LAW OF TORTS § 8, at 37–39 (5th ed. 1984).

22. For more discussion of the issue, *see* Ch. 5 *infra*.

ages to foreseeably present victims but not to unknown victims, especially where the exact same unreasonable conduct directly inflicted harm on both sets of victims, would be unjust.

While cases involving truly unknown and unknowable plaintiffs are rare, one situation that has a potential for recurrence involves the "flying pedestrian," the unfortunate intermediary struck by a carelessly operated vehicle, train or other instrumentality and rendered airborne, coming to rest only after impact with plaintiff-bystander, who might not have been foreseeably within the zone of danger. Applying risk-foreseeability, one could argue that when careless conduct foreseeably unleashes physical forces, the author of the conduct should anticipate that they might impact injuriously on anyone who might turn out to be within range. Thus, if a negligently operated train strikes a person unlucky enough to be in its way, as a matter of physics the collision will transfer a certain amount of energy to the object collided with, and whatever further damage results from the transfer should fall within the scope of defendant's liability. Here, the foreseeability inquiry should focus not on the presence of plaintiff but on the conversion of physical force. This would differ from a hindsight test based on directness, in that under risk-foreseeability, plaintiff would need to prove that defendant should have foreseen his conduct would produce the type of force that caused the harm, while a directness test would not require that defendant should have anticipated the particular kind of force that his conduct unleashed (as in *Polemis*, where defendant was held liable even though its employees could not have foreseen that the dropping of the plank would spark an explosion).

A hindsight test based on directness, as has just been noted, would also support a judgment in favor of the unknown plaintiff, since the harm inflicted was an immediate and direct consequence of defendant's carelessness. Moreover, notions of fairness and "rough justice" might also support compensating the innocent victim suffering a traumatic injury from forces unleashed by defendant and not yet coming to rest.

Duty-risk could likewise produce the same result, since a court might find that the scope of the duty owed by someone carelessly operating moving machinery extends not only to persons who might sustain injury upon impact with the machine, but also by anyone who might be struck by a person or thing set in motion by the collision.

Unknown-Kind-of-Damage Variant. Suppose defendant's conduct was careless because it risked property damage, and it not only damages property but also impacts it in a way that sends it in motion, with resulting injury to a plaintiff whose presence was unforeseeable. For example, the court might have concluded in *Fuentes* that there was no way the railroad workers might have detected the presence of a sleeping person, but that they had created an unreasonable and foreseeable risk of property damage when they let the train hit the stack of radiators. This would be a legitimate unforeseeable-plaintiff case, complicated by defendant's carelessness toward the integrity of the property of another.

Imposing liability here might not produce any meaningful deterrence, since defendant's duty to avoid property damage should be a sufficient inducement for the adoption of appropriate accident-avoidance measures. Moreover, the degree and nature of the culpability demonstrated by a failure to use due care for the protection of one person's property might not equal the blameworthiness we might attach to subjecting another person whose presence was undiscoverable to the risk of bodily harm. For that reason, a court might not want to extend liability to injuries inflicted on the undetected plaintiff.

These would be reasons why a court in a risk-foreseeability jurisdiction might insist that if liability for personal injuries is to be imposed, plaintiff must show that defendant should have foreseen risk to a human being. Thus, what would make the conduct of the railroad's employees potentially negligent was only the foreseeable risk that if they did not proceed with care, they might cause property damage. Injury to an unseen and unexpected person would fall outside the scope of this risk.

On the other hand, a court using a hindsight approach might conclude that plaintiff's injury resulted directly from a force set in motion by defendant's conduct, and therefore was a proximate consequence of that conduct, even though the consequence could not have been foreseen. The Supreme Court of Alabama took this approach in concluding that when defendant's train struck a cow on the tracks and hurled it through the air so that it bounced once and then hit plaintiff, an unforeseeable trespasser on defendant's right of way, the operation of the train might be found to have been a proximate cause of plaintiff's injuries.[23]

The Rescue Doctrine. A classic recurring scenario in which courts have been willing to extend the scope of liability to cover more persons than those immediately put at risk or injured by a defendant's negligence has inspired the so-called "rescue doctrine." The cases have consistently held that the duty of a defendant to use due care not to threaten or injure others extends to third persons who might suffer harm if they came to the aid of a person threatened or injured by defendant's substandard conduct.[24] The rule requires that there be an emergency, in the sense that the victim is in need of immediate help, so that if the risk of harm has abated, an injured plaintiff would not be allowed to recover.[25] In the case giving rise to the doctrine, Cardozo noted in dictum that the rescuer might recover whether or not defendant could have fore-

23. However, the court also concluded that hitting the cow under the circumstances was not a breach of any duty of care owed by defendant to the owner of the cow. Alabama G. S. R. Co. v. Chapman, 80 Ala. 615, 2 So. 738 (1887).

24. *See* W. PAGE KEETON ET AL., *supra* note 21, § 44, at 307–09.

25. For a case applying this gloss in a case involving the rescue of property, *see* Kiamas v. Mon–Kota, Inc., 196 Mont. 357, 639 P.2d 1155 (1982).

seen his presence,[26] a possibility we might exemplify with the far-fetched hypothetical of the hermit suffering injuries in an effort to rescue the occupants of an airplane that crashed in a remote and apparently uninhabited desert because of some negligence on the part of defendant. For Cardozo, the rescue doctrine would apply regardless of the foreseeability of the rescuer, which means that juries would not need to decide, on a case-by-case basis, whether defendant might have anticipated the intervention of the specific rescuer. Defendant would owe a duty to any rescuer, and might escape liability, in whole or in part, only under the doctrine of contributory or comparative negligence, if he could prove that the rescuer did not act as a reasonably prudent person under similar (emergency) circumstances.

The risk-foreseeability approach to rescue seems to emerge from the assumption that basic human urges make it highly likely that a rescuer will intervene. However, one can construct a continuum here, whereby the rescuer may or may not have a pre-existing relationship with the individual in need of help, and the decision to render assistance may be instinctive or deliberate. It is strongly foreseeable that someone who is a relative of the person in peril will make an impulsive rescue. At the other end of the spectrum is the total stranger who has time to make a considered choice about whether or not to intervene. Cardozo's noted rescue opinion contains another dictum relevant here, to the effect

26. Wagner v. International Ry. Co., 232 N.Y. 176, 180, 133 N.E. 437, 438 (1921).

that "The law does not discriminate between the rescuer oblivious of peril and the one who counts the cost. It is enough that the act, whether impulsive or deliberate, is the child of the occasion."[27]

Duty-risk has the advantage of permitting judges not only to take into account the general proposition that danger will invite rescue, but also the social utility of establishing incentives for rescue over and above the intangible rewards to be derived from altruistic activities. Thus, the possibility of recovering damages against the tortfeasor in the event of injury during the rescue might provide some enhanced degree of encouragement for would-be Good Samaritans, who are generally under no duty to go to the aid of strangers in peril. On the other hand, formulating a proposition permitting rescuers to recover would seem to contradict the essence of the test, at least as conceived by Leon Green, since it would require the judicial adoption of a general rule that would have to apply in all rescue cases.

If a person injured while performing the rescue of a third person falls within the scope of the risks created by a defendant whose carelessness made the intervention necessary, how should courts resolve the cases of a rescuer injured when the defendant's carelessness put himself, rather than a third party, at risk? or of a rescuer injured while trying to save defendant's or a third party's property threatened with destruction because of defendant's negligence? or the would-be rescuer who runs in the direction of

27. 232 N.Y. at 181, 133 N.E. at 438.

an accident and slips on a patch of ice (so that his injury occurs before he can begin a rescue attempt)?[28] or the person injured in an auto accident as he was taking to a hospital a companion injured because of defendant's carelessness?[29] or the mother who donates her kidney to a son whose need for an organ replacement resulted from negligent medical treatment?[30] or the bizarre scenario in which a rescuer removes two occupants from a vehicle set afire in an accident caused by defendant; he returns to the car to fetch a mat to use as a pillow for the head of one of the injured victims, and finds a pistol lying on it; removing the weapon, he hands the it to the other victim, whom, unbeknownst to plaintiff, has become temporarily deranged by the accident, and proceeds to shoot plaintiff in the leg.[31] These fact patterns, inviting efforts to expand the boundaries of the rescue doctrine and raising the issue of when, if ever, courts might logically cut off a rescuer's liability, illuminate the "slippery-slope" phenomenon, since it might be easy to justify a slight increment in the scope of the doctrine, but at the same time it might be difficult to justify the general proposition that there should be no limits at all on a rescuer's right to recover.

28. *See* Lambert v. Parrish, 467 N.E.2d 791 (Ind.Ct.App. 1984).

29. *See* Day v. Waffle House, Inc., 743 P.2d 1111 (Okla.Ct. App.1987).

30. *See* Sirianni v. Anna, 55 Misc.2d 553, 285 N.Y.S.2d 709 (1967).

31. These facts are taken from Lynch v. Fisher, 34 So.2d 513 (La.Ct.App.1947).

Risk-foreseeability does not seem to provide an adequate mechanism for determining extent of liability in these cases, since a jury might find that none of these scenarios falls outside the bounds of reasonable anticipation. If a tortfeasor might foresee risk to a rescuer when he carelessly puts a third person in danger, he certainly ought to foresee risk to a rescuer when he carelessly puts himself in danger. If a tortfeasor might foresee risk to a rescuer when he puts a third person or himself in danger, he certainly ought to foresee danger to a rescuer when he carelessly puts valuable property in danger of destruction. This mode of analysis would take us even as far as the case of the kidney donation, for which the tortfeasor might be liable to the donor, since in this age of advanced medical technology, organ transplants to save the lives of seriously injured persons have become increasingly commonplace.

Because it allows courts to consider more than just reasonable anticipation, the duty-risk approach would appear to have an advantage over risk-foreseeability in these cases. If the purpose of the rescue doctrine is to encourage humanitarian efforts to preserve life, it surely ought to apply to situations in which a defendant negligently (or even intentionally) put himself in peril. Moreover, a would-be rescuer might have no way of knowing whether a person was in a position of danger because of her own fault or that of another, so it would make little sense to apply the rescue doctrine in one case but not the other.

The Good Samaritan who intervenes in an effort to save valuable property from destruction presents a slightly more difficult case. Here, humanitarian instincts do not usually come into play, and hence the foreseeability factor is much less pronounced. However, courts may conclude that there is sufficient social utility in reasonable rescue attempts to warrant a rule that will furnish an incentive to undertake them, and may therefore permit property salvagers to recover.[32] The latter's legal obligation not to subject themselves to unreasonable risks of harm would operate as a limitation on the scope of liability.

Is there any valid reason to distinguish between, on the one hand, the rescuer injured in the throes of an effort to protect a victim from harm or to help a victim who has just suffered injuries, and on the other hand a would-be rescuer hurt en route to the scene of an accident? There may be cause-in-fact issue in the latter cases, depending on the identity of the rescuer and the time and place of his injury. In other words, it might not always be clear that plaintiff was really on his way to a rescue when he suffered harm. Should the fact that a proof problem relating to actual cause might arise in some cases weigh so heavily as to justify judicial limitation of the rescue doctrine to injuries suffered at the scene of the original accident during a rescue? Risk-foreseeability does not address this concern. Injuries to a would-be rescuer on the way to the scene of an

32. Some courts have taken this position. *See* W. PAGE KEETON ET AL., *supra* note 21, § 44, at 308.

accident might be as foreseeable as injuries during an actual rescue attempt. Duty-risk allows courts to take into account the administrative difficulties in proving cause-in-fact, and to balance them against the potential lessening of rescue incentives that a cramped version of the rescue doctrine might produce.

The accident-on-the-way-to-the-hospital case presents a similar extension problem, but without the potential cause-in-fact issue. Hence, the reasons favoring liability when a would-be Good Samaritan is hurt on the way to a rescue would similarly support an award of damages here. In addition, if, as I shall point out in the next Chapter, the primary-accident victim also suffered harm in the same mishap, he would be able to recover against the original tortfeasor whose negligence put him in a position of vulnerability. If the original accident made it reasonably necessary for a Good Samaritan to accompany the victim to the hospital, denying recovery to the Samaritan would seem to make little sense.

The kidney-donation case brings to center stage an altruist who has a close family relationship with the primary victim of defendant's negligence, and who acted not instinctively, but rather after careful deliberation and with full awareness of the consequences of her act. She loses a vital organ, and thereby becomes susceptible to future harm. Should these factors remove her from the embrace of the rescue doctrine?

If foreseeability alone determined extent of liability, what could be more predictable than a parent's unconditional willingness to donate a vital organ to a child in desperate need? Yet this is also not a garden-variety rescue situation. In the latter, the rescuer takes a chance; here, plaintiff knew exactly what harm she would incur when she made the decision to give up one of her kidneys. Moreover, in the usual case the rescuer suffers harm as a direct and immediate consequence of defendant's threatening conduct; here, the defendant's negligence had already inflicted harm on the primary victim. Finally, organ-donation cases are apt to arise often (but not necessarily always) in the medical-malpractice context.

The foregoing strongly suggests that courts ought to use the duty-risk approach in these kinds of cases. Judges need to address policy considerations such as the extent of potential liability that judgments in favor of organ donors might impose on medical-care providers, whether there is any need of a rule that would create incentives for organ donations in these situations (since humanitarian considerations would presumably provide sufficient motivation for close relatives), and the difficulty in making assessments of the damages suffered by the donor. Moreover, defendants will want to raise the argument that the issue is unsuitable for judicial determination, and therefore should be left for legislative resolution. Additionally, the need to draw principled limitations on liability requires a close look at whether it is proper for courts to treat medical-care providers more leniently than other defendants (such as pharmaceutical companies) whose negligence might necessitate donations to keep victims alive; whether it makes any sense to emphasize the conscious choice of the organ donor as a reason *not* to impose liability, when an ordinary rescuer who has time to think about what to do, decides to intervene and suffers harm *may* recover damages; and whether one can justify holding defendants liable for organ donations but not for a generous third party's donation of services or money.[33]

Finally, how should courts deal with rescuers who suffer injuries in freakish ways? The case of the plaintiff who artlessly hands a pistol to the person he has just pulled from a car wreck and for his efforts takes a bullet in the leg due to the momentary befuddlement of the victim illustrates nicely how the scenarios can overlap, inasmuch as one could classify what occurred as involving persons at risk, an unusual (to say the least) manner of occurrence, a different risk and a risk created by an injury to another. Plaintiff here would be a classic rescuer, caught up in a bizarre sequence of events, injured by a risk that might (or might not) have been different from the dangers unleashed by defendant's careless driving, and shot by a person whose confused mental state was a direct result of defendant's culpable conduct. I shall consider here all but

33. For cases denying recovery to organ donors, *see* Moore v. Shah, 90 A.D.2d 389, 458 N.Y.S.2d 33 (1982); Sirianni v. Anna, 55 Misc.2d 553, 285 N.Y.S.2d 709 (1967).

the last scenario, which will be the subject of discussion later in this Chapter.

The risk-foreseeability approach would clearly place plaintiff within the protection of the rescue doctrine. However, defendant might argue that the risks that made his driving negligent did not include the possibility of a deliberate (or even accidental) shooting. Depending on the geographical location of the accident, plaintiff might counter by insisting that the presence of firearms in motor vehicles was not uncommon, and their discharge after an accident was within the range of reasonable anticipation. Moreover, the increasingly widespread phenomenon of "road rage" nudges toward, if not into, the ambit of foreseeable risk the danger of violent conflict during highway travel.[34] It is perhaps more likely that the court's decision would turn on how it defines the risks of poor driving. If they encompass only the usual range of traumatic injuries associated with highway accidents and their normal sequelae, a shooting at the hands of a mentally confused crash victim would not appear on the list. On the other hand, if the court takes an expansive view of driving risks, they might embrace any traumatic injuries directly resulting from a collision or its immediate aftermath.

Note how the latter designation takes on characteristics of a hindsight test, which might turn on

34. *Contra* Bansasine v. Bodell, 927 P.2d 675 (Utah Ct.App. 1996) (driver firing gun into defendant's car not a foreseeable result of defendant's rude driving, and hence not proximate cause of passenger's death).

whether or not the shooting was a direct or immediate consequence of defendant's negligence. Another hindsight option would ask whether the manner of occurrence was so strange that it would be unfair to hold defendant liable.[35] On the other hand, does it not seem even more unfair to let the loss fall on the rescuer, and relieve the wrongdoer of liability, especially if the court determines that plaintiff's action in handing the gun to the accident victim was not unreasonable? In addition, as an administrative matter, by what principle might a court decide that the manner of occurrence was *so* outlandish that a careless defendant should not be responsible for the resulting harm? It would seem more appropriate, if a decision is to turn on gut feelings about fairness, to let jurors bring to bear the sense of the community on this question, especially in cases involving fact patterns that are not likely to repeat themselves.

Mirror-Image Cases. The flip side of the unforeseeably-present-plaintiff issue arises when an individual's presence might have been anticipated, but courts nonetheless refuse to include the harm inflicted within the scope of defendant's liability, often because of finding that defendant owed no duty to plaintiff. One example of this has given rise to the so-called "firefighter's rule," under which a defendant whose carelessness results in the setting of a fire will not be liable to firefighters injured in

[35]. *See* CLARENCE MORRIS & C. ROBERT MORRIS, JR., MORRIS ON TORTS 164–66 (2d ed. 1980).

an effort to extinguish the blaze,[36] even though few eventualities are less foreseeable than the presence of professional firefighters at a fire. The most logical justification for restricting the scope of liability here lies in policy reasons that might underlie a determination that tortfeasors creating rescue situations owe no duty to firefighters (or other public employees) whose presence is necessitated by defendants' careless conduct. The reasons include the fact that the firefighter's job is to fight fires, whether negligently set or not, and that tax-supported compensation and benefit programs available to firefighters provide a more appropriate way of compensating these public employees for fire-related injuries.

Policy reasons might also justify placing other classes of foreseeable plaintiffs on the far side of the ambit of liability. Recall two kinds of cases already discussed as part of the unforeseeable-risk, mirror-image scenario, involving emotional distress and financial loss. Suppose that this type of harm results when defendant allegedly breaches a duty of due care owed to a third person. A bystander suffers shock at seeing someone suffer serious harm because of defendant's carelessness; or a business suffers a loss of economic advantage as a result of property damage defendant inflicts on a third person's premises or transport facilities.

If a court decides, after weighing appropriate policy factors, not to award damages when plaintiff is a primary or direct victim of defendant's negli-

36. *See* DAN B. DOBBS, *supra* note 12, § 285 at 769–72 (2000).

gence, it would seem to follow as a matter of common sense and simple justice that secondary or indirect victims should not be permitted to recover. On the other hand, where courts have held that primary or direct victims might be able to recover for emotional distress or financial losses, there may be additional policy reasons that would justify turning away secondary or indirect victims. For example, the possibility that large numbers of people might foreseeably suffer emotional distress when they witness a horrible accident, or might foreseeably sustain financial loss from the destruction of property or transportation facilities might cut in favor of restricting defendant's liability. The availability of more efficient compensation mechanisms might also support a denial of liability in the financial-loss cases. A court might achieve such outcomes either by adopting a general no-duty rule,[37] or by recognizing a duty but limiting its scope by imposing the need for a more particularized finding of foreseeability.[38]

The Accidental-Self-Injury Scenario

A defendant's unduly risky activity may be a cause-in-fact of an injury that plaintiff accidentally brings on himself while trying to avoid harm threatened by defendant's original conduct. Suppose, for example, that defendant negligently causes the out-

37. *See* Barber Lines A/S v. M/V Donau Maru, 764 F.2d 50 (1st Cir.1985).

38. *See, e.g.,* Thing v. La Chusa, 48 Cal.3d 644, 257 Cal.Rptr. 865, 771 P.2d 814 (1989) (bystander emotional distress); People Express Airlines, Inc. v. Consolidated Rail Corp., 100 N.J. 246, 495 A.2d 107 (1985) (pure economic loss).

break of a fire that spreads toward a tank car delivering gasoline to a filling station; people begin to shout warnings; plaintiff, in a café across the street from the station, hears the cries, gathers up her child and hastens to leave the premises; in so doing, she trips over a chair and breaks a leg.[39]

Accidental Self–Injury and Risk–Foreseeability. Under the risk-foreseeability test, the factfinder might reasonably conclude that a defendant who creates an unreasonable risk of an explosion in a populated area might anticipate the possibility that some people might injure themselves in frantic efforts to escape from the ambit of danger. Any harm sustained in this manner might thereby fall within the scope of defendant's liability. Where a plaintiff's own carelessness may have contributed to the injury, defendant may raise the complete defense of contributory negligence, or the partial defense of comparative fault, depending on the jurisdiction.

The justification for extending liability to this type of risk is similar to the rationale that supports holding defendants liable in the unexpectedly-serious-harm scenario. Relieving wrongdoers from responsibility for the foreseeable consequences of their conduct, no matter how slight the possibility of actual harm might be, would reduce below an optimal level incentives to exercise care to avoid harm. This reasoning would support holding a defendant liable for the remotely foreseeable chance

39. These facts drew inspiration from Mauney v. Gulf Refining Co., 193 Miss. 421, 9 So.2d 780 (1942).

that a potential victim might accidentally hurt herself trying to avoid harm, to the same extent that it would justify holding defendant liable for the remotely foreseeable chance that a potential victim might be a hemophiliac.

Once again, the plasticity of the risk-foreseeability test manifests itself, since imposing liability requires a finding that defendant might have anticipated merely the general hazard that a person put at risk by defendant's careless conduct might suffer injury in an attempt to escape the risk, and not the specific risk (such as tripping over a chair) that in fact materialized. In this sense, the accidental-self-injury cases implicate an approach suggested for the unforeseeable-manner-of-occurrence scenario, where the impossibility of anticipating the exact way an injury came about might not insulate a defendant from liability, if a general risk of injury fell within the bounds of reasonable foreseeability.[40]

On the other hand, since accidental self-injuries might occur in a wide variety of factual contexts that might situate themselves at a considerable distance or time from defendant's careless conduct, defendants may argue that at some point their potential liability should terminate, even though their breach of duty might have been a but-for cause of the harm.

The risk-foreseeability test might leave it to the fact-finder to decide whether defendant could or should have anticipated the self-injury—not its spe-

40. *But see id.* (defendant not liable for harm resulting from remote possibility that plaintiff might trip over chair).

cific details, but rather the general circumstances under which it occurred (such as escape attempts in the immediate wake of the creation of a risk of explosion by defendant). This might produce uneven results, as well as uncertainty about how far a defendant's liability might extend in these types of cases.

Accidental Self–Injury and Duty–Risk. The duty-risk-approach would assign to the trial judge the task of determining how far defendant's responsibility should extend. In situations where the accidental self-injury was far removed from defendant's carelessness, the judge could in theory take policy factors into account, but it is not entirely clear what they might be. In the absence of relevant considerations of policy, fundamental fairness might serve as the most appropriate standard, which would in effect amount to a hindsight test based on justice and common sense. This in turn would raise the basic question whether trial judges or juries are better suited to make these kinds of decisions. As with risk-foreseeability, results would be unpredictable. However, if resolutions are to be *ad hoc*, it would seem preferable to base them on fairness grounds, rather than on manipulated findings of foreseeability.

Accidental Self–Injury and Hindsight. Hindsight tests based on directness or immediacy might exonerate defendants where the accidental self-injury was removed in time or space from the alleged careless conduct. Some courts might find the harm was "too remote" from the carelessness, although what they really mean is that under all the circumstances it would not be fair to hold defendant liable. If so, it would be preferable for them to talk in fairness rather than terms connoting time or distance. The basis for decision here would be identical to the criterion used under duty-risk. Again, there might be disagreement as to whether the trial judge or the jury should make the determination.

Subsequent Self–Injury. Plaintiff may have already suffered harm at the hands of a negligent defendant when he does something to aggravate his injury. For example, plaintiff has a broken leg, and while walking with crutches he falls and re-fractures it. The defendant responsible for the original break might assert as a defense the doctrine of avoidable consequences, which obliges us to use due care to minimize the effects of harm inflicted on us by a negligent defendant.[41] Hence, if plaintiff had been using the crutches carelessly and as a result toppled to the ground and aggravated his injuries, he would not be able to recover for the worsening of his condition (or he might be able to recover only in part, if the court applied comparative-fault principles).

But suppose plaintiff was acting with due care for his own safety when he slipped, and his fall was caused at least in part by his disabled condition. Such accidents might easily fall within the ambit of reasonable foreseeability. Indeed, courts in risk-foreseeability jurisdictions might conclude that reasonable minds could not differ on this point. Alter-

   41. *See* W. PAGE KEETON ET AL., *supra* note 21, § 65, at 458–59.

natively, the duty-risk test might reach the same result by positing that considerations of fundamental fairness and the policy of deterrence support the imposition of liability for accidents which occur during the healing process and which happen because of plaintiff's disability.

A more difficult case arises when the accident permanently disables plaintiff, and some considerable time afterward plaintiff injures herself in a manner that might be linked to her condition. Here, because of the passage of time, a finding of factual causation might be problematic. Moreover, courts might feel that the ambit of defendant's liability should have some limits. Hence, it is probable that a line might be drawn on the basis of pragmatic or commonsense considerations.

The Suicide Cases. Suppose that a defendant's careless conduct causes a person to take his own life. A legitimate extent-of-liability issue arises when the victim suffers actual harm that is so excruciating and prolonged that he takes his own life. Uncomfortable because of the lack of scientific knowledge about why people kill themselves and reflecting contemporary attitudes about the immorality of suicide, the first judges who had to resolve the issue tended to deny recovery for wrongful death, occasionally on the ground that defendant's negligence was not a proximate cause of the act of self-destruction. As understanding of the etiology of suicide increased, some courts began to impose liability where there was persuasive medical testimony that defendant's careless conduct was a contributing cause of the suicide and decedent killed himself because of an uncontrollable impulse, or did not understand the nature of his act.[42] Evidence of the latter would tend to support expert opinion about the cause of the suicide, and hence courts felt comfortable about sending the issue to the jury.

Suicide and Risk–Foreseeability. The risk-foreseeability test would not seem suitable here, since a defendant would have no way of anticipating whether and how a victim of his careless conduct might take her own life. Nor would hindsight tests work well in this context, because they would produce varying results based on case-specific findings of directness, immediacy or fairness. Duty-risk would be the most logical approach, but only if it recognized a general rule that the scope of a defendant's duty to protect others from unreasonable risks of physical harm extended to acts of self-destruction caused by such harm and perpetrated by an uncontrollable impulse or under circumstances where the victim did not comprehend the nature of her act.

Note that scope of liability is really not at issue where because of a pre-existing relationship or otherwise defendant has a duty of due care to protect an individual from harming himself. Here suicide would be the result of the very risk that made defendant's act or omission a breach of duty. Thus, courts have held mental institutions liable for fail-

42. *See* Victor E. Schwartz, *Civil Liability for Causing Suicide: A Synthesis of Law and Psychiatry*, 24 VAND. L. REV. 217 (1971).

ing to take reasonable precautions to prevent mentally unstable patients from taking their own lives.[43] On the other hand, the duty of an attorney to use due care in representing a client might not extend to the prevention of suicide by a client wrongfully convicted because of his lawyer's alleged negligence, a result supported by policy reasons such as a desire not to discourage attorneys from representing depressed or otherwise unstable clients.[44]

The Risk-or-Injury-to-Another Scenario

Defendant's carelessness might put at risk or injure a person who then injures plaintiff because of that injury or risk. We have already considered, under the unforeseeable-risk scenario, the fact pattern in which the victim of an automobile accident caused by defendant's careless driving becomes temporarily delirious and shoots a rescuer. A less problematic variant would involve an accident victim who becomes violent because of the pain he is suffering and lashes out blindly at a bystander, who suffers serious bruises as a result. By drawing an analogy to the suicide cases, courts might easily rule that defendant's liability should extend to the bystander's injuries if the third party acted in response to an uncontrollable impulse or did not understand what he was doing. In such a situation, what the primary victim did would be no different

43. *See id.* at 245–51.

44. *See* McLaughlin v. Sullivan, 123 N.H. 335, 461 A.2d 123 (1983); *see also* Cleveland v. Rotman, 297 F.3d 569 (7th Cir.2002) (tax attorney who gave decedent erroneous advice not liable for decedent's subsequent suicide).

from an explosion caused by defendant's negligence, or even a bite by a dog riding in the car and so terrified by the accident that it attacked plaintiff when he opened the door to the vehicle. In each of these instances, defendant unleashed a physical agency that inflicted harm on plaintiff.

A more difficult variant would arise if the injury to the third person did not result in harm to plaintiff for a considerable time. Suppose defendant negligently drives his automobile into a child, who suffers brain damage as a result; seven years later, the child shoots plaintiff, who alleges a cause-in-fact relationship between his injuries and the original accident.[45] Here, there would be an obvious cause-in-fact problem, and plaintiff would have to adduce sufficient evidence from which a jury could reasonably find that the original crash caused the brain damage, and the brain damage made the child shoot plaintiff.

The risk-foreseeability test provides no better answer here than in the case of the shooting of the rescuer. Indeed, in the New York decision involving the child with brain damage, the court gave a perfunctory tip of its cap to *Palsgraf* when it noted that the risk of shooting seven years after the original accident was not within the range of reasonable anticipation, but went on to emphasize that considerations of public policy and common sense dictated the conclusion that the shooting was too

[45]. *See* Firman v. Sacia, 7 A.D.2d 579, 184 N.Y.S.2d 945 (1959).

remote from defendant's careless conduct.[46]

Once again, duty-risk might provide a superior mechanism for resolving such cases, because it forthrightly encourages judges to take into account policy considerations. A court could find that the difficulties of establishing cause-in-fact in a particular case involving a third party who inflicts injury long after defendant's conduct had its impact justified a denial of liability. Thus, this would be a practical reason for limiting defendant's responsibility.

46. *Id.*

Chapter 4

Into the Crucible—Part II

Thus far we have considered instances of a single actor's careless conduct creating one or more risks to one or more persons: a failure to use due care brings about more harm than defendant might reasonably have expected, or foreseeable harm in an unexpected way, or a type of risk different from what he might reasonably have contemplated, or harm to a person whose presence he could not possibly have foreseen. Moreover, in each of these scenarios defendant's carelessness set in motion a force that was the sole cause of plaintiff's harm. We have also seen cases where a force generated by defendant affected plaintiff or a third party in a way that caused plaintiff to injure himself or the third party to inflict harm on plaintiff. In those situations we might view plaintiffs or the third parties as involuntary agents of defendants.

Now we take up the factually distinct issue whether to extend a defendant's liability to harm caused in part by forces generated by other persons or natural elements and interposing themselves between conduct potentially amounting to a breach of duty on defendant's part and the damage sustained by plaintiff. Our basic fact pattern involving the careless spillage of gasoline demonstrates that the intervention immediately precipitating the infliction of harm might be human or non-human in origin, and in the case of the former might amount to innocent, negligent, intentionally harmful, or even criminal conduct. Both defendant's act or omission and the intervention qualify as causes-in-fact of the injury, in that plaintiff would not have suffered harm in the absence of one or the other. The basic question to be resolved is whether the intervention should cut off, or supersede, defendant's liability, so that only a responsible third party might be liable to plaintiff, or whether the court should hold defendant and the third party jointly and severally (or proportionately) liable for the harm (or, in the case of non-human interventions, whether defendant should be totally responsible). I shall also analyze the issues that arise when the intervenor is not a third party, but rather the plaintiff himself or herself.

After distinguishing the invention and manner-of-occurrence scenarios, and after clarifying the relationship between duty and proximate cause in the intervention scenarios, I shall consider first the carrier whose carelessness causes a delay in the shipment of plaintiff's goods, and during the period of delay a storm destroys them. This will enable us to view the intervention issue in the context of a potentially recurring fact pattern rather than a happening unlikely to repeat itself, and to lay out some of the basic considerations that might help courts decide how far to extend a defendant's liability for harm to which an intervening act or force contributed. We shall then look at the rest of Chapter One's negligent-spillage hypotheticals and a host of related problems that implicate human intervenors.

Manner-of-Occurrence Scenario Distinguished. Recall that in my treatment of manner-of-occurrence cases in Chapter Three, I limited discussion to situations where harm was caused only by forces set in motion by defendant's careless conduct, and put aside for the moment consideration of cases where intervening acts or forces combined with defendant's prior negligence to cause harm. We saw there that the courts usually hold that even though an accident happens in an unanticipated way, defendant will still be liable if the injury was within the type of harms the risk created by defendant was likely to produce. However, where harm results from an unanticipated intervention, the courts, as we shall see, have been receptive to defense arguments that such an intervention should supersede defendant's liability.

There are several possible explanations for these different outcomes. In the first group of cases, an unbroken sequence linked defendant's carelessness with plaintiff's injury, while in the second a force generated by the intervenor interrupted the sequence. This would furnish a historical explanation for the divergent results, since courts were traditionally willing to impose liability when harm was a direct consequence of defendant's negligence, even though the linkage between the tortious conduct and the harm might have been unusual or even bizarre.

In addition, the first group involves situations where defendant should have foreseen that her carelessness might hurt someone like plaintiff, and it did, albeit in an unforeseeably strange way. In the second, defendant should have anticipated that her carelessness might hurt someone, but it took the unforeseeable intervention of another to supply an essential impetus that produced the harmful result.

Finally, there might be an efficiency-based explanation, in that relieving defendant of liability and placing it on the intervenor might conceivably create a more effective or less costly incentive for the latter to take precautionary measures to protect potential victims. Note, however, that this reasoning might shift liability to the intervenor even where defendant might have foreseen the intervention.

Duty vs. Proximate Cause. A defendant's act or omission might foreseeably bring into being the specific risk that plaintiff might suffer harm as a result of exposure to hazards created by acts or omissions of third parties, or by non-human interventions. If a court determines that the purpose of the legal duty owed by defendant to plaintiff is to protect plaintiff from these very risks and if the finder of fact concludes that defendant breached that duty, with resulting harm to plaintiff, logic mandates that there should be no need to make a separate finding of proximate cause, since defendant inflicted (or failed to prevent) the very kind of damage the recognition of the duty was meant to prevent. By resolving the duty issue, the court would have explicitly or implicitly indicated how far defendant's obligation should extend.

Thus, if a court holds that a tavern owner has a duty to use due care not to serve liquor to minors because they might operate a motor vehicle under the influence of alcoholic beverages and create risks of serious injury to third persons, the purpose of the duty is to protect the public at large from the risk of negligent or reckless driving by minors. Hence, there should be no need, in a suit by an injured third person against the tavern owner, for the court also to consider whether the negligence of the latter would be a proximate cause of plaintiff's harm, or whether the negligent driving of the minor would supersede defendant's liability. However, early cases took this position,[1] apparently because of a belief that criminal misconduct (*e.g.*, drunk driving) lies beyond the pale of reasonable expectation, a notion that would seem to fly in the face of human experience.[2] The more sensible approach, taken by many courts today, would be for the judge to ask whether the tavern owner, in serving an under-age patron, owed a duty to potential victims of a minor who became inebriated after having been served by defendant and as a result drove in an erratic and

1. *See, e.g.*, King v. Henkie, 80 Ala. 505 (1886). For a recent decision in accord, *see* Milligan v. County Line Liquor, Inc., 289 Ark. 129, 709 S.W.2d 409 (1986).

2. *See* Dan B. Dobbs, The Law of Torts § 190, at 471–72 (2000).

dangerous way, and if so, for the jury to consider, if reasonable minds might differ on the point, whether the tavern owner acted unreasonably under the circumstances, and whether such careless conduct was a cause-in-fact of plaintiff's injury.[3]

Similarly, a judge might rule that a manufacturer had a duty to provide reasonable warnings that reached the users of a product; the manufacturer might contend that it discharged its duty by providing warnings to an intermediary on whom it might justifiably rely to communicate the warnings to the actual users or consumers of the product; and a jury might find that under the circumstances the manufacturer should have foreseen that the intermediary might neglect to pass along the warnings, that the manufacturer might reasonably have inscribed cautionary language on the product itself, and that such an inscription would have prevented the injury.[4] In such a case the court does not need to consider, as a separate issue, whether the intermediary's careless failure to warn should supersede the manufacturer's liability for not inscribing the warnings (*i.e.*, whether the manufacturer's negligence was a proximate cause of the injury), since the jury's findings determined the matter of extent of liability.

Resolution of the duty issue in this way does not mean, however, that proximate cause will never be

3. For the pioneer decision imposing this kind of liability on a tavern owner, *see* Rappaport v. Nichols, 31 N.J. 188, 156 A.2d 1 (1959).

4. *See* AMERICAN LAW INSTITUTE, RESTATEMENT THIRD, TORTS: PRODUCTS LIABILITY § 2 cmt. i, at 29–30 (1998).

a disputed matter in intervention cases. The duty imposed by the court might oblige defendant to protect plaintiff from certain kinds of specific risks, but plaintiff might have suffered harm from different risks generated by the intervening act or force. This question would arise if defendant carelessly served intoxicating beverages to a customer and the customer subsequently committed an assault and battery on plaintiff. The duty imposed on vendors of alcoholic beverages might not extend to the protection of members of the public from risks other than negligent or reckless driving.[5]

Moreover, defendant's duty to plaintiff might be less precise in definition, such as would be the case with the general obligation to use due care imposed on transporters of flammable liquids in order to reduce or eliminate the range of risks that spillage might trigger. A court might then have to decide whether defendant's duty would extend to ignition of the liquid by natural forces, or by innocent, careless or malicious acts of a third party, and would need to apply one of the tests for proximate cause.

Non-Human Interventions

A defendant's negligent conduct might cause a plaintiff to be vulnerable to harm from the risk of acts of God (subsequent adverse natural events[6]) or

5. *See, e.g.*, Phan Son Van v. Peña, 990 S.W.2d 751 (Tex. 1999) (convenience store that sold alcohol to underage gang members not liable for subsequent rapes they committed while intoxicated).

6. This is the definition of act of God as adopted in the new Restatement of Torts. *See* AMERICAN LAW INSTITUTE, RESTATEMENT the actions of animals that inflict injury on her or damage her property. This conduct might put plaintiff in a location at a particular moment when the natural event sets in motion the forces that harm plaintiff, or it might make plaintiff particularly susceptible to or unable to protect herself from adverse natural phenomena or the harmful actions of an animal. The risk that the natural event might occur or that the animal might be present may or may not have been foreseeable to a reasonable person in defendant's shoes. Under which combination of these circumstances might non-human interventions relieve defendant of liability?

The Negligent–Delay-in-Shipment-of-Goods Cases. It is useful to begin with fact pattern capable of recurrence, that of carelessness on the part of a common carrier, which delays the shipment of plaintiff's goods while they are in transit, and as a result a flood destroys them.[7] Plaintiff argues that the delay was unreasonable, and that if defendant had not been careless, the goods would not have been in a position to be swept away by the rising waters; thus, both defendant's negligence and the flood were causes-in-fact of her loss. Defendant counters by insisting that the occurrence of the flood should sever its responsibility to plaintiff.

Is there really a proximate-cause issue here? To answer this question, we must inquire into the

THIRD, TORTS: LIABILITY FOR PHYSICAL HARM (BASIC PRINCIPLES) § 3 cmt. l (Tentative Draft No. 1, March 28, 2001).

7. Inspiration here comes from the facts in Green–Wheeler Shoe Co. v. Chicago, Rock Island & Pacific Ry., 130 Iowa 123, 106 N.W. 498 (1906).

nature of the duty of due care owed by defendant to plaintiff. If the specific purpose of imposing the obligation on the carrier was to protect goods in transit from the risks of particular natural disasters known to threaten shipments over the route taken and at the time of carriage, then clearly defendant should be liable if goods are destroyed or damages by one of these calamitous events. Hence, if the flooding at the place where it occurred was a normal, known hazard at a particular time, and if the goods would have avoided the risk if defendant had shipped them without a negligent delay, plaintiff should be allowed to recover damages on proof that defendant breached its duty to use ordinary care if the court finds that the shipper's obligations explicitly or implicitly encompassed protecting the goods from that very risk. What made defendant's conduct unreasonable was the fact that it subjected plaintiff's property to flooding, a foreseeable risk that would have been avoided if defendant had taken proper precautions. It should not be necessary even to think about proximate cause.

Negligent Delay and Risk–Foreseeability. As a matter of substance, risk-foreseeability analysis would posit that if possible loss in transit as a result of natural disaster was a foreseeable risk of delay and the delay was unreasonable at least in part because it subjected the goods to that risk, the carrier should be liable. Thus, if the flood was a normal hazard at the time when and the place where it occurred, plaintiff might recover damages. The court could reach this result as a matter of process by ruling that defendant had a duty to protect plaintiff from this expected hazard, or that the failure to take steps to protect the goods from this known danger amounted to unreasonable (*i.e.*, negligent) conduct, or that defendant's conduct was a proximate cause of damage resulting from a foreseeable risk.

Negligent Delay and Duty–Risk. Duty-risk might call for the same analysis and result, but it would also allow courts to consider on which party the risk of such losses ought to fall in a case where plaintiff and defendant stood in a contractual relationship that could very easily have specified which of them should bear the burden of purchasing insurance against natural hazards. The issue, of course, would be one of duty, but more broadly viewed than under risk-foreseeability. A court could consider the relative merits and disadvantages of first-party property insurance, which would cost the owner of shipped goods more if the carrier were not held liable for natural-hazard loss caused by negligent delay in transit, and would not require expensive litigation to determine responsibility, as compared to third-party liability insurance, which would cost the carrier more if the courts held them liable for negligent delays resulting in damage from acts of God, and thus might act as an incentive for careful conduct. The court could then fashion a rule that would encourage the purchase of the type of insurance deemed appropriate in this situation.

Suppose that the natural disaster was extraordinary and completely unanticipated, a once-in-a-life-time occurrence. Under the analysis suggested above, a risk-foreseeability court might find for defendant. A duty-risk court might extend its policy analysis to determine where the risk of unexpected loss should fall as between parties in a business relationship.

Plaintiff might argue here that the negligent delay made her goods vulnerable to any number of increased risks, since a journey of six days that becomes a journey of ten days because of a shipper's negligence exposes the goods to four additional days during which something—anything—might go wrong. The problem with this position is that it might make defendant liable for any loss occasioned by any sort of intervention, since if plaintiff's goods had not been where they were when they were, they would not have been damaged or lost. In order to recover, all plaintiff would have to prove is cause-in-fact, and defendant would be responsible for loss from *any* adverse happening—a falling meteor, a drunk driver, whatever—once plaintiff could establish that careless conduct on the part of a defendant put plaintiff in harm's way.

Since life is full of risks that are omnipresent and ubiquitous, merely shifting goods from one place to another or from one time frame to another might not in and of itself increase the hazards of everyday life. The same analysis could apply to instances of negligent interventions. Thus, a defendant whose carelessness blocks one avenue of transit and causes motorists to detour might not have exposed plaintiff to any increased highway risks when she took another route because of the obstruction and in so doing suffered injuries in a collision with a negligent driver. Hence, it seems inconceivable that a court would impose liability on a defendant whose carelessness did not increase plaintiff's exposure to risks that threaten anyone similarly situated.

But plaintiff in our negligent-delay case would stress that by keeping her goods in transit for several extra days defendant did in fact increase the possibility that her goods might suffer damage from some human or non-human intervention, and that any reasonable shipper should have known this. A court might respond by pointing out that the increased danger from the general risks that confront all of us was so infinitesimal that a prudent defendant might not take them into account in determining how much precaution to take.

Negligent Delay and Hindsight. How would a hindsight approach deal with these problems? When an adverse natural event intervenes between a defendant's carelessness and plaintiff's injury, by definition the latter is not a direct consequence of the former, and it may not be an immediate consequence either, depending on how literally one defines immediacy. (The same conceptual problem would arise in the case of third-party human intervenors.)

But courts using *Polemis* to hold that a defendant might be liable for the direct consequences of a careless act even though a reasonable person could not have anticipated those consequences are not necessarily postulating that a defendant can never be liable for the *indirect* consequences of a careless act. *Polemis* does not have to be the exclusive test for proximate cause or extent of liability. Courts could easily posit that a defendant might always be liable for direct consequences of a careless act whether or not it had been foreseeable, but would be liable for indirect consequences only if they could have been anticipated, which means that courts in a single jurisdiction would be using a hindsight for certain kinds of scope-of-liability issues, and the substance of the risk-foreseeability test for others.

Another hindsight approach would require struggling with the elusive distinction between causes and conditions, so that if defendant's negligence is deemed a mere condition and the intervening acts a cause, defendant would not be liable.[8] But it is not clear what this distinction means. If a "condition" is not a "cause" and defendant's conduct is deemed to have been a "condition" only, this would seem to be the equivalent of saying that the injury would still have occurred even if defendant had not been careless, and therefore the court could decide the case more properly and easily on cause-in-fact grounds.

As one commentator has observed, courts using the cause-vs.-condition test seldom define what they

---

8. For a trenchant criticism of the distinction, *see* 4 FOWLER V. HARPER, FLEMING JAMES, JR. & OSCAR S. GRAY, THE LAW OF TORTS § 20.6, at 172–74 (2d Ed. 1986); *see also* Jeremiah Smith, *Legal Cause in Actions of Tort*, 25 HARV. L. REV. 103, 110–11 (1911), reprinted in HARVARD LAW SCHOOL ASS'N, SELECTED ESSAYS IN THE LAW OF TORTS 649, 656–57 (1924).

mean by those terms, and often use them "to justify a judgment for defendant that is really thought valid on other grounds."[9] If these grounds amount to policy-oriented determinations, a sounder approach would be for courts to use the duty-risk approach and articulate clearly and fully the basis for their decisions.

The Negligent–Spillage Scenario. What about intervening adverse natural events that harm a plaintiff who does not have any pre-existing business relationship with defendant? Here we might look at our negligent-spillage hypothetical, in which defendant carelessly causes a quantity of highly flammable gasoline to spill. Before he can undertake any clean-up process or engage in any other precautionary measures, a force not controlled by or connected with him in any way—such as a bolt of lightning—ignites the liquid, and plaintiff, an innocent bystander, suffers serious injuries.

The *raison d'être* for the exercise of care in the transportation of gasoline derives from its combustibility. Causing it to escape its confines creates a risk that it might be ignited, with disastrous consequences to anyone unfortunate enough to be within the zone of danger. Thus, using either risk-foreseeability or duty-risk, a court might conclude that defendant should be liable whatever the cause of ignition might have been. The latter test would invoke the desirability of deterring a significant degree and amount of risk as a policy justification

9. Osborne M. Reynolds, Jr., *Proximate Cause—What If the Scales Fell in Oklahoma?*, 28 OKLA. L. REV. 722, 738 (1975).

for imposing liability, while the former might allow a court to posit that if defendant creates an unreasonable risk of ignition by failing to use due care, the way the spilled gasoline ignited should not be relevant—in other words, fact-of-occurrence trumps manner-of-occurrence. Hence, whether or not the lightning that sparked the disaster was or should have been foreseeable to defendant would not be in issue.

Extraordinary Natural Interventions. Courts have seemed somewhat reluctant to take this position, which would place no limits on the extent of defendant's liability. An early case using the traditional "natural-and-probable-consequences" hindsight test contains language suggesting that the "extraordinary manifestation of natural forces" might supersede defendant's responsibility in this type of case.[10] A workable distinction here might be between ignition by contact with a flaming meteor (an "extraordinary" event), and ignition by contact with lightning (not "extraordinary"), even if no lightning had ever before struck in the vicinity of the spillage.

How, then, might the courts deal with the hypothetical, loosely inspired by Alfred Hitchcock's classic film *The Birds*, of the avian that dropped a lighted cigarette into a pool of spilled gasoline? This would seem to be an extraordinary event of the first magnitude, and hence a potentially superseding cause under the test mentioned above. However,

10. Johnson v. Kosmos Portland Cement Co., 64 F.2d 193, 196 (6th Cir.1933).

two court faced with analogous, and equally mind-boggling fact patterns had no hesitation about imposing liability. No book about proximate cause would be complete without at least a nod to these extraordinary cases.

In *United Novelty Co. v. Daniels*,[11] defendant's employee, a minor, was using a gasoline-based liquid to clean a coin-operated machine in a room warmed by a gas heater with an open flame. The combination proved combustible in a most unimaginable way, as a rat who had been foraging inside the machine became doused with the cleaning fluid, and in the first of a pair of unwise decisions, darted out and sought sanctuary under the heater. This served only to ignite its gasoline-soaked fur, and to cause it to retrace its steps and take refuge back in the machine. The now-flaming rodent's return set the machine ablaze, and the unfortunate employee suffered fatal burns. In affirming a judgment for the deceased's family, the court treated the case as belonging to the manner-of-occurrence scenario, in that defendant, by not enforcing its own safety rules regarding the use of gasoline, and not providing adequate warnings to their young employee, created an unreasonable and foreseeable risk of fire. The agency of ignition, the court noted, was "incidental,"[12] which suggests that once defendant has carelessly spilled a highly flammable liquid, harm caused at least by any accidental ignition source would fall within the ambit of liability.

11. 42 So.2d 395 (Miss.1949).
12. 42 So.2d at 396.

In *Chase v. Washington Water Power Company*,[13] defendant maintained a power line 28 inches from an uninsulated guy wire that ran down the pole holding the line. A barbed wire fence near the pole leaned against the guy wire. In a strange concatenation of circumstances, two chicken hawks engaged in aerial combat above the power line. As the battle raged, their talons became interlocked in a deadly embrace, and they either flew or fell into the gap between the transmission line and the guy wire. One of the hawks touched the line, the other came into contact with the guy wire. Electricity surged from the line through the bodies of the two birds to the guy wire, down the latter and thence along the length of the barbed wire fence, and set fire to the dry grasses surrounding the metal barrier. The blaze destroyed property belonging to plaintiffs.

The Supreme Court of Idaho affirmed a jury verdict for plaintiffs. The majority noted that there was sufficient evidence from which the trier for fact could find that a reasonable power company would have insulated the guy wire or maintained its poles in such a way that barbed wire fences did not touch them. Using the "not-so-highly-extraordinary" test of the *Restatement (Second) of Torts*, as discussed in Chapter Two, the court found that in retrospect, the exact way the electricity went from the power line to the fences could not be considered unforeseeable as a matter of law. (How one can determine foreseeability retrospectively was a problem that did not occur to the court.)

13. 62 Idaho 298, 111 P.2d 872 (1941).

I would argue that the risk-foreseeability approach would have worked better here. The focus would be on the issue of breach. What made the failure to insulate the guy wire or to keep the fence from touching the guy wire unreasonable? A court would have to find that the cost of taking these precautionary measures was less that the cost of potential accidents that might happen if defendant failed to take the measures. In assessing the latter, the court would have to consider the risk that somehow electricity might escape from the power line on contact with the guy wire, and the seriousness of damage that might result. If defendant knew or should have known that this might happen in a variety of ways, the fact that it actually did happen in a freakish way that no one could possibly have predicted would be irrelevant, a point made by a concurring judge. Thus, the analysis used by risk-foreseeability courts dealing with manner-of-occurrence fact patterns would be applicable here as well.

Human Interventions

When a third party commits an intervening act that contributes to the injury suffered by plaintiff, under what circumstances should it supersede the liability of a defendant whose negligence was also a cause-in-fact of the harm? To what extent should the factual circumstances of the case influence its outcome?

The universe of human interventions provoking litigated extent-of-liability issues is vast, perhaps incapable of all-inclusive classification. However, certain characteristics seem to recur. One of the most common involves situations in which a defendant in control of an instrumentality or agency capable of causing harm fails to exercise due care, with the result that a third party has access to the instrumentality or agency and utilizes it in a careless way, with resulting injury to plaintiff. The so-called "key-in-the-ignition" cases, in which a defendant carelessly leaves keys in the ignition of his vehicle and a thief steals it, drives carelessly and causes an accident in which plaintiff is injured, typifies this type of case. In a second, a defendant carelessly does something (or fails to do something) that puts plaintiff in a position of vulnerability, thereby facilitating or permitting the negligent infliction of harm by a third party. A good example here would involve a defendant carelessly injuring a plaintiff who as a result requires hospital treatment and suffers further harm at the hands of a careless health-care provider.

One would expect that under the risk-foreseeability test, liability would turn on whether defendant anticipated, or should have anticipated, the intervening act, a question of fact for the jury unless reasonable minds could not differ. Under duty-risk, the issue would be more complex, involving consideration whether the scope of the duty owed by defendant encompassed the protection of plaintiff against risks of harm at the hands of a negligent third party, and requiring the court to take into account any relevant considerations of policy, morality and practicality, in addition to general foreseeability. Under a hindsight test based on directness or immediacy, there might be serious conceptual difficulties in determining extent of liability, since intervention would seem to obviate a finding that defendant's careless conduct was a direct or immediate cause of plaintiff's injury. A remoteness test might cut off a defendant's liability when the intervention occurred at a place or time far removed from defendant's act or omission. A cause-vs.-condition test might terminate defendant's responsibility on a finding that her unreasonable conduct was merely a condition providing a background for the infliction of harm, whereas the negligence of the intervening third party was the cause of the injury (although the basis for drawing such a distinction remains unclear). A fundamental-fairness test might work well in borderline cases that are not likely to recur. We can test these hypotheses in the context of innocent, negligent and intentionally wrongful intervening acts by third parties.

Innocent Human Interventions. Let us return to our gasoline-spillage hypotheticals and consider the explosion caused by the non-negligent act of a third party, unaware of the risk created by defendant's carelessness. This might happen when a smoker, under the reasonable belief that a puddle of careless spilled gasoline contained only water, throws his cigarette butt into the puddle. Defendant was transporting a dangerous liquid, and by carelessly spilling it created a dangerous situation that became disastrous because of an innocent human intervention. This seems a relatively simple case, at least for the risk-foreseeability and duty-risk tests. The foreseeable danger arising from discharged gasoline is that it might ignite, which is precisely what occurred. The rule that a court might fashion to deal with the case, on the basis of foreseeability of risk as well as the policy of deterring the preventable hazard associated with spilled gasoline, could easily impose liability in the innocent-intervention situation. Fortifying these results would be the fact that the negligent defendant is the only potentially responsible party available to plaintiff, since the intervenor did not breach any duty of due care to plaintiff.

Some hindsight tests, as has been suggested, might not work in the intervention cases. It would be difficult to find for plaintiff here if the court makes liability turn on whether the harm was a direct or immediate consequence of defendant's negligence. However, as has been noted, courts might decide that a test based on directness or immediacy was not the exclusive approach to limiting the scope of liability. A court might try to use the "cause-vs.-condition" distinction to decide the cases, but I have already suggested its elusiveness. Remoteness might be a factor justifying the denial of recovery, but only when considerable time or space separates the intervention from defendant's negligence. However, it would be difficult to craft a principled way to determine how much remoteness would be necessary before the outer limit of liability is reached. Drawing such a line ostensibly based on cause-vs.-condition or remoteness might be a cover for resort to considerations of "practical politics" or a "rough sense of justice," but again the issue whether judges or juries should make such a decision makes its presence felt. For these reasons, courts that in some situations use a hindsight approach switch to risk-foreseeability when an intervention scenario confronts them, and render decisions based on whether or not defendant should have foreseen the intervening innocent act.

Negligent Interventions: In General. In our spillage hypothetical, where a transporter carelessly discharges gasoline and a smoker carelessly ignites it, a party injured by the resulting explosion has the option of suing both. Her claim against the smoker would be uncomplicated, perhaps involving a dispute over whether or not his conduct amounted to a breach of his duty of due care, and in the absence of additional complicating facts should not give rise to an extent-of-liability issue. Her claim against the transporter would require her to establish not only a breach of duty but also that the risks created by the careless transporter were within the scope of the latter's liability, or that the breach was a proximate cause of her harm. The transporter would argue that the carelessness of the smoker should supersede its liability.

If plaintiff succeeds against both, the court will hold them jointly and severally liable, and plaintiff will have the option of satisfying her judgment in full against either defendant or the intervenor, or in part against each. The traditional common-law rule precluded a responsible party from obtaining contribution against the other. This bar against contribution gave way, as a result of decisions at common law or statutory reform, to a rule allowing contribution to be measured *pro rata*, and with the advent of comparative fault most jurisdictions permit allocation of the liability burden on the basis of percentages of negligence.[14]

What all this means is that the extent-of-liability issue will become critical in a real-world sense when plaintiff is not able to recover or collect a judgment against the smoker (or determines that the smoker is not worth suing in the first place). Therefore, if she is to recover any compensation, she must secure a judgment extending the transporter's responsibility to her injuries and imposing joint and several liability. The proximate-cause issue may also be crucial if plaintiff sues only the transporter, which then brings a third-party claim against the negligent smoker, in an effort to shift all or part of the liability burden. I shall discuss at the end of this Chapter the impact the statutory modification or elimination of joint and several liability may have on proximate-cause doctrine in intervention cases.

Negligent Intervention and Deterrence. Thus far, I have suggested as possible outcomes the exoneration of the first wrongdoer, so that plaintiff's only recourse would be against the negligent intervenor, or the imposition of joint and several

14. *See generally* Dan B. Dobbs, *supra* note 2, § 386 at 1078–79.

liability. Is there any argument to be made for exonerating the second wrongdoer?

Under an efficiency-oriented approach to scope of liability, a court might consider adopting a rule that would seek to provide the optimal level of deterrence at a minimal cost.[15] In other words, as between the first actor and the intervenor, liability should fall on the cheaper cost-avoider—the party better positioned to prevent harm at a lower cost. If we assume that a court could make this calculation, the available liability choice would be between the two wrongdoers, so it would be conceivable that only the first tortfeasor might be liable.

What complicates this method of assigning legal responsibility is that it works only when both parties have perfect information. Each would have to know not only what it would cost him to reduce or prevent foreseeable harm, but also what it would cost the other to prevent harm the other could foresee. If the first actor and the intervenor had this information and were aware that the applicable liability rule would make the cheaper cost-avoider liable, whichever of the two was the cheaper cost-avoider would take appropriate deterrent action. The unlikelihood of a perfect-information scenario probably explains why courts have not been tempted to try this approach in negligent-intervention cases. This does not mean, however, that deterrence should not be a factor that judges might take into

15. For an extended economic analysis of scope of liability, *see* Mark F. Grady, *Proximate Cause and the Law of Negligence*, 69 IOWA L. REV. 363 (1984).

account, along with other factors, in determining whether the risk that resulted in harm to plaintiff fell within the scope of the risks defendant was under a legal duty to prevent or minimize.

Negligent Interventions That Defendant Has a Specific Duty to Prevent. As has been suggested earlier in this Chapter, where the legal obligation imposed by the court requires defendant to use due care to protect plaintiff from a specific risk of harm emanating from the conduct of a negligent third party, the duty issue settles the matter of extent of liability. Thus, the purpose of imposing a duty of reasonable care on social hosts not to serve intoxicating beverages to minors at private functions would be to protect the motoring public, pedestrians and even persons near roads and highways from risks of harm that materialize when minors drive under the influence of alcohol. Here the dangerous instrumentality under defendant's control is the alcoholic beverage, which renders an instrumentality under the third party's control—a vehicle—highly dangerous to the traveling public. In dealing with a negligence claim brought against a social host by the victim of the drunken driving on the part of a minor whom defendant served alcoholic beverages, the court determines scope of liability when it decides whether or not to impose the duty, and thereafter should not have to wrestle with proximate cause or scope of liability. The general foreseeability of danger posed by young intoxicated drivers, plus the policy of reducing the toll of highway accidents, would support recognition of the duty, while the burdens such a rule would place on personal autonomy in the private sphere and problems in administering the rule (such as determining what conduct might meet the standard of reasonable care to which social hosts would be held, and the difficulty of proving cause-in-fact) would cut against it. Note that this seems to be a clear example of the strength of the duty-risk approach, which would mandate that courts weigh these various relevant considerations.

Negligent Interventions That Defendant Does Not Have a Specific Duty to Prevent. Our spilled-gasoline hypo represents a more complicated case, since the duty to use due care not to discharge the flammable substance would derive from the wide range of risks that might come into being when gasoline escapes its confines. One way of posing the critical question to be answered is whether the danger of negligent ignition would fall within those risks. Another way of putting it would be to ask whether a conscientious transporter, in deciding what quantum of care to use during shipment, would include in its calculations the possibility that some unknown third party might carelessly ignite gasoline if it spilled.

Note that framing the issue broadly, in terms of negligent ignition, would expand the ambit of liability. At the other end of the spectrum would be a narrow, liability-contracting delineation, asking whether defendant should have foreseen that a third party might carelessly drop a lighted cigarette into the spilled gasoline. Cutting against the latter would be the general proposition, as developed in our discussion of the manner-of-occurrence scenario in Chapter Three, that defendant need not be able to foresee the precise circumstances bringing about the harm in order to be held liable for it.

Negligent Interventions and Risk–Foreseeability. Many jurisdictions resort to the risk-foreseeability test in determining extent of liability in negligent-intervention cases. Perhaps concerned that with the benefit of hindsight some juries might find virtually any intervening occurrence foreseeable, the *Restatement (Second) of Torts* added as an element for consideration that if in retrospect it was extraordinary that the act of a third party intervened and contributed to the infliction of harm, defendant should not be liable.[16] Of course, extraordinary results are normally unforeseeable, so by using this as a gloss on risk-foreseeability judges would have at their disposal an additional tool for removing what they determine to be highly dubious claims from jury consideration.

Whether foreseeability alone is a satisfactory and sufficiently workable test in negligent-intervention (or even innocent-intervention) cases is open to debate. Take, for example, a New York case in which a landlord failed to repair a boiler in an apartment building and thereby breached its duty to tenants to furnish them with an adequate supply of hot water; a tenant heated a pot of water on the kitchen stove and was carrying it to the bathroom

16. *See* 2 AMERICAN LAW INSTITUTE, RESTATEMENT SECOND, TORTS § 442 (b) (1965).

when he spilled the scalding liquid on his infant son. This would exemplify the type of intervention that occurs after defendant's carelessness has made plaintiff vulnerable to harm provoked by the act or omission of a third party. The court denied liability on the ground that the act of the tenant was "unusual or freakish" and hence beyond the bounds of foreseeability as a matter of law, while a dissenting opinion argued that a jury might reasonably have found that failing to use due care to supply tenant with hot water created the foreseeable risk that heated water would be carried to the bathroom and that the person transporting the water might inadvertently spill it on children living in the apartment.[17]

Negligent Interventions and Duty-Risk. Compare the New York court's application of risk-foreseeability with the way duty-risk might have resolved this case. The determinant question would be whether the landlord's duty to supply hot water to its tenants was meant at least in part to protect tenants and their children from the risk of spillage accidents that might occur during the negligent (or even innocent) transport of heated water within the confines of an apartment during periods of time when as a result of the landlord's carelessness an apartment might be without a supply of hot water. The arguable advantage of duty-risk is that it keeps the court's eye on the appropriate ball, the task of determining the scope of a legal obligation, rather

17. Martinez v. Lazaroff, 66 A.D.2d 874, 411 N.Y.S.2d 955 (1978).

than on the somewhat disembodied question whether a particular risk or harm was reasonably foreseeable, and it assigns that task to judges rather than jurors, because the resolution of the issue might require more than just finding that defendant should have anticipated what happened.

The arguable weakness of duty-risk would be that it would require the trial judge in each individual case to make a policy-driven judgment about whether the liability of a landlord should extend to injuries caused by negligent or innocent third parties whom the carelessness of the landlord has placed in a position to inflict harm on plaintiff. The result would depend on the court's assessment of the mix of social, moral and practical concerns that the court finds relevant and applies to the specific factual context. Critics of the duty-risk test would argue that this places too much unbridled authority in judicial hands. The alternative, however, would be to allow each individual case to turn on a finding with respect to foreseeability alone, and judges would have broad authority to decide whether a particular risk was or was not foreseeable as a matter of law.

On the other hand, there are negligent-intervention cases that might lend themselves nicely to resolution under a modified version of duty-risk that imposed liability by creating and applying a general, rather than case-specific, extent-of-liability rule. Situations that are apt to recur would fall into this group. For example, whether a defendant who carelessly injures plaintiff should also be liable for further harm inflicted on plaintiff by a negligent rescuer or when she receives negligent treatment from a health-care provider should arguably not be decided on a case-by-case basis, and should not turn on whether a jury finds that subsequent carelessness was or was not reasonably foreseeable to the tortfeasor whose conduct put plaintiff in a position to suffer further harm, or whether a court determines that a specific defendant's duty in a specific case should extend to protecting plaintiff from the risk of additional injury at the hands of a negligent third party. It would not seem fair to hold some negligent defendants liable for such subsequent injuries, and exonerate others under similar circumstances.

A more logical way of dealing with these cases would be for the courts to decide once and for all whether the scope of a defendant's duty not to subject people to an unreasonable risk of injury embraces the danger that negligence by rescuers, emergency medical personnel (ambulance drivers, for example), and health-care providers might inflict further harm on a plaintiff rendered vulnerable by defendant's negligence. In the latter two types of cases, the fact that most emergency health-care personnel and health-care providers carry liability insurance would be relevant, because an extension of a tortfeasor's duty to cover these kinds of injuries might not saddle potential wrongdoers with the threat of an excessively onerous financial burden. Defendant can join the third party, and under rules of comparative fault would be allowed to share the burden of liability in accordance with the jury's allocation of percentages of fault. The only situation in which the original defendant might have to pay the entire amount of the judgment would be in the event he could not obtain contribution from the third party, in which case the rules of joint and several liability might require him to bear the entire economic burden. Thus, defining the duty to include injuries inflicted by careless emergency medical personnel and health-care providers merely assures innocent victims that they will receive full compensation for their injuries.

The rule suggested here might distinguish between vulnerability to risks greater in degree than those to which members of the public are ordinarily subjected to, and the general hazards we all face. Thus, the risks of injury at the hands of a careless rescuer, and of careless treatment by health-care providers, would be much more serious than those that members of the population confront in their ordinary lives, as would the perils of highway accidents resulting from high-speed emergency trips to a medical-care facility. On the other hand, harm suffered when an airplane crashes into a hospital where plaintiff has been interned as a result of defendant's negligence would fall outside the scope of defendant's liability because confinement in a hospital ordinarily does not increase the risk of harm from falling airplanes (depending, of course, on the location of the hospital).

A defendant's careless conduct might make plaintiff vulnerable to third-party negligence in other contexts that might also suggest the appropriateness of using a similar general rule to resolve the extent-of-liability issue. For example, defendant might heedlessly obstruct a public roadway, and the blockage might expose plaintiff to risks of third-party negligence that inflicted harm on her. One way to decide such cases would be to adopt and apply a rule imposing liability when defendant's carelessness exposed plaintiff to special or extra risks generated by the negligence of others. Thus, if plaintiff merely had to take an alternative route to avoid the obstruction, a collision between his vehicle and that of an inadvertent third party would qualify as an ordinary risk of highway travel, and faced equally by other members of the traveling public. Hence, defendant would not be liable for causing plaintiff to be in the wrong place at the wrong time. But if the obstruction forced plaintiff to leave the relative safety of his automobile and made her particularly vulnerable to risks of harm because of the location, weather or time of day, it might be appropriate to hold defendant liable for injuries that resulted directly from the negligent driving of a third party.[18]

The facts of *Ventricelli v. Kinney System Rent a Car, Inc.*[19] help illustrate the point. Defendant, a

18. For a decision refusing to imposing liability in this kind of case because defendant's negligence was merely a "condition" or "occasion" and not a "proximate cause" of plaintiff's injuries, *see* Kopriva v. Union Pac. R. Co., 592 P.2d 711 (Wyo.1979).

19. 45 N.Y.2d 950, 411 N.Y.S.2d 555, 383 N.E.2d 1149, *modified,* 46 N.Y.2d 770, 413 N.Y.S.2d 655, 386 N.E.2d 263 (1978).

rental agency, supplied plaintiff with an automobile with a defective trunk lid. Plaintiff parked the vehicle on a street, and while he was attempting to fix the problem, a driver who had parked several car lengths behind carelessly caused his automobile to lurch forward and strike plaintiff. In denying liability, the New York Court of Appeals pointed out that the same misfortune might have befallen plaintiff if he had been loading or unloading the trunk. Thus, what caused the accident was an ordinary risk that anyone making normal use of the street might have had to confront. On the other hand, suppose plaintiff had been on a busy freeway when the trunk flew open because of the defect and obstructed his visibility; he stopped on the shoulder and got out of the car in an effort to secure the lid; and a negligently operated vehicle hit him. Here, defendant's negligence would have exposed him to a highly hazardous situation, and one might plausibly conclude that the rental agency ought to be at least partially responsible.

Gazing, Janus-like, in the direction of both the majority and dissenting opinions in *Palsgraf*, the court in *Ventricelli* found that the happening of the accident as a result of a vehicle defect was not "foreseeable" as a matter of law, and that considerations of convenience, public policy and a "rough sense of justice" would not justify the imposition of liability on defendant. However, the concept of foreseeability seems overworked to the point of meaninglessness in this context, since the careless operation of motor vehicles is one of the true constants in our modern motorized society. Policy and fairness considerations might acceptably justify the general rule I have suggested, but the court seemed to be using the terms as standards by which to determine the liability of the individual defendant. As a matter of administrative convenience, it would appear preferable to decide this issue consistently, rather than to weigh considerations of process, policy and justice afresh on the facts of each individual case.

Negligent Interventions: Key-in-the-Ignition Cases. A recurring negligent-intervention scenario involves the defendant who leaves keys in the ignition of a vehicle, or who otherwise fails to secure it from unauthorized use; a third party seizes the opportunity created by defendant's heedlessness, steals the vehicle, drives it carelessly and injures plaintiff.[20] Defendants in the cases are usually owners or authorized users of the stolen vehicles, but they might also be car dealers or valet-parking services. Note the unique factual aspect here—the need for the third party to commit two intervening acts, (1) the theft of the vehicle, and (2) negligent operation that resulted in harm to someone on or near the roadway.

A further complicating factor is that, depending on the criminal law of the jurisdiction, plaintiff may be able to assert, in addition to a common-law count alleging breach of duty, a negligence *per se* claim. The latter would depend on proof that defendant violated a statute making it illegal to abandon a

20. For an illustrative decision, *see* McClenahan v. Cooley, 806 S.W.2d 767 (Tenn.1991).

vehicle with keys left in the ignition. Negligence *per se* requires a judicial determination that one of the purposes of the statute was to protect a class of victims to which plaintiff belonged, from risks caused by the careless driving of a vehicle thief. If so, then the unexcused violation of the statute would in and of itself amount to a breach of duty. Note the similarity between a negligence *per se* analysis and the duty-risk approach to a common-law claim. Duty-risk would require a court to decide whether it should burden drivers or others in control of vehicles with the duty to use due care not to facilitate the unauthorized use of the vehicle by leaving keys in the ignition, for the protection of anyone whom the careless driving of an unauthorized user might put at risk.

An interesting issue that arises at this point relates to the extent of the benefits that accrue from recognition of the duty. Might a court properly take into account statistics about the incidence of car thefts when keys have been left in the ignition, and the rate of accidents involving stolen vehicles? These would be so-called legislative or policy facts, bearing on the desirability of creating a rule of law (or recognition of a duty) and brought to the court's attention by judicial notice (as opposed to adjudicative facts, which the parties must allege and introduce at trial in order to establish the elements of plaintiff's case and any defenses asserted by defendant).[21] The argument in favor of considering these

21. For debate on the propriety of using such statistics in a key-in-the-ignition case, *see* Cruz v. Middlekauff Lincoln–Mercu-

kinds of statistics is that they bear upon the social costs exacted by a particular type of vehicle-related carelessness and presumably susceptible to reduction through the incentives a liability rule would create.

A court that imposed a duty in a key-in-the-ignition case would next have to focus its attention on breach. At this point the specific facts of the case would be relevant, since plaintiff would have to prove that by leaving keys in the ignition, defendant engaged in conduct that fell below the standard of reasonable care under the circumstances. It is at this point that foreseeability comes into play, as the finder of fact would have to determine whether a reasonable person in defendant's shoes should have anticipated that someone might steal the vehicle if keys were left in the ignition. Courts have considered, as bearing on proof of foreseeability, the time and place where defendant left the vehicle, the kind of people known to frequent the area, how long the vehicle was left unattended, and whether the model, age and condition of the vehicle was likely to attract unauthorized users.[22]

More problematic is whether defendant should have foreseen that a thief would drive the vehicle negligently. If defendant should have anticipated that teenagers might take the car for a "joy ride"

ry, Inc., 909 P.2d 1252 (Utah 1996); *see also* Cornelius J. Peck, *An Exercise Based on Empirical Data: Liability for Harm Caused by Stolen Automobiles*, 1969 WIS. L. REV. 909.

22. *See, e.g.,* Hosking v. Robles, 98 Cal.App.3d 98, 159 Cal. Rptr. 369 (1979); Smith v. Shaffer, 395 N.W.2d 853 (Iowa 1986).

(because, for example, defendant left the car near a high school on a weekday afternoon), then careless driving could easily be found to lurk within the ambit of foreseeable risk. If defendant should have anticipated that a professional thief might take advantage of the presence of the keys (because, for example, the vehicle was especially valuable), it would seem likely, on the one hand, that the thief would drive carefully to avoid detection, but on the other hand would drive recklessly if discovered and pursued by the police. Note that statistics about thefts of vehicles with keys left in the ignition and accidents resulting from car thefts would not seem to be relevant to the breach-of-duty issue, which requires consideration of what a specific defendant should have foreseen at a particular place and time.

Suppose the car thief intentionally harms a police officer in the immediate aftermath of the theft. A court would need to decide whether a rule intended to protect against traffic accidents caused by third parties who steal vehicles with keys left in their ignitions was also meant to protect law-enforcement officials who attempted to apprehend them. Risk-foreseeability would be problematic here, since efforts to resist arrest would not seem to lie beyond the range of reasonable anticipation. A New Jersey court wrestling with this issue affirmed a summary judgment for defendant, on the dubious ground that as a matter of law such an assault could not have been foreseen.[23] However, an alternative basis for the decision was that as a matter of policy individu-

23. Berko v. Freda, 172 N.J.Super. 436, 412 A.2d 821 (1980).

als whose careless conduct facilitates the commission of a crime owe no duty to police officers injured in attempting to apprehend the perpetrator, perhaps because it would be overly burdensome to impose this kind of liability on members of the public, and the salaries and benefits received by law-enforcement officers reflect the increased risks of their job and thereby provide a basis for allocating loss that is superior to tort liability. This would bring the decision in line with the "firefighter's rule," noted in the discussion of liability to rescuers in Chapter Three, and would amount to duty-risk in action.

The hindsight tests would not seem to work well in key-in-the-ignition cases, except that if the traffic accident caused by the thief occurs long after or at a considerable distance from the spot where defendant left the vehicle, courts might resort to the type of analysis, described above, that seeks to distinguish ordinary risks from special or increased risks generated by defendant's negligence. Thus, if the exigencies of escape have passed and the thief is going about his normal activities, damage produced by his careless driving should fall outside the ambit of defendant's liability.

Some courts might succumb to the temptation to use the remoteness test in these kinds of cases, but query whether remoteness *per se* should suffice as a standard here. If the thief is 100 miles from the spot of the original theft and local police, informed of his crime, discover his presence and give chase, a court might properly find that injuries suffered by third parties as a result of the negligent driving of the thief were within the scope of defendant's responsibility.

Intervention by Inaction. Thus far, we have seen extent-of-liability issues arising when the *conduct* of a third party intervenes between defendant's carelessness and the infliction of harm on plaintiff. Indeed, the word "intervention" connotes the act of intervening. But consider a factual variant involving a third party who by doing nothing *fails to perform* a duty owed to plaintiff and thereby contributes to the harm that plaintiff suffers. *Petition of Kinsman Transit Company*[24] suggests an example, the failure of employees to raise the drawbridge over the Buffalo River, despite timely warning by the Coast Guard, with the result that the unmanned vessels collided with the structure and caused a bridge tower to topple in a way that inflicted personal injuries and property damage. It would seem an orgy of illogic for courts were to extend liability to the owner of the first ship if the employees raised the bridge before the vessels arrived but did so in a careless way, with the result that it fell and blocked their passage, but to deny liability if the employees simply failed to raise the span when they had ample time to do so.[25] Hence, it would make eminent sense for courts to treat intervention by negligent inaction no differently from active negligent interventions.

24. 338 F.2d 708 (2d Cir. 1964).

25. *See* 4 Fowler V. Harper, Fleming James, Jr. & Oscar S. Gray, The Law of Torts § 20.5 at 161 (2d ed. 1986).

Plaintiff as Intervenor. I have excluded from the intervention scenario cases in which it was the plaintiff's carelessness that intervened between defendant's negligent act and the infliction of harm, and the conduct of both parties qualified as causes-in-fact of the injury. Some courts apply proximate-cause principles here, which means that plaintiff's negligence might operate as a complete bar to recovery if the court determines that it superseded defendant's negligence (in other words, that defendant's conduct was not a proximate cause of the harm).[26]

Note that in a contributory-negligence jurisdiction a court could reach the same result by invoking the doctrine of contributory fault. However, in a comparative-negligence jurisdiction, a great deal will turn on which approach the court chooses, since plaintiff will recover nothing if the court treats his careless conduct as a superseding cause, but will recover a percentage of his monetary damages if the court treats his careless conduct as comparative negligence.

Note also the problem facing plaintiffs if courts first ask whether their carelessness is a superseding cause relieving defendant of liability, and secondly, if plaintiff's negligence is deemed not to cut off defendant's liability under proximate-cause principles, they apply the doctrine of contributory or

26. *See generally* Christopher Dove, Note, *Dumb as a Matter of Law: The "Superseding Cause" Modification of Comparative Negligence*, 79 Tex. L. Rev. 493 (2000).

comparative fault.[27] In a jurisdiction that still recognizes contributory negligence as a complete defense, defendant would have two strings to his defensive bow—first, the argument that his negligence was not the proximate cause of plaintiff's injury, and then the assertion that plaintiff's contributory fault should act as a total bar to recovery. However, in a comparative-negligence jurisdiction, plaintiff will be able to obtain a partial recovery in situations in which proximate-cause principles do not cut off defendant's liability, since the court will treat her subsequent negligence as a form of comparative fault.

In cases involving interventions by plaintiffs, an alternative approach would be to abandon proximate cause and to apply comparative-fault doctrine exclusively. A "what's-good-for-the-goose" argument here might invoke the analogy of the fate of the last-clear-chance rule after the adoption of comparative-fault principles. Under last-clear-chance, plaintiff's careless conduct would not operate as a bar to liability under contributory negligence if defendant had an opportunity to avoid the accident subsequent to the breach of the obligation of self-protection on plaintiff's part. The rule modified the perceived harshness of "all-or-nothing" contributory fault by treating defendant's subsequent negligence as superseding plaintiff's carelessness. However, recognition of comparative fault brought with it a consensus that courts should abolish last-clear-

27. For a recent decision adopting this position, *see* Torres v. El Paso Elec. Co., 127 N.M. 729, 987 P.2d 386 (1999).

chance, and that the negligence of plaintiff and the subsequent negligence of defendant should fall within the ambit of comparative-negligence principles, so that plaintiff might receive a partial rather than a full recovery.[28] Thus, the lure of logic would fortify the suggestion that in the reverse of the last-clear-chance situation, where it is the negligence of plaintiff that comes into play after defendant has acted carelessly and where the activities of both are causes-in-fact of plaintiff's injury, comparative fault should trump proximate cause, just as it has trumped last-clear-chance.

On the other hand, such treatment of plaintiff's negligence might produce inequitable results. Suppose two hypothetical cases in which defendant performs the same careless act; in the first, plaintiff also acts carelessly, in a way no one could have foreseen, and in the second, it is a third person who intervenes carelessly and defendant could not have anticipated the intervention; in both cases the conduct of each party contributes to plaintiff's injury. In a comparative-negligence jurisdiction treating negligent interventions of plaintiffs as a form of comparative fault, a plaintiff whose negligence could not have been anticipated would still be able to obtain a partial recovery from defendant. But a blameless plaintiff injured by the carelessness of defendant and the unforeseeable intervening negli-

28. *See, e.g.,* Sumpter v. City of Moulton, 519 N.W.2d 427 (Iowa Ct.App.1994). *See, generally,* VICTOR E. SCHWARTZ, COMPARATIVE NEGLIGENCE § 7–2(f) (3d ed. 1994).

gence of a third party would recovery nothing from defendant.

One way to avoid this anomaly would be to permit the blameless plaintiff to recover from both the negligent defendant and the negligent intervenor, whether or not the intervention was foreseeable, but eliminate joint and several liability, a solution that the latest version of the *Restatement* suggests.[29] I shall consider this idea in greater detail at the end of this Chapter.

Intervention Involving Aggravated Negligence. Suppose that the conduct of an intervenor is more culpable than mere negligence, and would qualify as grossly negligent, reckless, wilful or wanton. If in a similar factual setting a negligent intervention would supersede a negligent defendant's liability, *a fortiori* an intervention amounting to an aggravated form of negligence should logically have the same effect. Thus, if the court found that defendant had no duty to protect plaintiff from the negligence of a third party, it should surely not saddle defendant with the legal obligation to take measures to safeguard plaintiff from gross negligence, or reckless, wilful or wanton misconduct on the part of the third person. However, if the scope of defendant's duty extended to the use of reasonable care to prevent harm that might result from an intervenor's negligence, should the fact that the intervenor behaved in a highly irresponsible way

29. AMERICAN LAW INSTITUTE, RESTATEMENT THIRD, TORTS: LIABILITY FOR PHYSICAL HARM (BASIC PRINCIPLES) § 33 and cmt. c (Tentative Draft No. 2, March 25, 2002).

relieve defendant of liability? Our hypothetical man with the cigarette in the spilled-gasoline scenario might have been fully aware of the dangers of combustion but might have evidenced a total indifference to the consequences of flipping his glowing butt into the pool, circumstances that might justify even an award of punitive damages against him in a suit by a victim of the resulting explosion. How might a court deal with the case?

The duty-risk test would focus on whether the scope of defendant's duty to use due care in the transporting of a highly flammable liquid should extend to protecting bystanders from the risk of explosion resulting from aggravated negligence on the part of a third party. The foreseeability of highly blameworthy behavior on the part of third persons causing ignition of the particular liquid being transported under defendant's control would be an important consideration, as would the volatility of the substance under shipment and the general nature of the route the shipment would follow.

Risk-foreseeability would zero in on the act of aggravated negligence and inquire whether defendant should have anticipated it and therefore should have taken extra precautions to prevent spillage or otherwise guard against ignition by highly culpable third parties.

A leading case dealing with intervening aggravated negligence suggests that courts have not had an easy time dealing with the issue. In *McLaughlin v.*

Mine Safety Appliance Company,[30] a young girl who had nearly drowned suffered burn injuries when a volunteer nurse pressed heat blocks that should have been covered with insulating material directly against her skin. Defendant, the distributor of the product, had placed written instructions, calling for the use of insulation, in the boxes containing the heat blocks, but the firefighter who gave the blocks to the nurse did not pass along the instructional literature, even though he had received training in the safe use of the blocks five or six years earlier, and he knew the nurse was unaware of the danger. The New York Court of Appeals held that on retrial the jury should be instructed that if they found that the firefighter had actual knowledge of the risk associated with the use of the blocks yet did not warn the nurse and stood quietly by while she applied them to plaintiff's skin, such conduct would have been "so gross" that it superseded the liability of defendant for failing to provide better warnings and instructions for use. Defendant, in the view of the majority of the court, could not possibly have foreseen that a third party would disregard what he had learned and fail to give the nurse either the pamphlet or a verbal warning. A dissenting opinion pointed out that the possibility that a pamphlet containing cautionary language would not reach the person actually applying the product was one of the risks that might make it a breach of the duty of due care not to inscribe a warning on the surface of the blocks themselves.

30. 11 N.Y.2d 62, 226 N.Y.S.2d 407, 181 N.E.2d 430 (1962).

It seems unwise to draw a liability line as the New York court did, on the basis of degrees of grossness. Certainly if the firefighter consciously withheld information from the nurse for the purpose of harming the girl, a strong case might be made for cutting off defendant's liability, as we shall see in a moment. But mere forgetfulness, even if totally inexcusable under the circumstances, falls close enough to the penumbra of negligence to place it within the bundle of foreseeable risks that might qualify the failure to inscribe a warning as negligent marketing.

Interventions as Intentionally Wrongful Misconduct. An intervenor may commit an intentional wrongful act, which may or may not amount to a crime, and both his misconduct and defendant's prior negligence may be factual causes of plaintiff's harm. Within the universe embraced by this scenario, there might be cases in which defendant and plaintiff had a relationship that predated the criminal intervention. This relationship might give rise to a duty to provide reasonable preventive measures against intentionally harmful conduct, or not to make plaintiff vulnerable to risks of harm from such conduct. Alternatively, there may be criminal-intervention cases in which defendant had a prior relationship with the intervenor, or control over an instrumentality or agency which, if falling into the hands of an ill-intentioned third party, might be used for the purposeful infliction of harm on plaintiff. Finally, in some situations defendant might not have had any prior relationship with plaintiff, or the third person, or the instrumentality that caused the harm.

Criminal Interventions and Prior Relationships with Plaintiffs. Courts originally held that intervening criminal acts superseded a careless defendant's liability as a matter of law, ostensibly on the dubious ground that such conduct was unforeseeable.[31] However, in some situations they began to recognize duties to protect against criminal misconduct when defendant had a prior relationship that justified the imposition of such an obligation. The courts addressed these issues by weighing the general benefits that might accrue to society from the reduction of injuries, deaths and property damage or loss that might result from the intentional misconduct of third parties, against the general burdens such a duty would place on defendants subjected to it, and any other social costs the obligation might entail. The relationship between the parties might have made potential victims particularly vulnerable to criminal assaults, or might have brought into being some kind of justifiable expectation that defendant would take preventive measures. Courts have typically wrestled with this problem in suits by invitees or tenants against occupiers of business premises or landlords.[32]

In these situations, courts might deny the existence of any duty as a matter of law, or they might recognize a duty of care, with or without limita-

31. DAN B. DOBBS, *supra* note 2, § 190 at 471–72.

32. *See* JOSEPH A. PAGE, THE LAW OF PREMISES LIABILITY Ch. 11 (2d ed. 1988).

tions. Thus, exemplifying limited duty, the obligation imposed on a commercial invitor might come into play only when a criminal assault had begun and defendant was or should have been aware of it,[33] or if defendant knew or should have known of prior similar incidents.[34]

Plaintiff's argument with respect to the breach-of-duty element in these cases would stress the existence of a specific untaken precaution that would have protected her against intentionally wrongful misconduct that defendant might reasonably have foreseen; for example, defendant-invitor should have provided private security guards or better lighting; or defendant-landlord should have installed better locks. Thus, without the commission of intentional or criminal wrongdoing, there could be no actionable breach of duty.

Some prior-relationship cases have raised the issue whether a legal duty owed to plaintiff required defendant to take reasonable steps not to render plaintiff vulnerable to intentional wrongdoing by a third party. Thus, a railroad might be under a duty not to discharge a passenger in a dangerous area known to be frequented by individuals who might inflict harm on her;[35] and an insurance company might have a duty not to issue a life-insurance

33. *See, e.g.*, Henley v. Pizitz Realty Co., 456 So.2d 272 (Ala.1984).

34. *See, e.g.*, Timberwalk Apartments, Partners, Inc. v. Cain, 972 S.W.2d 749 (Tex.1998) (no duty to protect plaintiff from risk of rape where only prior criminal incidents on premises involved tire-slashing, car burglary and car theft).

35. *See* Hines v. Garrett, 131 Va. 125, 108 S.E. 690 (1921).

policy to someone who had no insurable interest in the life of the insured, because it might furnish the purchaser with the incentive to make herself the beneficiary and thus have a motive to murder the insured.[36] In both instances, the foreseeable risk of intentionally inflicted harm by third persons should have influenced defendant to take appropriate preventive measures. On the other hand, a car-rental agency might not be under a duty to protect a customer from the risk of harm from the explosion of a bomb placed in one of defendant's vehicles by an unknown third person, if defendant had no reason to suspect the criminal intervention, and therefore no reason to protect against it.[37]

Does this mean that in these intentional-wrongdoing intervention cases, once a court had decided to impose a duty of care, there will never be any need to address the extent-of-liability issue, since the resolution of the duty issue will have settled the matter? Certainly defendants should not be permitted to argue a lack of proximate cause *solely* on the ground that the wrongful intervention superseded defendant's negligence, inasmuch as an obligation to protect a class of potential victims against the wrongdoing of a third party should not evaporate just because the third party has engaged in the very sort of wrongdoing that gave rise to the duty. That would be totally irrational.

36. *See* Liberty Nat'l Life Ins. Co. v. Weldon, 267 Ala. 171, 100 So.2d 696 (1957).

37. *See* Danielenko v. Kinney Rent A Car, Inc., 57 N.Y.2d 198, 455 N.Y.S.2d 555, 441 N.E.2d 1073 (1982).

However, even when courts might in principle recognize that defendant had a duty to exercise ordinary care to protect a class of potential plaintiffs from the risk of harm from intentionally wrongful misconduct on the part of third persons, extent-of-liability issues might still arise. For example, the type of wrongdoing perpetrated by the third party might be completely different from the misconduct against which defendant might have been obliged to protect plaintiff. This would raise problems discussed in our consideration of the different-risk scenario in Chapter Three.

Criminal Interventions and Prior Relationships with Third Persons. A plaintiff injured by the criminal misconduct of a third person might argue that defendant had a prior relationship from which a court might derive a duty to use due care to prevent the third party from harming plaintiff. This issue arises in suits by persons injured by violent individuals over whom defendants exercised some measure of responsibility or control.[38] Once again the court will have to weigh the societal burdens and benefits of recognizing a duty in the context of particular relationships, and to determine, if such a duty is to be imposed, whether any limits should be placed upon it. Thus, the duty arising from control or other responsibility over potentially violent individuals might arise only if the individuals had

38. *See, e.g.*, Dudley v. Offender Aid and Restoration of Richmond, Inc., 241 Va. 270, 401 S.E.2d 878 (1991) (halfway house under duty to use due care to control convicted felon).

threatened specific identifiable victims,[39] or might be satisfied by a warning only.[40]

Criminal Interventions and Relationships with Third Persons: Remoteness. Once again, even when courts recognize the obligation, there may be extent-of-liability issue that arise in particular cases. For example, the infliction of harm might have far removed in time or space from defendant's original negligence. Suppose that a person prone to commit acts of violence escapes confinement because of the carelessness of the person or institution that had the responsibility to restrain him, and he inflicts harm on a victim a considerable time after the escape, or at a considerable distance from the place where he had been held. A risk-foreseeability approach might suggest that defendant's liability should have no limits, since it is surely within the bounds of reasonable anticipation that if a violent individual who should have been kept in confinement is allowed to flee and regain his freedom, he may give vent to his anti-social propensities at any moment and wherever he happens to be.

A court applying the duty-risk test might ask whether the scope of defendant's responsibility to use due care to keep the individual confined extends to the risk that he might commit violent acts on innocent victims while he is at large. Would there

39. *See* Thompson v. Alameda County, 27 Cal.3d 741, 167 Cal.Rptr. 70, 614 P.2d 728 (1980).

40. *See* Tarasoff v. Regents of the University of California, 17 Cal.3d 425, 131 Cal.Rptr. 14, 551 P.2d 334 (1976) (therapist under duty to warn person threatened by patient).

be any policy reasons for concluding that defendant's duty should not extend *ad infinitum*? The purpose of imposing a duty to exercise due diligence in keeping dangerous people retained is the judgment that if such individuals were allowed to roam freely, they would pose a danger to society-at-large, or some identifiable portion thereof. A violent act perpetrated on an innocent victim and similar in kind to the misconduct that justified the original confinement would arguably fall within the scope of the risks giving rise to the duty of care. Moreover, to relieve defendant of responsibility for the intentionally wrongful misconduct of individuals who escaped from their care or control might decrease incentives to exercise appropriate levels of precaution.

On the other hand, defendant might contend that general risks associated with a violent individual and resulting in intentionally harmful misconduct after he has settled into a more or less normal life following a successful escape would be identical to the dangers posed by the person after a lawful release from confinement; humans with violent tendencies are not like wild animals with inherent dangerous propensities, in that the former exercise free will when they decide on courses of conduct; therefore, the ambit of risk created by carelessly letting them escape does not include the dangers they might pose to members of the public when they engage in conventional criminal misbehavior. A court receptive to this argument might limit the responsibility of defendant to harmful acts intentionally committed during the escape.[41]

Courts using a hindsight approach might resort to remoteness as the deciding factor. Given the miracles of modern transportation, distance in and of itself should not justify cutting off defendant's liability. An escapee could drive a vehicle or fly a plane hundreds of miles in one day, and commit a violent crime on the next. The time element, however, might be a dispositive factor. Thus, suppose the dangerous person inflicts harm on plaintiff months or even years after the escape. A court might conclude that the harm was "too remote" from defendant's negligence, but as is usually the case with remoteness, the question will always arise as to how the line should be drawn. This may be a situation where the court (or the jury) might utilize common sense or fundamental notions of fairness to make the determination. There would not seem to be any need to fashion an arbitrary limit for all similar cases, because one of the factors that merits consideration is the degree of danger posed by the individual third party. (Another would be the vulnerability of potential victims.)

Criminal Interventions and Control Over Instrumentalities of Harm. Defendant may have under his control a substance or instrumentality that would be potentially dangerous if an ill-intentioned third party obtained access to it. Defendant might carelessly allow the substance or instrumen-

---

41. *See* Nelson v. Washington Parish, 805 F.2d 1236 (5th Cir.1986) (applying Louisiana law).

tality to escape his control, after which a stranger happens along and makes criminal use of it to injure plaintiff. For example, as our spilled-gasoline hypothetical demonstrates, defendant might be in the process of transporting a dangerous liquid and might fail to use due care, with the result that the substance escaped from the vehicle in which defendant was shipping it and formed a pool into which an arsonist tossed a lighted cigarette. A variant involves the situation where defendant carelessly fails to prevent a third person from taking possession or control of the instrumentality from defendant, as would be the case where defendant's carelessness allows someone to steal a gun, with which he subsequently shoots plaintiff.

In the first example, plaintiff would contend that if defendant had not carelessly caused the spill, she would not have suffered burns. Defendant's position would be that he should not have to bear responsibility for the results of another person's volitional lawless misconduct. A subtext here might be the suspicion that a defendant with a mind to inflict harm or damage will do so whenever the opportunity arises, and if defendant had not presented one, another would eventually materialize, with similarly deleterious results; thus, defendant merely facilitated the commission of a wrongful act that might have occurred sooner or later.

As has been already suggested, some of the hindsight tests would seriously disadvantage plaintiffs, because the harm was not directly inflicted, nor did it flow in an unbroken sequence from defendant's careless conduct. Moreover, these do not seem to be cases that lend themselves to *ad hoc* dispositions on the basis of "rough justice," "practical politics" or even judicial common sense. They involve fact patterns that might happen again, and therefore consistency in results would be appropriate.

An early Kentucky decision arising from facts similar to our hypothetical took a risk-foreseeability approach and held that defendant would not be liable because as a matter of law defendant could not have anticipated the criminal act of another.[42] If the court meant that intervening criminal acts are never foreseeable (perhaps on the dubious grounds that people are presumed to obey the law), the holding is open to question. On the other hand, the court may have meant that on the facts of the specific case, no reasonable person could find that defendant should have foreseen the type of criminal conduct that occurred, in which case the decision would be defensible. If the transporter was passing through an area known to be frequented by persons likely to engage in destructive mischief, however, the logic of the risk-foreseeability approach would seem to call for sending the case to the jury.

Another way of looking at these kinds of cases would be as instances where defendant has control over an instrumentality that might be used to inflict harm on others if it fell into the hands of someone disposed to make criminal use of it; a third

42. Watson v. Kentucky & Ind. Bridge & Ry. Co., 137 Ky. 619, 126 S.W. 146 (1910).

party gains access to or possession of the instrumentality and uses it to injure plaintiff.

On the issue whether defendant breached a duty of due care in allowing the third party to gain control of or access to the instrumentality, would the danger of criminal misuse of it by a third person fall within the ambit of foreseeable risk that defendant should have considered in deciding how much precaution to exercise against such an eventuality? In a case involving the theft of an ordinary kitchen knife or a tool-kit hammer that was later used in a criminal assault, a court could decide as a matter of law that defendant did not breach a duty of ordinary care in allowing the knife or hammer to fall into the assailant's hands. The fact that the general public would not expect, under ordinary circumstances, that people will violate the criminal law would operate powerfully in defendant's favor.[43] Only if there were special facts that should have put defendant on notice that the instrument or agency in his possession or control might be used criminally would a jury question arise on this point. An example of the latter might arise in the context of the possession of certain dangerous instrumentalities such as firearms or ammunition that in an urban setting might be so related to criminal activity that a possessor might be found obliged to take this risk into account in taking measure to prevent them from falling into the wrong hands.

43. *See* W. PAGE KEETON ET AL., PROSSER AND KEETON ON THE LAW OF TORTS 201 (5th ed. 1984).

Under a duty-risk approach, a court might find that certain instrumentalities or agencies carry such a high degree of risk or have the potential to inflict such a substantial amount of harm that the obligation of the possessor is to keep them under control in order to minimize the danger that might arise from their criminal misuse, and that such a burden would not amount to an unreasonable infringement of the personal autonomy of those who make legal use of these products. Thus, a court might rule as a matter of law that the duty of sellers of firearms or ammunition encompassed using reasonable precautionary measures to keep them away from third persons who might put them to illegal use.

Criminal Interventions Without Prior Relationships. Thus far, we have considered situations in which defendants had a preexisting relationship with either plaintiff or the third party who engaged in the intentionally wrongful misconduct. But suppose no such relationship existed. A defendant might carelessly place a stranger in a position of vulnerability, which then enables an unknown third party to inflict harm on her. An exemplary fact pattern might feature a young woman whom an assailant accosts, forces into an apartment building whose door has a broken lock on it and rapes. The unfortunate victim sues the owner of the building and alleges that the failure to provide proper locks amounted to negligent conduct that caused her harm. If plaintiff had lived in the building and her attacker had gained entrance because of a faulty lock and then harmed her, she might have claimed that her landlord breached a duty to use due care in providing security for tenants and their guests. However, in our case there was nothing except the assault to link the victim and the owner.

The New York Court of Appeals confronted these facts in *Waters v. New York City Housing Authority*,[44] and held that plaintiff could not recover. In an opinion notable for the way it first invoked and then discarded *Palsgraf*, the court posited that defendant was not within the ambit of foreseeable risk, but then articulated policy and commonsense considerations that had little to do with foreseeability and justified the refusal to extend to a stranger the protection of the duty defendant owed to its tenants. They included the inability of urban landlords to control what happens on public streets, the limitless liability recognition of such a duty might impose on landlords, and the fact that it is unlikely that the imposition of the duty would reduce street crime, since people with a mind to commit criminal assaults have numerous alternative methods available to them.

Note that with respect to the last point, the court might have said that even if this defendant had properly secured its doors, plaintiff would still have suffered the same harm. Such a finding would have to have been made in the context of cause-in-fact, an issue properly for the jury unless reasonable minds could not differ. Instead, the court was invoking the general difficulty of proving cause-in-fact

[44]. 69 N.Y.2d 225, 513 N.Y.S.2d 356, 505 N.E.2d 922 (1987).

in these types of cases as a practical factor cutting against the imposition of a legal duty.

The court in *Waters* was plainly using a duty-risk approach to reach its holding. Its analysis may be open to criticism. For example, the thrust of plaintiff's claim had nothing to do with the landlord's ability to control what occurred on the street, but rather with its ability to control access to the building. However, the strength of duty-risk lies in the way it requires courts to spell out carefully and openly all the considerations behind their decisions to extend, or not to extend, the scope of a defendant's duty to the kind of risk that caused harm to a plaintiff. This exposes holdings to the type of reasoned criticism that can either solidify or eventually modify them.

Termination of Responsibility for Risk. A variation on the intervention scenarios implicates Able, who breaches a duty he owed to a foreseeable class of victims by creating a foreseeable risk of harm; but before the risk actually causes harm, Baker assumes a duty, or does something to give rise to a duty on his part, to protect potential victims from that very same hazard. Able argues that in so doing Baker should be held to have taken full responsibility for protecting against or eliminating the risk, and that if the risk should thereafter result in harm, the victim's sole recourse should be against Baker. The court would then have to determine whether to terminate Able's responsibility for the risk because of Baker's intervention.

Note that if Able's termination argument were to prevail, plaintiff would recover compensation only if Baker had negligently failed to prevent the harm. If Baker had assumed responsibility and the risk originally created by Able caused damage because of non-negligent ineffectiveness on Baker's part, plaintiff would be left without any remedy.

Able's contention might be that the harmful potential originally created by his conduct came to an end when Baker assumed responsibility—the termination-of-risk argument. But Baker's counter would be that the harm suffered by plaintiff would not have occurred but for Able's negligence. So the real question for the court would be whether Able's responsibility *ought* to terminate.

Thus, suppose a physician negligently treats a patient in a way that puts the latter at risk of serious complications.[45] Let us consider three variants that might flow from these basic facts. First, she thereafter makes every reasonable effort to prevent the risk from taking effect, but to no avail. The prevailing view is that she will still be liable for the harm resulting from the risk she negligently created,[46] which seems an intuitively sensible and just result. Second, the complications from her careless treatment inflict actual physical injury that

45. I have adapted this hypothetical from an example discussed in DAN B. DOBBS, *supra* note 2, § 194 at 484.

46. *See* 2 RESTATEMENT, SECOND, TORTS, *supra* note 16, § 437. The same rule applies to a manufacturer who unsuccessfully makes a reasonable attempt to eliminate a product defect caused by its negligence. *See* AMERICAN LAW INSTITUTE, RESTATEMENT, THIRD, TORTS: PRODUCTS LIABILITY § 11 cmt. d (1998).

requires the intervention of a specialist, who then carelessly inflicts additional harm on the unfortunate patient. We have already seen earlier in this Chapter that courts would hold both health-care providers jointly and severally liable for the aggravation caused by the specialist. The mere fact that the specialist owed and breached a duty of due care to the patient would not in and of itself supersede the liability of the first physician. Third, the physician puts the patient in danger of grave complications, again she calls in a specialist, and this time he negligently fails to prevent the risk she created from causing harm to the patient. Is there any compelling reason to reach a different result in this third variation and exonerate the physician merely because instead of inflicting an injury and making plaintiff vulnerable to additional harm, or reasonably but unsuccessfully trying to reduce or eliminate the risk she originally and negligently created, she called in a specialist who then negligently failed to eliminate the risk? It would seem difficult to justify a different outcome in these cases.

What if the specialist explicitly agreed with the physician to assume full responsibility for protecting the patient from the risk created by the physician? As a general proposition, courts have been reluctant to permit potentially responsible parties to shift or delegate duties to safeguard the personal safety of others.[47] It would seem to follow logically from this that courts would be even more reluctant

47. For examples, *see* 2 RESTATEMENT (SECOND) OF TORTS, *supra* note 16, §§ 396, 423, 424.

to terminate a defendant's responsibility *after* he has already breached a duty. The more appropriate solution both here and in the case of a non-contractual assumption of duty by the specialist would be to leave intact plaintiff's remedy against the original physician and allow the latter to obtain indemnity, either under the contract or in tort, against the specialist for any damages she might have to pay to the victim.[48]

Suppose that defendant creates an unreasonable risk and without his knowledge a third party enters the picture and because of her relationship to potential victims or as a result of actions she takes, she assumes legal responsibility to protect others from harm that might result from that risk; the third party's intervention turns out to be ineffectual, and plaintiff suffers harm as a result. The paradigmatic case here presents a defendant who allows a child access to a dangerous instrumentality, such as a gun or a dynamite cap. If the child injures himself or another, defendant may be liable. But instead, a parent learns of her child's possession of the device and takes it away from him. Defendant contends that the parent had assumed control of the dangerous situation, and had undertaken a duty to use due care to protect the child and others; in so

---

48. The *Restatement of Torts (Second)* recognized that in special cases courts might allow an original tortfeasor to shift a duty of care and thus relieve himself of responsibility for subsequent harm, but added that "[i]t is beyond the scope of this Restatement to attempt to state when the duty can be shifted, and when it cannot." *See* 2 RESTATEMENT (SECOND) OF TORTS, *supra* note 16, § 454(2) cmt. e.

doing she should be considered also to have relieved defendant of responsibility if somehow the child regained possession of the instrumentality because the parent was careless or even under circumstances not amounting to negligence on the part of the parent, and harm subsequently resulted either to the child himself or to another.

Note how this scenario differs from others we have considered. The intervening act or omission here fails to reduce or eliminate a risk previously created by defendant. In the other scenarios we have examined, the risk created by defendant was in making possible the negligent, injury-producing act of an intervenor (as in, for example, the key-in-the-ignition cases). In addition, in the usual negligent-intervention case, a crucial question is whether defendant should have increased the amount of precaution he will exercise by taking into account the foreseeable possibility of negligence by a third party. But in termination cases, if defendant could have foreseen that an intervenor might eliminate or reduce a risk he (the defendant) created, this might justify a reduction in the amount of precaution on his part, although a court might decide that such a reduction was improper on the ground that defendant was the cheaper cost-avoider.

The courts have tended to struggle with these cases. Early decisions exonerated defendants on the ground that the action of the parent constituted an independent causal force that broke the link between defendant's negligent and the injury, so that defendant's negligence was not a proximate cause of the harm.[49] But this "rationale" was no more than a conclusory statement, lacking in reasoned justification for relieving defendants of liability in these types of cases. What the courts seemed to be doing here, at least in cases where plaintiff was the child from whom parent had taken the instrument and who later regained possession of it, involved imputing the negligence of the parent to the child, and then barring the child under the doctrine of imputed contributory negligence, in the words of one treatise a "barbarous rule" that in effect "visited the sins of the father upon the children."[50] Perhaps stern judicial notions of parental responsibility lurked behind the decisions. In any event, this reasoning could not even facially justify barring an innocent injured victim other than the parent's child, since no negligence could possibly be imputed to him.

Termination of Responsibility: Risk–Foreseeability. How would risk-foreseeability work here? A court using this approach might ask whether a defendant who carelessly puts a dangerous instrumentality into the hands of a child could

49. *E.g.*, Pittsburg Reduction Co. v. Horton, 87 Ark. 576, 113 S.W. 647 (1908). For a case indicating that if defendant's negligence intensified a sense of curiosity that strengthened the child's determination to regain possession of the dangerous instrumentality and as a result the child frustrated his parent's attempt to keep that object away from him, the forces generated by defendant had not come to rest when the victim ultimately suffered harm. Calkins v. Albi, 163 Colo. 370, 431 P.2d 17 (1967)(reversing a judgment for plaintiff because of an error in jury instructions relating to an alleged statutory violation).

50. W. PAGE KEETON ET AL., *supra* note 43, § 74 at 531.

reasonably have anticipated that a parent might intervene ineffectively. But since these cases are apt to recur, putting the foreseeability to the jury in each case might produce different results on similar facts.

A good example of the divergent results that might be reached under risk-foreseeability may be found in a pair of products-liability decisions involving a product defect caused by the negligence of defendant-manufacturer, and the intervening negligence of someone who knew about the flaw yet failed to take available precautions against it, with resulting injury to an innocent victim. In *Comstock v. General Motors Corporation*,[51] the intervenor knew of a brake problem but momentarily forgot about it, drove the vehicle toward plaintiff and was unable to stop in time to avoid hitting him. In *Ford Motor Company v. Wagoner*,[52] there were two intervenors who were aware of a defect in the catch mechanism of a vehicle's hood but did not install a new catch the defendant-manufacturer offered to provide. The court in *Comstock* held that there was sufficient evidence from which a jury might have found that defendant could reasonably have foreseen the negligent intervention, while in *Wagoner* the court held that no reasonable person could have anticipated the conscious unwillingness of the intervenor to remedy the defect.

It seems difficult to understand why the negligent forgetfulness of an intervenor might raise a ques-

51. 358 Mich. 163, 99 N.W.2d 627 (1959).
52. 183 Tenn. 392, 192 S.W.2d 840 (1946).

tion of foreseeability for the jury, but an intervenor's refusal to fix a known defect might not.[53] This is yet another example of the tendency of the risk-foreseeability test to focus on the wrong factor—foreseeability—instead of what would appear to be the real issue here, the scope of the legal duty owed by defendant.

Termination of Responsibility: Duty–Risk. Duty-risk might operate more effectively in these cases, in the sense that a court might consider the desirability of adopting a rule that would prevent possessors or sellers of dangerous instrumentalities from reducing precautionary measures aimed at keeping such objects from children in the expectation that in a certain percentage of cases parents might take the hazardous instruments away from their offspring. In addition, the duty-risk approach would force judges to explain openly why the value of enhancing parental responsibility outweighed the value of deterrence, if that is what they believed. Likewise, in the products-liability field, courts might consider factors such as deterrence by the cheaper cost-avoider in determining the scope of the duty owed by manufacturers in cases where third parties learn of a defect yet take no steps to avoid it.

These kinds of cases may raise close questions, as demonstrated by the *Restatement (Second) of Torts*, which seemed to adopt a *de facto* duty-risk approach

53. For a discussion of the two cases, *see* Dix W. Noel, *Manufacturer's Negligence of Design or Directions for Use of a Product*, 71 YALE L. J. 816, 869–72 (1962).

for the termination-of-responsibility scenario and stated in black letter that "Where, because of lapse of time or otherwise, the duty to prevent harm to another threatened by the actor's negligent conduct is found to have shifted from the actor to a third person, the failure to prevent such harm is a superseding cause,"[54] and in a comment indicated that no governing rule could be stated, and therefore the decision when the duty shifts is one for the court, which should weigh factors such as the degree of risk, the amount of danger threatened, the identity of the third person, his relation to the parties, the amount of time that has lapsed between defendant's negligence and the assumption of control by the third party and perhaps other considerations.[55]

Effect of Comparative Fault and the Reform of Joint and Several Liability. We have thus far examined how courts have resolved scope-of-liability issues arising from interventions by third parties and acts of nature. There remains for consideration the possibility that the adoption of comparative fault and the (mostly legislative) elimination or modification of joint and several liability might furnish reasons for considering whether the courts should change the way they have traditionally addressed these problems.

A preliminary draft of the new *Restatement of Torts* has suggested such a change. The Reporters

54. 2 AMERICAN LAW INSTITUTE, RESTATEMENT, SECOND, TORTS § 452 (1965).

55. *Id.* at cmt. f.

argue that the doctrine of superseding cause, by which a defendant escaped liability if the intervening act of a third party was unforeseeable, originated in judicial unwillingness to impose liability on a defendant whose tortious conduct combined with that of an intervenor to cause harm to plaintiff, where the culpability of the defendant was a small fraction of that assignable to the intervenor, and the rule of joint and several liability might make defendant responsible for the entire amount of plaintiff's damages; even where defendant could obtain contribution from the intervenor, he could recover only a *pro rata* share of the damages paid, which might be considerably more than a proportional share measured by degrees of fault; hence, according to the Reporters, the courts developed the doctrine of superseding cause as a way to relieve defendants of the risk of having to pay a disproportionate share of the damages in cases where the intervening act had been unforeseeable; however, the spread of the doctrine of comparative fault has meant that defendants could recover from the intervenor not a *pro rata* share of the recovery, but an amount proportionate to culpability; this has undercut the need to apply the principle of superseding cause to unforeseeable interventions.[56]

Hence, they have proposed a black-letter rule that would impose liability on defendants whose tortious conduct combined with an intervening act, even one that could not have been anticipated, to cause harm

---

56. *See* AMERICAN LAW INSTITUTE, RESTATEMENT THIRD, TORTS: LIABILITY FOR PHYSICAL HARM (BASIC PRINCIPLES) § 33 cmt. c (Tentative Draft No. 2, March 25, 2002).

to plaintiff, as long as the harm was among the harms whose risks made defendant's conduct tortious.[57] This would mean that in our hypotheticals of the negligently spilled gasoline and the negligent or intentional ignitions of third persons, the transporter would be liable whether or not the ignition could have been foreseen, because the risk of ignition by third parties was within the scope of the risks that made it a breach of the duty of due care to cause the liquid to spill.[58] Thus, one could say that the Reporters seem to be considering these cases as falling within the manner-of-occurrence scenario.

On the other hand, if the ultimate harm inflicted by the intervenor was not one of the risks that made defendant's conduct negligent, defendant would not be liable.[59] Thus, if as a result of the diversion of attention created by the accidental ignition of carelessly spilled gasoline, teenagers were able to slash the tires of cars parked in the vicinity, the transporter would not be liable for the vehicular damage inflicted by the young vandals.[60] This kind of case would be treated as falling in the different risk category.

The Reporters argue that their position gains support not only from the widespread adoption of

57. *Id.* § 33.

58. *See id.*, Illust. 5, at 294.

59. *Id.* § 33 (b).

60. *See id.* § 33 cmt. g, Illust. 9, at 297–98, for a similar example involving a hot-air balloonist who imprudently decided to fly in bad weather and crashed near a picnic area.

comparative fault, but also from legislative abolition or revision of the rule of joint and several liability. Jurisdictions that have kept a modified version of the rule have taken compromise positions, such as maintaining the rule as it would apply to damages for pecuniary losses (medical expenses and lost earnings, both past and future), while eliminating the rule as it might affect non-pecuniary loss (pain and suffering), for which defendants would be liable severally under allocative principles of comparative fault.[61] This means that even though defendants might be liable for unforeseeable intervening acts, their liability might be limited by rules of apportionment under comparative-fault principles. But it is important to keep in mind that only a relatively small number of jurisdictions have opted for the outright abolition of joint and several liability and have instead adopted several liability;[62] most of the changes in joint and several liability have kept the basic rule with modifications.

Thus, under this approach victims would be able to recover fully in all intervention situations if they are able to sue both the original negligent tortfeasor and the culpable intervenor, and both parties are sufficiently solvent to satisfy the judgments. Plaintiff would recover total compensation, and the original tortfeasor and the culpable intervenor would

61. *See* AMERICAN LAW INSTITUTE, RESTATEMENT THIRD, TORTS: APPORTIONMENT OF LIABILITY § 17, Reporters' Note at 149–59 (2000).

62. *See id.* at 154. Some of the jurisdictions that have adopted several liability have limited the switch to certain classes of cases, such as toxic torts or medical malpractice.

pay amounts in proportion to the percentages of fault the jury assigns to them. However, the intervenor may be judgment-proof, not amendable to suit or even unknown. In such cases, where joint and several liability has been abolished, plaintiffs would be able to recover for only a portion of their damages, calculated solely on the basis of comparative-fault principles, against the original negligent defendant; where joint and several liability has been modified, plaintiffs can collect from defendant not only the percentage of their damages allocable to defendant's degree of fault, but also a portion of the damages allocable to the intervenor.

This solution seems to embody a *quid pro quo*, in the sense that plaintiff might be able to recover either full or partial damages in cases where the intervening act was totally unforeseeable (under existing rules, the original defendant might not be liable in such a case, so that plaintiff's only recourse would be against a culpable intervenor, who may or may not be amenable to suit or financially capable of satisfying an adverse judgment). However, plaintiff would not be able to recover full damages even though the intervening act had been foreseeable, if the intervenor was not amenable to suit or able to satisfy the proportionate amount of the judgment, as determined by comparative-fault principles (under existing rules of joint and several liability, the original defendant would be liable for the full amount of the judgment if the culpable and foreseeable intervenor was not amenable to suit or able to satisfy his proportionate share of the judgment).

One area where this approach might be problematic is where the specific purpose of the duty imposed on defendant is to protect a class of potential victims from the negligence or intentional misconduct of third persons. The proportionate amount of fault allocated to a negligent intervenor is likely to be at least as high as that allocated to a defendant whose negligence put plaintiff in a position to be harmed by the third party's negligence; the proportionate amount of fault allocated to a criminal assailant is apt to be substantially higher than the fault attributed to an inadvertent or careless defendant who made it possible for the assailant to harm plaintiff.

Hence, the abolition of joint and several liability might have two unfortunate consequences. First, where the intervenor is insolvent or not amenable to suit, plaintiff will not be permitted to collect full compensation from the defendant whose negligence enabled the injury to be inflicted. As between a negligent defendant whose carelessness was a cause-in-fact of the harm and an innocent victim, it would seem to be a matter of simple justice that the defendant should have to bear the loss, even though someone else might have been more at fault. Second, the incentives for defendants to use care to fulfil their legal duty to protect potential victims from harm at the hands of negligent or intentional wrongdoers will be reduced substantially if defendants know that their liability might amount only to a fraction of the loss incurred by victims.

Chapter 5

Beyond Negligence

Thus far I have examined how courts determine the extent of the liability of a defendant who violated a duty of due care he owed to plaintiff and therefore was negligent. However, other causes of action inhabit the mansion of tort law. Hence, in order to complete our story of proximate cause, we shall have to consider the approaches courts might take to decide whether and how to limit liability when plaintiff's tort suit rests on claims other than negligence. Among these would be intentional torts, such as assault, battery, false imprisonment and outrage, as well as strict tort liability, which courts have imposed on defendants who, *inter alia*, keep livestock or dangerous animals, engage in abnormally hazardous activity or put defective products into the stream of commerce.

Proximate Cause and Intentional Torts

As every torts novice quickly learns, a critical difference between negligent and intentional torts is that the former impose responsibility for conduct that is merely careless or inadvertent, while the latter require, in most instances, proof that defendant invaded a legally protected interest with an intent to do so, or with knowledge to a substantial certainty that such an invasion would occur as a result of his act. Unsurprisingly, the degree of moral culpability society attaches to the conduct of the intentional tortfeasor is in general much greater than the blame directed at negligent defendants.

In Chapter Two we saw that one of the arguments for limiting the scope of a defendant's liability was that there should be some proportionality between blameworthiness and the scope of a defendant's responsibility; therefore, it might not be fair to hold defendant liable for the remote consequences of inadvertence, when the harm resulting from those consequences was far more extensive than anyone could reasonably have foreseen.

In intentional-tort cases, the proportionality factor would seem to cut the other way and work in favor of extending a tortfeasor's liability a good bit further than in negligence cases, because of the considerably greater culpability of defendant's conduct. But the question still remains, how far? Where the malfeasance of an intentional tortfeasor produces attenuated harmful consequences, judicial opinions imposing liability have occasionally suggested, without much explanation, that liability for intentional wrongdoing should follow all its consequences, apparently *ad infinitum*.[1] An advantage flowing from the adoption of this sort of bright-line rule would be ease of administration, but one suspects that this dictum touches the hem of hyperbole, and that courts might not actually follow it in

1. *See, e.g.,* Wyant v. Crouse, 127 Mich. 158, 86 N.W. 527 (1901).

cases involving truly remote or bizarre results. So, if a court were to reject an absolute rule stretching the liability of intentional tortfeasors wherever the ripples of cause-in-fact may radiate, it would have to face the challenge of devising some way to draw a line beyond which responsibility will not stretch.

I shall explore this problem first in the context of an arguably easy case involving aggravated harm. I shall then consider how courts might handle questions of proximate cause in several of the other scenarios that have served as focal points for discussion in Chapters Three and Four, and might realistically produce disputes about scope of liability in intentional-tort cases.

Intentional Torts and the Aggravated–Harm Scenario. An intentional tortfeasor might mean to put a hurt on plaintiff, and because of some pre-existing weakness or condition in plaintiff's physical make-up, the harm might turn out to be much greater in extent that defendant could reasonably have expected. For example, Charlie intentionally pushes Delta, who falls backward and hits her head on a protruding object; unbeknownst to Charlie, Delta has a steel plate in her skull because of a war wound, and she dies from the relatively mild trauma to her cranium.

It would seem beyond cavil that Charlie should be liable for Delta's death. If he had carelessly pushed Delta to the ground under circumstances that might have given rise to liability in negligence, he would be liable for the entire extent of the harm he caused, for reasons already discussed at length in Chapter Three, no matter which approach to proximate cause the court opted to use. The same reasons supporting liability in negligence would apply even more cogently in cases involving intentional infliction of personal injury. If fundamental fairness would require that as between an innocent plaintiff and a negligent defendant, the latter ought to pay for the unexpectedly serious consequences of his carelessness, so much the more compelling is the argument that a defendant who has committed a battery producing far more harm than he might reasonably have anticipated should be liable for whatever harm the battery in fact caused, because of the intentional tortfeasor's greater moral culpability. If the goal of optimal deterrence is best met by a rule that imposes on a negligent tortfeasor liability for unforeseeably extensive harm resulting from conduct that may have some social utility, the same rule should apply to tortfeasors whose conduct is morally reprehensible and of minimal or no social utility.

The foregoing suggests a broader proposition, to the effect that in any intentional-tort case raising an issue of extent of liability, if plaintiff might have recovered on similar facts against a negligent tortfeasor, she should *a fortiori* recover against an intentional tortfeasor. However, this still does not solve the problem of how to deal with cases in which a defendant would have escaped liability if his culpable conduct had amounted to mere negligence. If the scope of liability ought to extend further in intentional-tort cases than in negligence cases but should not be unlimited, we are still left with the task of determining how to draw the outer boundary.

Intentional Torts and the Self–Injury Scenario. One type of scope-of-liability issue that might arise in intentional-tort cases is whether the survivors or the estate of a victim who committed suicide as a result of the tort should be permitted to recover damages against the tortfeasor.

Suppose the tortfeasor acted for the purpose of provoking the victim to take his own life. Here it would seem eminently logical that extent of liability should not even be an issue, since decedent's death would clearly fall within the scope of defendant's tortious intent, and hence imposing liability would serve the ends of both deterrence and corrective justice. The same would be true in the assisted-suicide scenario, although plaintiffs might have some difficulty establishing a threshold intentional tort, overcoming the defense of consent (perhaps the illegality of attempted suicide might nullify decedent's assent[2]), and, as a practical matter, proving damages substantial enough to justify bringing a lawsuit.[3]

2. On whether assent to criminal conduct may amount to a legally operable consent, *see* W. PAGE KEETON ET AL., PROSSER AND KEETON ON THE LAW OF TORTS § 18, at 122–24 (5th ed. 1984).

3. On liability for conduct meant to induce suicide, *see* Victor E. Schwartz, *Civil Liability for Causing Suicide: A Synthesis of Law and Psychiatry*, 24 VAND. L. REV. 217, 220–22 (1971).

Suppose defendant intentionally inflicted physical injuries, emotional distress or even harm to some property interest, and as a result the victim took his or her own life. Plaintiffs would have to establish cause-in-fact by proving by a preponderance of the evidence that the suicide in fact resulted from the defendant's tortious conduct—potentially a problematic burden. Moreover, even if plaintiff makes out the element of factual causation, defendants may still argue that the self-inflicted harm should fall outside the ambit of liability.

We have already seen, in Chapter Three, how some courts have imposed liability for the death of a person who suffered injuries as a result of defendant's negligence and subsequently committed suicide under the influence of an uncontrollable impulse traceable to those injuries. It would seem appropriate to apply at least this same rule in cases where intentional wrongdoing caused the original injuries.

A quite plausible argument can be made that because of the greater degree of culpability in the latter cases, plaintiffs should not be required to prove that the act of self-destruction resulted from an uncontrollable impulse, but merely that there was a cause-in-fact relationship between the intentional tort and the suicide. A court might take the position that defendants should be liable any time a suicide results from injuries intentionally inflicted by a tortfeasor. In the alternative, defendants in these kinds of cases might be held liable only when the moral culpability of an individual defendant is sufficient enough to justify imposing liability, a position taken in an early discussion draft of the new *Restatement of Torts*.[4] The former approach has the advantage of providing a rule that would be simple to administer and would produce consistent results (since different courts might reach different results about moral culpability on substantially similar facts), while the latter gives courts the kind of flexibility that would not be problematic in an area where factual variations might justify variations in results, and where, in any event, there are not likely to be cases with substantially similar facts.

Where a defendant has engaged in outrageous conduct for the purpose of inflicting extreme emotional distress on a plaintiff and not only provokes acute mental suffering but also causes the victim to take his own life, the same alternatives present themselves. A court might permit plaintiff to recover upon proof that decedent took his own life while in the throes of an uncontrollable impulse,[5] or upon proof simply that defendant's outrageous, morally reprehensible conduct was a cause-in-fact of the suicide.[6]

Finally, in a case involving the conversion of personal property under circumstances that caused decedent to commit an act of self-destruction result-

---

4. AMERICAN LAW INSTITUTE, RESTATEMENT, THIRD, TORTS: LIABILITY FOR PHYSICAL HARM (BASIC PRINCIPLES) § 32(b) (Tentative Draft No. 2, March 25, 2002).

5. *See* State ex rel. Richardson v. Edgeworth, 214 So.2d 579 (Miss.1968).

6. *See* Tate v. Canonica, 180 Cal.App.2d 898, 5 Cal.Rptr. 28 (1960).

ing from an irresistible impulse that precluded decedent from realizing what he was doing, a court permitted recovery for wrongful death because defendant committed an intentional wrong that was a direct cause of the suicide.[7] Here, perhaps because of the lesser degree of culpability where interference with property rights gave rise to the cause of action, the requirement of both an uncontrollable impulse and directness served as limits on the scope of liability.

Intentional Torts and Different Risks. In Chapter Three, we saw how courts have confronted cases in which defendant creates a foreseeable and unreasonable risk of harm, but plaintiff suffers injury or damages as a result of a different, unforeseeable risk also brought into being by defendant's careless conduct.

In the area of intentional torts, liability attaches not because of the careless creation of risks, but rather from purposeful conduct aimed at producing particular harmful consequences. In most cases defendant brings into being not a risk but a virtual certainty of harm. The analogous case, then, would arise when defendant intends to cause one type of harm, but her conduct in fact causes another. An alternative way of looking at the problem would frame it as one in which defendant intends to violate one kind of legally protected interest enjoyed by plaintiff, but ends up unwittingly violating a different interest.

7. Cauverien v. De Metz, 20 Misc.2d 144, 188 N.Y.S.2d 627 (Sup.Ct.1959).

One illustrative situation implicates the defendant who intends to perpetrate an offensive contact on plaintiff, but inadvertently causes a harmful contact. *Vosburg v. Putney*,[8] occasionally used as a curtain-raiser in torts courses, presents facts that might fall into this category. A mischievous schoolboy kicked a fellow student on the shin after their teacher had called class to order. The impact aggravated a pre-existing condition that converted what otherwise would have been a minor bruise into a serious injury. The victim and his parents sued for battery, and in response to defendant's contention that he should answer only for those injuries he might reasonably have foreseen, the court held that he would be responsible for all injuries directly resulting from the wrongful kick, whether or not he might have anticipated them. Thus, one interpretation of *Vosburg* would be that it falls within our aggravated-harm scenario. However, what made the kick wrongful? If defendant did not mean to hurt plaintiff, the conduct was tortious because of defendant's intent to commit an offensive battery, in that he knew that the kick amounted to an unpermitted contact at the time and place he delivered it.

Similarly, where defendant intends to invade a plaintiff's legally protected interest in physical security and inadvertently invades a different protected interest, courts have not hesitated to hold defen-

---

8. 80 Wis. 523, 50 N.W. 403 (1891). For a fascinating account of *Vosburg* and its historical context, *see* Zigurds Zile, Vosburg v. Putney: *A Centennial Story*, 1992 WIS. L. REV. 877.

dant liable for the second invasion. Thus, if defendant intends to inflict an offensive contact on plaintiff but inadvertently perpetrates a harmful contact, he will be held liable for the latter under a theory of battery, even if he did not intend to injure plaintiff.[9] If defendant intends merely to make plaintiff apprehensive of an immediate bodily contact but ends up inadvertently inflicting such a contact, even if he did not intend the latter he will be held liable for battery.[10] The courts treat a defendant as though he had meant to violate the legal interest that was actually violated, a legal fiction fortified by the fact that there was a direct cause-in-fact relationship between defendant's act and the infliction of harm. There are several possible justifications for the fiction. It brings about results consistent with the early rule that imposed liability for directly inflicted harm. It also reflects a moral condemnation of intentional wrongdoing. In addition, the influence of the criminal law seems to loom large here, in the sense that the rule enables society to punish wrongdoers who may otherwise escape liability.

In these cases, the courts resort to a legal fiction because otherwise they might not be able to justify holding defendant liable at all. This would be true where defendant intends a harmful contact and fails to do so, but instead inadvertently makes plaintiff apprehensive of the contact, or intends to

9. *See* Dan B. Dobbs, The Law of Torts § 40, at 75 (2000).

10. *See* Manning v. Grimsley, 643 F.2d 20 (1st Cir.1981) (pitcher warming up in Fenway Park bullpen threw ball at fence behind which hecklers had positioned themselves; spheroid unexpectedly sailed through small hole in fence and hit one of them).

make plaintiff apprehensive and fails to do so, but instead inadvertently causes a harmful contact. The important point here is that if defendant had not invaded the interest he ended up unintentionally invading, he would not have committed an actionable intentional tort. Hence, the use of the fiction became necessary in order to make defendant answer for the harm plaintiff actually suffered.

However, there may be other situations in which defendant intentionally violates one kind of protected interest and inadvertently violated another. For example, defendant intends to imprison plaintiff, who then suffers physical injury in a reasonable attempt to escape. Here a court would not necessarily have to resort to a fiction in order to hold defendant liable for the harm plaintiff incurred while escaping, since it could include within plaintiff's recovery for false imprisonment damages not only for the wrongful confinement, but also for the injuries sustained as a direct result of it.[11]

Thus far, I have discussed intentional torts requiring proof of a state of mind that would justify a conclusion that defendant was morally blameworthy. However, not every intentional tort requires proof of this kind of culpability. For example, the tort of trespass to land necessitates only that defendant acted, and that as a result of his action he disturbed the possessory interest of another. Even though he failed to realize he was violating this

11. This occurred in Sindle v. New York City Transit Auth., 33 N.Y.2d 293, 352 N.Y.S.2d 183, 307 N.E.2d 245 (1973).

legally protected interest, he will be held liable for trespass.[12]

Suppose as a result of a trespass plaintiff suffers harm greatly in excess of or different from what might reasonably have been expected. For example, defendant does something that causes water to accumulate on plaintiff's land and form a fetid pool, in which mosquitoes subsequently breed. One of these insects bites plaintiff, who sustains a serious personal injury as a result.[13] Clearly defendant would be liable for trespass to land, and plaintiff could recover for the violation of his right to the exclusive possession of his property. But should plaintiff also be permitted to recover substantial damages for the unanticipated physical harm he sustained? One way of dealing with the extent-of-liability issue would be to examine defendant's state of mind when he committed the trespass. If he meant to damage plaintiff's possessory interest by casting water he knew to be contaminated onto plaintiff's land, his conduct might be found to have a sufficient degree of moral culpability to justify imposing liability for any harm that resulted, no matter how unexpected. On the other hand, if he had no reason to believe that the water would invade plaintiff's premises, even though he might have committed an actionable trespass, what he did might not be blameworthy enough to warrant holding him responsible for unforeseeable damage.

12. *See* DAN B. DOBBS, *supra* note 9, § 51 at 98.

13. For a decision imposing liability on these facts, *see* Wardrop v. City of Manhattan Beach, 160 Cal.App.2d 779, 326 P.2d 15 (1958).

Intentional Torts and the Persons-at-Risk Scenario. In cases where defendant intends to commit an intentional tort on a specifically targeted individual, and instead violates a legally protected interest of someone else whose presence was not and could not reasonably have been anticipated, should defendant be liable to the actual victim? Where defendant's misconduct is directed at one person and a different person suffers harm, an initial conceptual problem arises, in that courts would have to determine what type of cause of action plaintiff can assert.

In claims based on the ancient common-law torts of assault, battery and false imprisonment, courts have solved this problem by resorting to the same kind of legal fiction they have used in cases where defendant intends to violate one kind of protected interest enjoyed by plaintiff and ends up violating another. Suppose a tortfeasor means to assault, batter or imprison a particular target. However, instead of harming her intended victim, she causes harm to a third person of whose presence she was completely unaware. Such harm might take the form of an injurious or offensive contact, or the immediate apprehension of such a contact, or even confinement. In such situations, courts have invoked the doctrine of transferred intent to permit the actual victim to recover for battery, assault or false imprisonment.[14] They accomplish this result

14. *See* W. PAGE KEETON, *supra* note 2, § 8 at 37–39.

by taking the wrongful intent of defendant *vis-à-vis* her intended target and "transferring" it, as if by magic, to the plaintiff. Thus, defendant is treated as though she had meant to violate plaintiff's interest, even though she had no reason to suspect plaintiff would be put at risk by her conduct. The same reasons supporting recovery when defendant meant to subject plaintiff to one type of risk but instead subjected him to another would apply equally as well in this type of case. Note that the transferred-intent doctrine obviates the need for any analysis of proximate cause, since the fiction used by the courts performs the function of extending defendant's liability to an unknown victim.

What about cases that do not involve the old common-law intentional torts? Suppose that in reaction to outrageous misconduct defendant directs at a third party, plaintiff suffers no harmful contact, is not apprehensive of such an immediate contact and has no restrictions placed on his freedom of movement, but instead suffers extreme emotional distress. Here courts have mechanically refused to apply the doctrine of transferred intent. A likely reason for this derives from a desire to prevent the possibility of open-ended liability for emotional distress, since there might be a large number of eyewitnesses to a defendant's egregious misconduct.

One approach to restricting the extent of liability here would be to posit that a third party might recover for the tort of outrage (or intentional infliction of emotional distress) upon proof that defendant knew with substantial certainty that his conduct, even though directed at another, would subject the third party to substantial mental suffering. Such a finding could be made only if defendant knew or had good reason to know of plaintiff's presence. Hence, if defendant was unaware that plaintiff was witnessing the misconduct aimed at the third party, plaintiff's distress would fall outside the scope of liability. The Second Edition of the *Restatement of Torts* goes even further and would place additional limits on the extent of liability for intentional infliction of distress on a third-party witness; either plaintiff must sustain some actual bodily harm as a result of the fear, fright or shock, or she must be a member of the primary victim's family.[15]

Intentional Torts and Rescuers. Suppose an intentional tortfeasor places his victim in peril or in need of medical attention, and a rescuer injures herself while trying to help the latter. Certainly if plaintiff might have recovered against a defendant whose negligence created the need for a rescue, she should be able to recover against an defendant whose intentional wrongdoing created an identical need.

A more interesting question is whether on the particular facts of a rescue case plaintiff could not have recovered against a negligent tortfeasor, she might still be permitted to recover against an intentional wrongdoer. Consider the case of the plaintiff

15. 1 AMERICAN LAW INSTITUTE, RESTATEMENT, SECOND, TORTS § 46 (2) (1965).

who donates an organ to the victim of a battery at the hands of defendant. Courts have refused to permit organ donors to recover against defendants whose negligence caused serious injuries necessitating the donation.[16] Might they take a different tack in the battery scenario?

One feasible approach would be to ask whether, on the specific facts of the case, defendant's moral culpability was of a sufficient degree to justify extending the scope of his liability to harm suffered by an organ donor. This should probably be a question for the jury, since it requires the application of community standards of fairness.

Intentional Torts and Other Extent-of-Liability Scenarios. Although actual cases may be quite rare, it is conceivable that other kinds of proximate-cause issues might arise in intentional-tort cases. The victim of an intentional tortfeasor, for example, might be injured in a traffic accident on the way to the hospital. Defendant might intend to inflict one kind of harmful contact, but the way it actually happens might be bizarre and totally unforeseeable.

The approach suggested above is that if defendant might be liable for extended or unusual consequences if his conduct had been negligent, he should be liable for them when his conduct was intentionally wrongful. If liability for negligence would not have extended to the particular results in the case at bar, the court might still hold defendant

16. *See* cases cited in Ch. 3, n. 33.

liable if it judged his conduct sufficiently blameworthy so as to make it fair to make him pay for the damage plaintiff incurred.

Proximate Cause and Strict Liability

Suppose a defendant maintains livestock that intrude on a neighbor's property and cause damage; or harbors a tiger that escapes confinement and mauls an innocent passerby;[17] or performs an abnormally dangerous activity that goes awry and causes harm to people in the vicinity; or markets a flawed product that inflicts injuries on consumers. In each of these scenarios, if defendant had been careless and his substandard conduct was a cause-in-fact of the damage or injury, the victims can assert a straight-forward claim in negligence. If defendant argues that his carelessness was not a proximate cause of the resulting harm, the courts will apply normal scope-of-liability rules and doctrines, as discussed in the preceding Chapters.

When defendant used reasonable care in performing the activities listed above but plaintiff still suffered damage, courts have imposed liability under somewhat eclectic principles of strict tort, for reasons rooted in both efficiency and corrective-justice concerns. This is not an appropriate venue to rehearse the detail of these concerns: that strict tort

17. This is not so far-fetched a hypothetical as one might imagine. There are an estimated 5,000 pet tigers in the United States, "a number believed to be at least equal to the world's wild tiger population." Helen Rumbelow, "A Cat–Fight Brews Over Backyard Wildlife," WASHINGTON POST, Sept. 3, 2002, at A3; for more details on pet tigers, see Susan Orlean, "The Lady and the Tigers," THE NEW YORKER, Feb. 18 & 25, 2002, at 95.

can reduce accidents by making it easier for plaintiffs to recover in cases where it might be overly difficult or costly to prove negligence, and by reducing levels of dangerous activities; that it can shift and spread accident costs to parties better able to absorb or distribute them; and that it can bring about achieve corrective justice by imposing strict liability on defendants who subject others to risks of harm that are qualitatively and quantitatively much more serious than the risks to which others subject defendant. Our task is to consider how courts might limit the scope of responsibility in these cases.

One might surmise that the absence of moral culpability on the part of a defendant subject to liability without fault might push in favor of placing narrower limitations on extent of liability than would be drawn in intentional-tort cases. But it is still necessary to consider how courts might define these limitations.

Animals and Proximate Cause: Different Risks. The common law has traditionally imposed strict tort liability for harm or damage resulting from the possession of three kinds of animals: livestock that intrude on the land of others, wild animals, and pets or other domesticated animals (generally dogs) that have demonstrated dangerous propensities.[18] The courts have limited liability in these cases to the risks that made it both efficient and just to hold defendants responsible without fault in the first place. Hence, straying livestock generally create the risk of property damage to

18. *See* W. PAGE KEETON, *supra* note 2, §§ 76, 78.

adjacent possessors of land. Wild animals and dogs who have taken their first bite generally create a risk of injury to persons unfortunate enough to encounter them at inopportune moments. What this suggests is that someone who inadvertently trips over a sleeping dog or lion and suffers only a broken leg would not be permitted to recover in strict tort from the owner, since the risk of traumatic injury from a fall is not one of the bundle of hazards that makes these animals so dangerous as to justify imposing strict tort liability. On the other hand, tripping and breaking a leg in an effort to escape from a wild animal or vicious dog might be well within the scope of foreseeable risks that make such animals extremely dangerous.[19] Extent of liability in these cases would be governed by the contours of the obligation owed by those responsible for the control of inherently vicious beasts or domesticated animals that have demonstrated hazardous tendencies, rather than by a separate rule of proximate cause.

Note that this might be considered a *de facto* application of the risk-foreseeability approach, limiting the scope of defendant's liability to the foreseeable risks that make it appropriate to impose strict liability on the owner of the offending animal. A tiger has certain characteristics that make it extremely dangerous and frightening to humans. A person who keeps a tiger as a pet should be respon-

19. *See* 3 AMERICAN LAW INSTITUTE, RESTATEMENT, SECOND, TORTS § 507 cmt. g (1965).

sible for any tiger-inflicted harm associated with these characteristic risks.

Animals and Proximate Cause: Interventions. Hollywood-inspired hypotheticals serve to illustrate the kinds of issues that might arise where the acts of animals combine with natural or human (or even animal) interventions to inflict harm or damage. The first, courtesy of "The Greatest Show on Earth," evokes the circus train wreck caused by a flood or other natural disaster, with the result that various lions, leopards or other similarly inclined creatures escaped from their cages and cause harm to persons or property in the immediate neighborhood of the accident. The second draws inspiration from "King Kong," in which negligently aggressive photographers provoked the title character to break loose from his chains and create havoc in parts of New York City.

If the owner or possessor should have foreseen the kind of intervention that occurred and might have prevented the escape of the animals by the exercise of due care, plaintiffs injured by the animals might be able to recover from him in negligence, and there would be no need for them to assert strict tort liability.

Suppose, however, that the intervention could not have been anticipated by a reasonable person in defendant's position. One approach would be to consider how strict we would want this particular kind of strict liability to be. Given the potential for serious harm that might befall innocent victims at the teeth, horns, claws or coils of a dangerous animal, a court might want to hold the possessor strictly liable no matter what kind of an intervention caused them to gain their freedom. The *Restatement (Second) of Torts* took this position, except that it expressed no opinion about the effect of intervening acts done with the intent of causing the animal to inflict personal injury or property damage.[20] A preliminary draft of the new *Restatement* posits in a comment that a defendant should not be liable when the intentional misconduct of a third party enables the animal to cause harm, on the ground that it would be unfair to impose liability on someone who no longer has control over the animal.[21] This does not seem entirely convincing, since the possessor of a wild animal might lose control of it because of a negligent human intervention or natural causes, yet the *Restatement* would still hold defendant strictly liable. Thus, the control element does not provide an adequate explanation for limiting liability in animal cases.

If capability to inflict serious harm or damage is the appropriate criterion, the lack of it would justify not imposing liability for harm caused by straying livestock when the unforeseeable intervention of natural forces or third persons causes them to roam at large and they damage a neighbor's property. Thus, the hazards posed by meandering livestock

20. *Id.* § 510.

21. *See* AMERICAN LAW INSTITUTE, RESTATEMENT, THIRD, TORTS: LIABILITY FOR PHYSICAL HARM (BASIC PRINCIPLES) § 24 cmt. b (Tentative Draft 1, March 28, 2001).

might not be so serious as to warrant extending the scope of liability in intervention cases.

Animals and Other Extent-of-Liability Scenarios. Again, although actual cases are sparse, one might visualize other kinds of proximate-cause issues developing in animal strict-liability cases. For example, an attack might occur long after the escape or at a place far removed from where defendant had kept the beast. Presumably a court might want to draw the line somewhere. One solution in these kinds of remoteness cases would be to absolve a defendant from responsibility if the animal eventually reaches a natural environment approximating its native habitat.[22]

The strict liability of an animal owner might extend to rescuers injured in efforts to protect the immediate victim of a dangerous beast, for the same reasons that would apply in negligence cases. Whether fringe "rescuers," such as organ donors, should also be permitted to recover in strict tort is a closer question, although one might argue that because of the high degree of risk associated with defendant's conduct, the scope of liability might extend further than it would for a negligent defendant.

Abnormally Dangerous Activity and Proximate Cause: Different Risks. When defendant engages in an abnormally dangerous activity, defined as one that brings into being a foreseeable and highly significant risk of physical harm even though

22. This is the position taken in 3 AMERICAN LAW INSTITUTE, RESTATEMENT, SECOND, TORTS § 508 (1965).

reasonable care is exercised and that is not a matter of common usage,[23] courts have imposed strict tort liability for harm resulting from the hazard that makes what defendant is doing extremely hazardous. As with animals, defendant will not be strictly liable for harm resulting from a danger not within the parameters of the recognized, highly significant risk.

Suppose that a logging company uses dynamite in its operation; on a nearby farm, mother minks who had just given birth to kittens become so agitated by the noise that they kill their young, a not unnatural reaction on the part of these high-strung fur-bearing creatures.[24] The risk of the destruction of new-born minks by their mothers was not one of the foreseeable hazards that made the dynamiting an abnormally dangerous activity, so the logger should not be held strictly liable in tort to the owners of the mink farm. Thus, the court would not have to address the extent-of-liability issue here, because the rule of strict liability will not apply on the facts of the case.

Note once again how nicely this approach meshes with the risk-foreseeability test in negligence cases. What determines the extent of a defendant's liability is the same as what determines whether or not his conduct was tortious. The only significant differ-

23. This is the definition adopted by a preliminary draft of the new Restatement. *See* AMERICAN LAW INSTITUTE, RESTATEMENT, THIRD, TORTS: LIABILITY FOR PHYSICAL HARM (BASIC PRINCIPLES) § 20(b) (Tentative Draft No. 1, March 28, 2001).

24. These facts come from Foster v. Preston Mill Co., 44 Wash.2d 440, 268 P.2d 645 (1954).

ence is one of procedure, in that where plaintiff asserts a cause of action in negligence, whether or not a risk was foreseeable would be a jury question, unless reasonable minds could not differ. However, under strict liability, it is the function of the trial judge to determine whether or not an activity is abnormally dangerous,[25] which would require the court to decide what foreseeable risks defendant's activity generated.

Does the duty-risk approach have any role to play here? The actual cases involving the infanticidal mother minks might be interpreted as applying duty-risk, since plaintiff had in fact informed defendant of how the mothers would react to the noise from charges of dynamite, and defendant nonetheless went ahead with the operation. In finding for defendant, the court stated that as a matter of "sound policy," plaintiff should bear the risk of loss.[26] What the court seemed to be saying was that the duty of the logging company did not extend to the particular kind of damage sustained by plaintiff, even though it was to be expected. The criticism one can level at the opinion was that the court failed to explain what those considerations of policy might be.

Abnormally Dangerous Activity and Proximate Cause: Interventions. The miscarriage of an abnormally dangerous activity may result from a

25. *See* AMERICAN LAW INSTITUTE, RESTATEMENT, THIRD, TORTS: LIABILITY FOR PHYSICAL HARM (BASIC PRINCIPLES) § 20 cmt. i (Tentative Draft No. 1, March 28, 2001).

26. 44 Wash.2d at 446, 268 P.2d at 648.

natural or human intervention. If a reasonable person in defendant's position should have anticipated the intervention and could have prevented it in the exercise of due care, defendant ought to be liable in negligence for resulting harm sustained by plaintiffs.

However, the intervention might have been totally unforeseeable. As in the case of strict liability for dangerous animals, the *Restatement (Second) of Torts* took the position that the unexpected intervening acts of third parties, animals and forces of nature would not supersede defendant's responsibility, except that the document explicitly left open, without discussion, whether the acts of an intervening third party who intended to cause harm would relieve defendant of liability.[27]

The latest draft of the new *Restatement* thus far adopts the same view, except that it would absolve defendants when the harm resulted from the conduct of a third party who meant to cause damage. The justification offered is that it would be unfair to hold defendant strictly liable in such cases, and that liability for the miscarriage of dangerous activities should fall on the person who has "basic control over the relevant danger."[28] On the matter of fairness, as between the innocent victim and the person responsible for an abnormally dangerous activity

27. 3 American Law Institute, Restatement, Second, Torts § 522 (1965).

28. American Law Institute, Restatement, Third, Torts: Liability for Physical Harm (Basic Principles) § 24 cmt. b (Tentative Draft No. 2, March 25, 2002).

that miscarried because of the intervention of an intentional wrongdoer, it would arguably be just to place the loss on the shoulders on the party who created the activity and thereby made the intervention possible. Moreover, the defendant had control that might have prevented the intervention from happening, even though he would have had to have exercised a greater amount of precaution that reasonable care would have required (or might even have had to discontinue or relocate the activity).

Proximate Cause and Products Liability: In General. A manufacturer owes a duty to exercise due care in the design and construction of a product for the benefit of anyone who might foreseeably be put at risk if the duty is breached. In addition, manufacturers have an obligation to use adequate precautions when they provide information that will enable consumers to make an informed choice about whether or not to consume or handle a product, and to use in a reasonably safe way those products to which they decide to expose themselves. A breach of any of these duties might result in the imposition of liability for negligence.[29]

Courts have held that a defendant who places a defective product in the stream of commerce may also be strictly liable for harm that occurs as a result of the defect. As product-liability doctrine has evolved, courts and commentators have reached a near universal consensus that genuine strict tort liability (that is, liability without fault) should apply

29. *See, generally*, 1 DAVID G. OWEN, M. STUART MADDEN & MARY J. DAVIS, MADDEN & OWEN ON PRODUCTS LIABILITY Ch. 2 (2000).

if a product flawed because of some miscarriage in the process of manufacture causes harm to a user, consumer or bystander.[30] The policies supporting this kind of strict liability include cost-spreading (it is better to spread the costs of product-related losses by making consumers pay higher prices for risk-generating products than forcing victims injured by those products to bear the expense), and deterrence (strict liability forces manufacturers to raise loss-prevention levels that might remain less than reasonable if only negligence liability applied, because they might predictably avoid the full measure of liability for negligence[31]). One might even combine these policies by noting that manufacturers normally control levels of risk and are in a superior position to decide either to take precautionary measures that would reduce or eliminate defects or pay for losses caused by their flawed products. Thus, the focus of plaintiff's claim under strict liability is on the condition of the product, and he does not have any need to prove culpability on defendant's part.

However, where the product defect comes into being because of an alleged design flaw or the alleged inadequacy of warnings or instructions for use, although courts may say they are imposing strict liability, in fact they often use the same test that would determine liability for negligence, by

30. *See* 1 *id.* § 7.10, at 423–28 (2000).

31. This might occur if manufacturers could foresee that injured consumers might not be able to prove negligence even though defendants in fact acted unreasonably, or were willing to settle at less that a claim was worth because of difficulties in proving breach of duty or because of pressing financial needs.

weighing the foreseeable costs of avoiding harm by adopting an alternative design, warnings or instructions for use, against the foreseeable costs of accidents that might happen if defendant failed to adopt the alternative urged by plaintiff.[32] This is the balancing approach taken by the new *Restatement of Products Liability*, which specifically eschews labels and refrains from indicating whether the theory it proposes sounds in negligence or strict liability.[33] On the other hand, a number of courts impose a genuine form of strict liability for defective design if the product inflicts harm because it fails to meet the reasonable expectations of the ordinary consumer (the so-called consumer-expectations test, under which plaintiff might recover even though the manufacturer may have exercised due care).[34]

It seems logical that when courts decide products cases under a theory of negligence, they should resolve any proximate-cause issues in the same way they would in any negligence case. Thus, jurisdictions that have adopted a hindsight or risk-foreseeability test would apply it in a straightforward way to determine whether to limit the scope of liability of an allegedly negligent manufacturer for harm caused by a product. The duty-risk approach, on the other hand, might take into account the factual

32. *See, e.g.*, Seattle–First Nat'l Bank v. Tabert, 86 Wash.2d 145, 542 P.2d 774 (1975).

33. *See* AMERICAN LAW INSTITUTE, RESTATEMENT, THIRD, TORTS: PRODUCTS LIABILITY § 2(b)-(c) (1998).

34. *See, e.g.*, Vincer v. Esther Williams All–Aluminum Swimming Pool Co., 69 Wis.2d 326, 230 N.W.2d 794 (1975).

context and unique features of mass production and marketing as relevant to the parameters of the obligations owed by manufacturers and sellers, since the special risks associated with consumer products, their importance to the economy and quality of life, and the nature of the relationship between manufacturers and consumers might implicate policy factors that could bear on the scope of liability for negligence in products cases.

When plaintiff sues in strict tort and there is an issue of extent of liability, the courts would need to decide whether to hold manufacturers and sellers responsible beyond the limits that might be imposed under negligence. The culpability of defendants would be irrelevant in genuine strict tort (as applicable to manufacturing defects and in design cases where courts use the consumer-expectations test), which might support an argument that the scope of liability should be at least co-extensive with (and perhaps narrower than) in negligence, because of the notion that extent of responsibility should be proportionate to the degree of wrongfulness of a defendant's conduct. But the goal of cost-spreading that supports the adoption of strict liability for defective products might cut the other way, in favor of imposing liability for harm that falls even beyond the outer limits of responsibility for negligence.

I shall consider here some typical extent-of-liability problems that have arisen in products cases and compare how a court might resolve them under negligence and strict liability. The first pair of fact patterns will present the sort of issues discussed in

Chapter Three, involving product defects giving rise to one or more risks to one or more persons. Next I shall discuss products liability and intervening acts. Finally, I shall touch upon the special case of product misuse.

Proximate Cause and Products Liability: Multiple Risks. A common scenario places on the table defects that might foreseeably give rise to one type of hazard, but in fact plaintiff suffers a product-related harm that defendant argues was not within the bundle of risks that would have provided justification for considering the product defective. To use a somewhat indelicate yet apt example, suppose a restaurant customer eats some shrimp that is unfit for human consumption and throws up in a nearby restroom; shortly thereafter, a customer enters the same restroom, inadvertently slips on what plaintiff has left on the floor and breaks a leg.[35] Plaintiff alleges that a reasonable inspection by the supplier of the food would have revealed that the product was not fit to eat. Defendant insists that its alleged negligence in putting unwholesome food into the stream of commerce was not a proximate cause of plaintiff's fall.

This fact pattern would situate itself within our different-risk scenario. As we have seen, the most common approach courts have taken in these kinds of cases is the risk-foreseeability test, under which a court would need to determine whether the possibility of this type of accident was one of the hazards

35. For a case on these facts, *see* Crankshaw v. Piedmont Driving Club, Inc., 115 Ga.App. 820, 156 S.E.2d 208 (1967).

that made it negligent for defendant to serve defective shrimp. Would a reasonable person in defendant's position have anticipated that this kind of mishap might result from the marketing of defective shrimp? Certainly the risk that a consumer might become nauseous and vomit was well within the scope of the risk. What happened to plaintiff presents a more difficult issue. If defendant had marketed a defective automobile, the chance that it might become disabled and cause a collision with another vehicle (and injure the latter's occupants) would be foreseeable. Indeed, a court might easily find that if the defect ended up causing a highway accident, the victim could recover even though the exact way the accident occurred could not have been anticipated.[36] But the environment of use of unwholesome shrimp is much less likely to create risks to parties other than the consumer. Whether the trial judge should let the issue go to the jury or should decide that what happened was unforeseeable as a matter of law and hence not a result within the risk would be a close question.

How might a hindsight approach resolve the extent-of-liability issue here? In the actual case from which I have borrowed these facts, the court upheld the dismissal of plaintiff's claim on the ground that the harm was no more than the conceivable or possible result of defendant's carelessness, which

36. For an example of a negligence case taking this position, *see* Ferroggiaro v. Bowline, 153 Cal.App.2d 759, 315 P.2d 446 (1957) (defendant's careless driving caused vehicle to strike pole and disable traffic lights, as a result of which two cars collided at intersection and passenger suffered injury).

was therefore too remote and not the proximate cause of the injury.[37] However, this language merely expresses a conclusion and does not adequately explain why plaintiff should not recover. Indeed, none of the various versions of the hindsight test seem to present a workable, principled approach to these kinds of cases.

Suppose plaintiff's theory of recovery was that the court should hold defendant strictly liable in tort for supplying unwholesome (i.e., defective) food, and defendant raised the proximate-cause issue. One judicial approach might be to use the functional equivalent of the risk-foreseeability test and ask whether what happened to plaintiff occurred as a result of one of the foreseeable risks that would justified classifying unwholesome shrimp as defective. This would present the same close question as would arise if plaintiff had sued in negligence.

Duty-risk might be more flexible in strict tort cases, inasmuch as to determine the scope of duty, the court might take into account the policies that support holding manufacturers and sellers liable for harm caused by defective products, even though defendants may not have been negligent. Thus, whether or not extending liability to include remotely possible risks would advance the goals of deterrence and cost-spreading that undergird the theory of strict tort liability for flawed products could be the focus of the court's inquiry.

37. *Crankshaw, supra* note 35.

A particularly unique scope-of-liability issue in the products field has arisen in cases involving harm to the children of women who developed defects in their reproductive systems as a result of their mothers' consumption of the drug DES during pregnancy. The drug had caused cancers in a number of the daughters, whose suits against the manufacturers have generated a number of difficult issues.[38] Equally problematic, if not more so, is the extent-of-liability conundrum that has arisen as a consequence of the discovery that the drug might also have caused serious harm to the second generation of offspring of the original consumers of the product.[39]

Although the temptation exists to invoke the talismanic phrase "remoteness" or to draw analogies to *Palsgraf*, the duty-risk approach seems much better suited to deal with this issue. The basic question to be resolved is whether as a matter of sound policy liability should extend to (and perhaps even beyond) the second generation of victims of dangerous prescription drugs. To reach an answer, courts should carefully consider the possibility that liability might financially overwhelm defendants,

38. *See, e.g.,* Payton v. Abbott Labs., 386 Mass. 540, 437 N.E.2d 171 (1982) (suit by DES daughters for emotional harm caused by worry about the increased risk of developing cancer in future); Sindell v. Abbott Labs., 26 Cal.3d 588, 163 Cal.Rptr. 132, 607 P.2d 924, *cert. denied*, 449 U.S. 912 (1980) (imposition of so-called market-share liability for harm caused to DES daughters).

39. For illustrative cases, *see* Enright v. Eli Lilly & Co., 77 N.Y.2d 377, 568 N.Y.S.2d 550, 570 N.E.2d 198, *cert. den.*, 502 U.S. 868 (1991); Grover v. Eli Lilly & Co., 63 Ohio St.3d 756, 591 N.E.2d 696 (1992).

the impact the imposition of liability might have on pharmaceutical research and development, the implications of leaving innocent victims without a remedy against tortfeasors, and practical problems such as the difficulties of proving causation in individual cases.

Proximate Cause and Products Liability: Interventions. A product defect and a force generated by a third person or an animal may combine to cause harm to plaintiff. Suppose defendant manufactures a large, heavy mask that caricatures the face of President Bill Clinton or George Bush and fits over the entire head of the wearer; a nightclub entertainer is wearing one of them when a patron shoves him violently from behind; he falls to the floor and the weight of the mask causes his neck to twist; he suffers a serious strain that disables him for weeks.[40] Let us further postulate two possible product defects that might have contributed to the injury: (1) a flaw in the safety harness built into the mask for the purpose of providing support for the neck and head of the wearer; or (2) a design defect, in that the manufacturer failed to incorporate such a harness into the structure of the mask. In suits for negligence and strict tort liability, how should the court deal with defendant's claim that neither alleged flaw was a proximate cause of the injuries?

With respect to the claim based on the manufacturing defect, plaintiff would argue that the func-

40. Inspiration from this example comes from Price v. Blaine Kern Artista, Inc., 111 Nev. 515, 893 P.2d 367 (1995), involving a mask that reproduced the features of President George Herbert Walker Bush.

tion of the harness was to maintain sufficient stability so as to prevent the mask from causing the wearer to lose his balance and from subjecting the wearer to excessive pressure in the event of a fall; the harm suffered by plaintiff resulted from one or both of these risks; and the reason why an outside force caused plaintiff to fall (a malicious shove) should be irrelevant. The fact that the harness was incorporated into the design of the product indicated an awareness on the part of the manufacturer that users might be subjected to outside pushes, pulls or even traumas that might destabilize them. Plaintiff would then attempt to convince the court to treat this as a manner-of-occurrence scenario, and would insist that the risk contributing to his injury was the very risk that would justify concluding that the mask had a manufacturing defect. Plaintiff could invoke either the risk-foreseeability or the duty-risk test as the basis for his argument.

Defendant would have to concede the foreseeability of a risk that the mask might create instability problems for the wearer if he tripped or otherwise lost his balance, but would contend that the danger of a deliberate push by a third person was outside the scope of the risks that might foreseeably arise from a defective harness.

Plaintiff could counter, first, by urging that defendant should have foreseen the risk of a deliberate push by a third person, because of the strong emotions a Clinton or Bush mask might provoke in a politically excitable person (especially in the environments where such masks might be worn). However, this argument might lead to results that depended on whether the caricature depicted a highly controversial public figure or a lovable icon such as Mickey Mouse.

A second line of argument, as suggested above, would posit that the result—neck injuries—was within the scope of the risks arising from the failure of the harness to function properly, and the fact that defendant may not have reasonably anticipated that an aggressive third party would push the mask wearer and cause him to fall should not remove what happened from the scope of liability.

Would this case be on all fours with our spilled-gasoline hypothetical, where a third party intentionally and unforeseeably tosses a cigarette butt or match into a highly combustible puddle? Would strong considerations of fairness support defendant's position that it should not bear responsibility for harm caused by a battery committed by plaintiff's assailant? In the mask case, the product arguably furnished a specific motivation and occasion for the third-party intervention. Without the mask there would have been no reason for the shove. On the other hand, it is conceivable that the unknown intervenor who set the gasoline on fire might well have found other ways to inflict damage. What this suggests is that if defendant could prove that the assailant had a personal grudge that would have motivated an attack even without the presence of defendant's mask, this might properly supersede liability on defendant's part.

Should the result differ depending on whether plaintiff's claim sounds in negligence or strict liability? Once again, a court might justify a more expanded scope of liability under strict tort, on the ground that the policy of loss spreading would justify placing on the manufacturer the costs of injury from intervening criminal acts.

To confront the second factual version requiring a claim of defective design where the injured victim sought recovery under negligence or strict liability that requires proof of what would amount to negligence, plaintiff would have to establish that there was a foreseeable risk of harm from the weight of the mask and that a safety harness was technologically feasible and not excessively expensive. Whether the danger of a malicious shove fell within the scope of the risks that defendant should have anticipated, and whether the foreseeability of an intentional push should be irrelevant would raise the same problems discussed above.

In the actual case from which I have derived these facts, the court strained to develop a different justification for reaching a result in plaintiff's favor under strict liability as well as under negligence. Drawing an analogy to the crashworthiness doctrine, under which courts have held automobile manufacturers liable for failing to protect passengers from impacts with the interior of a vehicle during a collision, the opinion pointed to judicial language suggesting that the motivation of a third person who caused the original collision would be irrelevant (so that the intentional ramming of plaintiff's vehicle by someone seeking to injure him would not relieve the manufacturer from liability). However, the sentence that the court cited, to the effect that the crashworthiness doctrine applies "whatever the cause of the accident,"[41] is clearly dictum and might be read as referring to accidental causes only. Moreover, the court never really explained why it was extending the scope of a manufacturer's liability to cover these kinds of cases, other than by alluding to the desirability of having a more expansive rule in strict liability cases.

Proximate Cause and Products Liability: Misuse. One extent-of-liability issue that recurs in manufacturers-liability cases involves product misuse that results in harm when the misuser is the injured plaintiff or when the misuser's conduct contributes to the infliction of harm on an innocent plaintiff.

In both situations, the initial question that the court must resolve is whether the product was defective. A negative finding would mandate a dismissal, whatever theory of liability plaintiff asserts. The approach courts generally take is to consider whether the misuse was reasonably foreseeable, and whether defendant should have modified the design of the product, or included warnings, in order to protect against the risks that might arise if someone used the product in a manner not intended by the manufacturer. If the misuse could not have been anticipated, or if it could have been foreseen

41. Soule v. General Motors Corp., 8 Cal.4th 548, 34 Cal. Rptr.2d 607, 882 P.2d 298, 303 (1994).

but there was no reasonable way to design out or caution against the risk, the court would have no option but to rule that the product was not defective, and hence neither an injured misuser nor a plaintiff injured by a misuser would be able to recover damages.

If, on the other hand, the court were to rule that the manufacturer should have incorporated an alternative design or issues warnings that would have negated or reduced the risk of misuse, defendant might still raise the affirmative defense of contributory fault against an injured misuser. In a jurisdiction that still recognized contributory negligence, this would be a complete bar to recovery, while in a comparative-negligence jurisdiction plaintiff might receive compensation, reduced by the percentage of fault attributed to him. The fault of the misuser, however, would not in and of itself bar a victim of the misuser from recovering all or part of the damages sustained.

Chapter 6

Whither Proximate Cause (Scope of Liability)?

Our trip with gun, camera and divining rod through the hills and valleys of proximate cause has enabled us to peruse the factual landscape as well as the various ways courts and commentators have reacted to it. As I indicated in Chapter One, and have sought to demonstrate in subsequent Chapters, there are no easy answers to the problem of how to fix just and sensible limits on the scope of a tortfeasor's liability. One important insight that our odyssey has produced is that this may be in large part due to the varieties of context that may give rise to the extent-of-liability conundrum. Hence, it should come as no surprise that there is no simple, "one-size-fits-all" approach that neatly solves the entire range of issues that gather under the rubric of extent of liability.

What we have seen on our journey is that each of the tests we have examined has something positive to offer. Certain kinds of cases seem amenable to resolution through the application of the duty-risk test, while for others the risk-foreseeability approach works smoothly and effectively. There are even scope-of-liability issues that a hindsight test can best resolve. Thus, it may well be that judges could use any one of the three, depending on which performs best under the circumstances.

This, of course, does not mean that courts should decide in an unprincipled way, on the basis of personal whim, political preference or otherwise, how far liability should extend in a particular case (*i.e.*, the bottom line), and then choose the approach that will enable them to reach the result they have foreordained. It does mean that courts might determine on a principled basis the kinds of cases each test handles best, and then apply that test consistently when the appropriate scenario requires considering whether to limit the extent of liability.

My own conclusion on this point is that courts could do this most efficiently by using as their starting point a modified version of duty-risk. The first question they should address would be whether the particular extent-of-liability issue before them might be addressed according to existing rules or new rules worth developing as part of the formulation of defendant's legal duty and its scope. In other words, is there, or should there be, a generally applicable rule of law that specifically defines the extent of defendant's liability? An affirmative answer would require the court either to apply a pre-existing rule that speaks directly to the scope issue, or create a new rule by using the tools traditionally available to courts when they address the duty element in any torts case.

If there is no existing rule defining scope and applicable to the case at bar, and if the court determines that creating a new scope-of-duty rule would be inappropriate because of the difficulty or undesirability of crafting a proposition that would have general applicability (here *Palsgraf* comes most readily to mind), the court should then seek to determine extent of liability by considering whether the risk that harmed plaintiff was one of the risks that made defendant's conduct negligent. This would amount to an invocation of the risk-foreseeability test, which would focus attention on specifics such as the dangers likely to arise from particular conduct. The critical difference between duty-risk as I envision it here (and I shall have more to say on this point in a moment) and risk-foreseeability is that the latter requires the court to focus on the facts of the case before it, and to determine whether the specific risk that cause specific harm to a specific plaintiff was within the scope of the risks that made a specific defendant negligent, whereas duty-risk requires a more general look at classes of plaintiffs, defendants, risks and harms.

As a final, fall-back position, if risk-foreseeability failed to work well (as might occur in certain non-recurring freak-accident contexts), the court might resort to an appropriate hindsight test, based on considerations such as fundamental fairness or "rough justice," which would resolve the dispute between the parties in a sensible way.

We have already seen that duty-risk as originally conceived would require judges to define the reach of a defendant's responsibility by determining as a matter of law both the existence and the scope of his or her legal duty. This they would do by taking into account not only relevant policy, moral and practical factors but also the specific factual background of the dispute before them. Hence, determinations of duty and its scope might vary, depending on whether, for example, defendant was in the business of providing transportation, or medical services, or products for consumption or use.[1] However, under this approach it is conceivable that different judges might reach different conclusions when they fashioned the scope of a defendant's duty on the basis of similar elements to which they might give different weights, and factual circumstances would never be quite the same in each case. This gives traditional duty-risk a certain formlessness and plasticity that would make it very difficult for anyone to predict ahead of time how judges might decide cases, and creates the possibility that courts might decide similar cases in different ways. Both the stability essential to the smooth functioning of the judicial system and the protection of justifiable reliance interests, as well as to the promoting of the goal of equal justice under law, would be difficult to achieve under pristine duty-risk, which perhaps helps explain why courts have been on the whole quite reluctant to embrace it.

However, there may be a way to rescue duty-risk from what are perceived as its shortcomings, and to build on its strengths. Recall that at the end of

1. Indeed, the one torts casebook utilizing a legal-realist approach and embracing duty-risk organizes its chapters according to factual context. *See* LEON GREEN ET AL., CASES ON THE LAW OF TORTS (2d ed. 1977).

Chapter Two, in our discussion of duty-risk, we saw that the approach has roots in legal realism, a jurisprudential movement that looked with great skepticism on legal rules. This is because the legal realists were reacting against formalism, the dominant legal theory of the late nineteenth and early twentieth centuries. Formalism, or mechanical jurisprudence as some called it, saw law as a self-contained science, unaffected by and unconcerned with the society in which it operated. In deciding cases under the common law, courts using formalism took the view that they could derive rules to solve any issue before them by rigorously reasoning from precedent.

The realists, on the other hand, argued that legal rules and principles were and should be the creation of judges, rather than the dictates of some "brooding omnipresence in the sky," and that for the most part they consciously or unconsciously reflect judicial policy preferences. Under formalism, the realists maintained, judges hid what they were doing behind reasoning that often manipulated precedent as a way of promoting the policy goals that appealed to them; instead, courts should openly decide cases by carefully weighing considerations of policy, as well as morality and practicality. The duty-risk approach derives directly from this aspect of legal realism.

The legal realists were undoubtedly correct in faulting formalism for taking an extreme position by insisting that courts could solve all legal problems on the basis of rules and principles they extracted from prior holdings. However, it seems equally obvious that legal realism went to the other extreme in its intransigent averseness to all legal rules. Duty-risk, in its pure form, reflects this extremism by holding in effect that each dispute should be decided on the basis of judicial applications of policy, morality and practical factors to a particular factual context.

There may be a middle ground here. But to reach it, we would first have to set aside the realists' unyielding hostility to rules and accept the possibility that courts are capable of creating and refining generally applicable and acceptable propositions of law to delineate scope of liability in recurring situations, and that factual variations in subsequent cases need not always exert decisive influences on determinations of scope of duty. If we limit duty-risk to cases that courts can decide by either applying or fashioning such propositions or rules, the approach becomes more manageable and escapes the criticism that it is excessively *ad hoc*. We have already seen a number of examples where courts have actually done this, such as when they have extended liability to rescuers, or have held tortfeasors responsible for aggravated harm caused by the negligent provision of medical services made necessary by them, or have made defendants responsible for failing to protect victims against the criminal acts of unknown third parties. These are situations where courts have been able to utilize the various considerations (policy, morality and practicality) that properly serve as justifications for recognizing or not recognizing legal duties, or for recognizing them with specific limitation on their scope.

Suppose there is no existing rule of law that speaks directly to the extent-of-liability issue in dispute, nor is there any new general proposition that a court might fashion on the basis of policy, moral or practical considerations, and that would adequately determine scope of liability as a matter of law. In such situations plaintiff would often have to assert that defendant is under a general duty to protect foreseeable plaintiffs against foreseeable risks of foreseeable kinds of harm, and a general standard of negligence governs. If a legitimate scope-of-liability issue then presented itself, the court could turn to risk-foreseeability, or the risk rule, and ask whether the actual risk that caused harm to plaintiff fell within the range of the risks that would justify a finding that defendant's conduct fell below the standard of reasonable care.

What role might a hindsight test properly play? I have not attempted to conceal my belief that most hindsight tests do not work well, in large part because of the difficulty in articulating them in a way that makes sense and is consistent with the goals of tort law, and in framing instructions that will be meaningful to a jury. However, there *are* instances in which it is impossible to frame a generally applicable scope-of-duty rule, and risk-foreseeability fails as a mechanism for limiting liability. These problems often arise in freak-accident cases that are highly unlikely to repeat themselves. Since the scope issue may be a close one in these situations, making the call based on the community's sense of fairness or the common sense of the ordinary person seems to be to be a just and sensible solution. The jury would be the appropriate body to render such a decision. Strict judicial control of the types of issues juries might resolve under the standard of "rough justice" would minimize the risk of unfair verdicts.

The approach I have suggested is in large part consistent with the direction being taken in a preliminary draft of the new *Restatement of Torts*. The Reporters posit that duty is a primary mechanism for limiting liability, and assert it "is a preferable means for addressing limits on liability when those limitations are clear, are based on relatively bright lines, are of general application, do not usually require resort to disputed facts in a case, and implicate policy concerns that apply to a class of cases that may not be fully appreciated by a jury deciding a specific case."[2] They also include black-letter provisions adopting the rescue doctrine[3] and a rule imposing liability for enhanced injury due to the efforts of others to help a plaintiff harmed as a result of defendant's tortious conduct.[4] One might

2. AMERICAN LAW INSTITUTE, RESTATEMENT OF TORTS: LIABILITY FOR PHYSICAL HARM (BASIC PRINCIPLES) § 29 cmt. d at 195–96 (Tentative Draft No. 2, March 25, 2002).

3. *Id.* § 31.

4. *Id.* § 34.

easily interpret these sections as scope-of-duty rules.

For scope issues that courts cannot resolve in the context of the duty element, the *Restatement* proposes what it refers to as the "risk standard,"[5] exculpating actors from "harm different from the harm whose risks made the actor's conduct tortious."[6] This is essentially the risk-foreseeability test, which the Reporters point out "has the virtue of relative simplicity,"[7] and "can be employed to do justice in a wide range of cases in which the particular facts require careful consideration and thereby resist any rule-like formulation."[8]

Finally, the Reporters recognize that in some situations, characterizing risks may be a highly debatable question and might "lead to different outcomes and require the drawing of an evaluative and somewhat arbitrary line. Those cases are left to the community judgment and common sense provided by the jury."[9] This permits, in a limited number of situations, resort to a hindsight test based on "rough justice."

Thus, a flexible, pragmatic and somewhat eclectic approach may in the end prove to be the most consistently just and efficient way to deal with scope of liability. An unidentified French savant is supposed once to have said, "What you suggest may

5. *Id.* § 29 cmt. e at 199.
6. *Id.* § 29.
7. *Id.* § 29 cmt. j at 210.
8. *Id.* § 29 cmt. j at 211.
9. *Id.* § 29 cmt. i at 209.

be all very well in practice, but it will never work in theory." Since applicability to the real-life problem of setting limits to the extent of a tortfeasor's responsibility is what is at stake here, I would argue that the Gallic philosopher's apocryphal dictum identifies a strength rather than a weakness.

TABLE OF CASES

References are to Pages.

Alabama G.S.R. Co. v. Chapman, 118
Albala v. City of New York, 112
Anthony v. Slaid, 57
Atchison, T. & S.F.R. Co. v. Stanford, 53

Bansasine v. Bodell, 127
Barber Lines A/S v. M/V Donau Maru, 130
Berko v. Freda, 176
Blue Shield v. McCready, 12
Bunting v. Hogsett, 96

Calkins v. Albi, 203
Carroll Towing Co., United States v., 21, 69
Cauverien v. De Metz, 219
Chase v. Washington Water Power Co., 156
Christianson v. Chicago, St. P., M. & O. Ry. Co., 53
Cleveland v. Rotman, 137
Comstock v. General Motors Corp., 204
Crankshaw v. Piedmont Driving Club, Inc., 241
Cruz v. Middlekauff Lincoln–Mercury, Inc., 175

Danielenko v. Kinney Rent A Car, Inc., 188
Day v. Waffle House, Inc., 121
Dellwo v. Pearson, 71
Dewey v. A. F. Klaveness & Co., 24
Di Ponzio v. Riordan, 103
Doughty v Turner Manufacturing Co, 105
Dudley v. Offender Aid and Restoration of Richmond, Inc., 189

TABLE OF CASES

Enright v. Eli Lilly & Co., 10, 244

Ferroggiaro v. Bowline, 242
Firman v. Sacia, 138
Ford Motor Co. v. Wagoner, 204
Foster v. Preston Mill Co., 10, 234
Fuentes v. Consolidated Rail Corp., 113

Gallick v. Baltimore & Ohio R. Co., 11
Gorris v. Scott, 101
Green-Wheeler Shoe Co. v. Chicago, R.I. & P.R. Co., 147
Grover v. Eli Lilly & Co., 244

Healy v. Hoy, 59
Henley v. Pizitz Realty Co., 187
Hill v. Lundin & Associates, Inc., 80
Hill v. Winsor, 95
Hines v. Garrett, 187
Hines v. Morrow, 96
Holmes v. Securities Investor Protection Corp., 12
Hosking v. Robles, 175
Hughes v. Lord Advocate, 104

Johnson v. Kosmos Portland Cement Co., 154
Jorgensen v. Meade Johnson Laboratories, Inc., 112

Kiamas v. Mon-Kota, Inc., 118
King v. Henkie, 144
Kinsman Transit Co., Petition of, 58, 73, 178
Kopriva v. Union Pac. R. Co., 171

Laborers Local 17 Health & Benefit Fund v. Philip Morris, Inc., 58
Lambert v. Parrish, 121
Larrimore v. American Nat. Ins. Co., 100
Liberty Nat. Life Ins. Co. v. Weldon, 188
Lynch v. Fisher, 121

Manning v. Grimsley, 221
Marshall v. Nugent, 60
Martinez v. Lazaroff, 167
Mauney v. Gulf Refining Co., 131
McClenahan v. Cooley, 173

McLaughlin v. Mine Safety Appliances Co., 183
McLaughlin v. Sullivan, 137
Milligan v. County Line Liquor, Inc., 144
Milwaukee & St. P.R. Co. v. Kellogg, 52
Moore v. Shah, 126

Nelson v. Washington Parish, 192

Overseas Tankship (U.K.) Ltd. v. Miller Steamship Co., 69
Overseas Tankship (U.K.) Ltd. v. Morts Dock & Engineering, 67

Palsgraf v. Long Island R. Co., 22, 43
Payton v. Abbott Labs, 244
Pennsylvania R. Co. v. Hope, 63
People Exp. Airlines, Inc. v. Consolidated Rail Corp., 130
Petition of (see name of party)
Phan Son Van v. Peña, 146
Pittsburg Reduction Co. v. Horton, 203
Polemis & Furness Withy & Co. Ltd., In re, 41
Price v. Blaine Kern Artista, Inc., 245

Rappaport v. Nichols, 145
Renslow v. Mennonite Hospital, 112

Schilling v. Stockel, 9
Seattle–First Nat. Bank v. Tabert, 239
Sindell v. Abbott Laboratories, 244
Sindle v. New York City Transit Authority, 222
Sinram v. Pennsylvania R. Co., 73
Sirianni v. Anna, 121, 126
Smith v. London and South Western Railway Co, 33
Smith v. Shaffer, 175
Soule v. General Motors Corp., 249
State ex rel. Richardson v. Edgeworth, 218
Steamfitters Local 420 v. Philip Morris, Inc., 12
Steinhauser v. Hertz Corp., 87
Sumpter v. City of Moulton, 181

Tarasoff v. Regents of University of California, 190
Tate v. Canonica, 218
Thing v. La Chusa, 130
Thompson v. Alameda County, 190
Timberwalk Apartments, Partners, Inc. v. Cain, 187
Torres v. El Paso Elec. Co., 180

TABLE OF CASES

Union Pump Co. v. Allbritton, 64
United Food and Commercial Workers Unions v. Philip Morris, Inc., 58
United Novelty Co. v. Daniels, 155
United States v. _____ (see opposing party)

Ventricelli v. Kinney System Rent A Car, Inc., 171
Vincer v. Esther Williams All–Aluminum Swimming Pool Co., 239
Vosburg v. Putney, 220

Wagner v. International Ry. Co., 119
Wardrop v. City of Manhattan Beach, 223
Waters v. New York City Housing Authority, 197
Watson v. Kentucky & Indiana Bridge & R. Co., 194
Wyant v. Crouse, 213

INDEX

References are to pages.

ABNORMALLY DANGEROUS ACTIVITY
Different risks, 233–235
Duty-risk test, 235
Interventions, 235–237
Risk-foreseeability test, 234–235

ACCIDENTAL SELF–INJURY
Generally, 15, 130 et seq.
Duty-risk test, 133
Hindsight test, 133–134
Risk-foreseeability test, 131–133
Subsequent self-injury, 134–135
Suicide, this index

ACTS OF GOD
Generally, 146 et seq.

AGGRAVATED NEGLIGENCE
Intervention involving, 182 et seq.

ALCOHOLIC BEVERAGES
Social host serving liquor to minor, 164
Tavern owner serving liquor to minor, 144–145

ANIMALS
Different risks, 229–231
Interventions, 147, 231–233
Other extent-of-liability scenarios, 233

ANTI–TRUST
Proximate cause, application of, 12

INDEX
References are to pages.

ASSAULT
Persons-at-risk scenario, 224

AUTOMOBILES
Defective trunk lid, 172
Key-in-ignition cases, 173 et seq.

BACON, FRANCIS
Proximate cause maxim, 29–30

BATTERY
Persons-at-risk scenario, 224

BIRTH DEFECTS
DES children, 244

BREACH OF CONTRACT
Proximate cause, application of, 12

BREACH OF DUTY
Duty, this index
Duty–Risk Test, this index

BURDEN OF PROOF
Shifting, 13

BYSTANDERS
Emotional distress, recovery for, 108 et seq., 129, 225–226
Flying pedestrian, impact with plaintiff-bystander, 115–116
Risk-or-injury-to-another scenario, 137

CARDOZO, BENJAMIN
Loaded gun hypothetical, 110
Palsgraf opinion, 45 et seq.
Rescue doctrine, 119

CAUSATION–IN–FACT
Differentiation from proximate cause, 5 et seq.

CHAIN REACTION CASES
Fairness test, 60

CHILDREN
Birth defects, DES children, 244
Loaded gun hypothetical, 108 et seq.

CHRISTIANSON CASE
Unbroken sequences rule, 53 et seq.

COMMON CARRIERS
Negligent delay in shipment of goods, 147 et seq.

COMPARATIVE FAULT
Contributory or Comparative Fault, this index

COMPOUNDED BAD LUCK CASES
Fairness test, 61

CONSEQUENCES
Direct Consequences Test, this index
Natural and probable consequences test, 19

CONTRACT, BREACH OF
Proximate cause, application of, 12

CONTRIBUTORY OR COMPARATIVE FAULT
Affirmative defense, 9
Interventions by third parties, effect of comparative fault, 206 et seq.
Plaintiff as intervenor, 179 et seq.

CONVERSION OF PROPERTY
Self-injury scenario, 218–219

CORRECTIVE JUSTICE
Generally, 7 et seq.
Historical background, 30
Manner-of-occurrence scenario, 94
Unexpectedly-serious-harm scenario, 85

CRIMINAL INTERVENTIONS
Intervention, this index

CRIMINAL OFFENSES
Broken locks, liability of building owner to rape victim, 198
Intervention, criminal interventions, this index
Proximate cause, application of, 11
Third party, criminal act of, 16

DAMAGES
Unexpectedly-serious-harm scenario, 85 et seq.
Unknown Kind of Damage, this index

DANGEROUS ACTIVITY
Abnormally Dangerous Activity, this index

DEFINITIONS
Proximate cause, 3 et seq.

INDEX
References are to pages.

DELAY
Negligent delay in shipment of goods, 147 et seq.

DETERRENCE FUNCTION
Generally, 8
Intentional torts and aggravated harm scenario, 214–216
Negligent intervention, 162–164
Products liability, 238
Unknown kind of damage, 117

DIFFERENT–RISK SCENARIO
Generally, 14, 99 et seq.
Abnormally dangerous activity, 233–235
Animals, 229–231
Duty-risk test, 101
Hindsight test, 101–102
Intentional torts, 219 et seq.
Manner-of-occurrence scenario, distinguished from, 103 et seq.
No recovery, rationales for, 102–103
Risk-foreseeability test, 99–101
Trespass to land, 222–223

DIRECT CONSEQUENCES TEST
Generally, 20
Historical background, 31
Polemis case, 39 et seq.

DOUGHTY V. TURNER MANUFACTURING
Generally, 105 et seq.

DRUNK DRIVING
Serving liquor to minor, 144–145, 164

DUTY
Breach of duty, 5 et seq.
Duty–Risk Test, this index
Intervention, duty vs. proximate cause, 143 et seq.
Limitation of liability as function of duty element, 74 et seq.

DUTY–RISK TEST
Generally, 24 et seq.
Abnormally dangerous activity, 235
Accidental self-injury, 133
Aggravated negligence, intervention involving, 183
Broken locks, liability of building owner to rape victim, 198
Criminal interventions, 190 et seq.
Different risk scenario, 101

DUTY–RISK TEST—Cont'd
Flying pedestrian, impact with plaintiff-bystander, 115–116
Green (Leon) theory, 79 et seq.
Key-in-ignition cases, 174–175
Manner-of-occurrence scenario, 98–99
Modified version of test, proposed, 252 et seq.
Negligent delay in shipment of goods, 149 et seq.
Negligent interventions, 167 et seq.
Palsgraf, distinguished from, 80
Products liability, 243 et seq.
Rescue doctrine, 120, 122, 125
Risk-or-injury-to-another scenario, 139
Termination of responsibility for risk, 205–206
Unexpectedly serious harm scenario, 88–90

EGG SHELL SKULL
Pre–Existing Weakness, this index
Unexpectedly–Serious–Harm–Scenario, this index

EMERGENCIES
Rescue Doctrine, this index

EMOTIONAL DISTRESS
Bystanders, 108 et seq., 129
Intentional infliction, 217–218, 225–226
Liability for, 17, 106 et seq., 129 et seq.

EXTRAORDINARY EVENTS
Natural interventions, 154 et seq.

EXTRAORDINARY RESULTS
Not-so-highly-extraordinary result test, 64–66

FAIRNESS TEST
  Generally, 59–62
Chain reaction cases, 60
Compounded bad luck cases, 61
Questions of law and fact, 60 et seq.

FALSE IMPRISONMENT
Persons-at-risk scenario, 224

FINANCIAL HARM
Recovery for, 106 et seq., 129–130

FIREARMS
Loaded gun hypothetical, 108 et seq.

References are to pages.

FIREFIGHTER'S RULE
Generally, 128 et seq.

FIRES
Hindsight test, application to spreading fire cases, 53

FLAMMABLE LIQUID
Accidental ignition, 155
Criminal interventions and control over instrumentalities of harm, 192 et seq.

FORESEEABILITY
De facto foresight approach, 36
Duty–Risk Test, this index
Hindsight Test, this index
Interventions, this index
Manner-of-Occurrence Scenario, this index
Multiple Foreseeable Risks, this index
Palsgraf v. Long Island Railroad Co., 43 et seq., 70–71
Persons-at-Risk Scenario, this index
Policy factors, 23–24
Rescue Doctrine, this index
Risk–Foreseeability Test, this index
Smith v. London and South Western Railway, 36
Unexpectedly–Serious–Harm Scenario, this index
Wagon Mound case, 70–71

GOOD SAMARITANS
Rescue doctrine, 120, 123, 124

GOODS
Negligent delay in shipment of goods, 147 et seq.

GREEN, LEON
Damage to property of extraordinary worth, 92–93
Duty-risk test, 24 et seq.
Limitation of liability as function of duty element, 74 et seq.
Rescue doctrine, 120

GROSS NEGLIGENCE
Intervention involving, 182 et seq.

GUNS
Loaded gun hypothetical, 108 et seq.

HAND FORMULA
Risk-foreseeability test, 21–22, 70

HEALTH CARE PROVIDERS
Complications from negligent care, 199 et seq.
Negligent intervention cases, 168 et seq.

HIGHWAYS
Negligent obstruction, 171

HINDSIGHT TEST
Generally, 19–20
Accidental self-injury, 133–134
Arbitrary line, 63
Causes vs. conditions, 64
Criminal interventions, 192 et seq.
Different risk scenario, 101–102
Emotional harm, 107
Financial harm, 107
Fire cases, 53
Flying pedestrian, impact with plaintiff-bystander, 115–116
Innocent human interventions, 159 et seq.
Jury instructions, 20
Key-in-ignition cases, 177
Loaded gun hypothetical, 111
Manner-of-occurrence scenario, 96–98
Natural-and-continuous-sequence test, 51 et seq.
Negligent delay in shipment of goods, 151 et seq.
Not-so-highly-extraordinary-result test, 64–66
Palsgraf dissent, 50
Polemis case, 42
Products liability, 239, 242 et seq.
Questions of law and fact, 20
Smith v. London and South Western Railway, 37
Spreading fire cases, 53
Suicide cases, 136
Unexpectedly serious harm scenario, 90–91
Unknown kind of damage, 117–118
Variants, 50 et seq.

HUGHES V. LORD ADVOCATE
Generally, 104 et seq.

HUMAN INTERVENTIONS
Generally, 157 et seq.

IGNITION
Key in ignition cases, 173 et seq.

References are to pages.

INACTION
Intervention by inaction, 178

INSTRUCTIONS
Jury instructions, hindsight test, 20

INSTRUMENTALITIES OF HARM
Control over, criminal interventions, 192 et seq.

INSURANCE COVERAGE
Proximate cause, application of, 11–12

INTENTIONAL TORTS
    Generally, 212 et seq.
Aggravated harm scenario, 214–216
Assault, 224
Battery, 224
Conversion of personal property, 218–219
Different risks, 219 et seq.
Emotional distress, 217–218, 225–226
Extent-of-liability scenarios, 227–228
False imprisonment, 224
Interventions as intentionally wrongful misconduct, 185
Persons-at-risk scenario, 224–226
Proximate cause, application of, 10 et seq.
Rescuers, 226–227
Self-injury scenario, 216–219
Third party, intentionally tortious act of, 16
Transferred intent, 225
Trespass to land, 222–223

INTERVENTION
    Generally, 15–16, 140 et seq.
Abnormally dangerous activity, 235–237
Aggravated negligence, 182 et seq.
Animals, 147, 231–233
Comparative fault, effect of, 206 et seq.
Criminal interventions
    Control over instrumentalities of harm, 192 et seq.
    Plaintiffs, prior relationships with, 186 et seq.
    Remoteness, 190 et seq.
    Third persons, prior relationships with, 189 et seq.
    Without prior relationships, 196 et seq.
Duty vs. proximate cause, 143 et seq.
Extraordinary natural interventions, 154 et seq.
Human interventions, 157 et seq.
Inaction, intervention by, 178

INTERVENTION—Cont'd
Intentionally wrongful misconduct, 185 et seq.
Joint and several liability, reform of, 206 et seq.
Manner-of-occurrence scenario distinguished, 142–143
Negligent interventions
    Generally, 161 et seq.
  Aggravated negligence, 182 et seq.
  Deterrence, 162–164
  Duty-risk test, 167–168
  Gross negligence, 182 et seq.
  Key-in-ignition cases, 173 et seq.
  No specific duty to prevent, 165–166
  Risk-foreseeability test, 166–167
  Specific duty to prevent, 164–165
Non-human interventions, 146 et seq.
Plaintiff as intervenor, 179 et seq.
Products liability, 245 et seq.
Spillage scenario, 153–154
Termination of responsibility for risk
    Generally, 198 et seq.
  Duty-risk test, 205–206
  Risk-foreseeability test, 203–205

JOINT AND SEVERAL LIABILITY
Reform of, effect on intervention issues, 206 et seq.

JURY INSTRUCTIONS
Hindsight test, 20

JURY QUESTIONS
Questions of Law and Fact, this index

KEYS
Key-in-ignition cases, 174–175

KINSMAN TRANSIT CASE
  Generally, 71 et seq.
Analysis of holding, 73–74
Palsgraf, distinguished from, 73–74

LAST CLEAR CHANCE
Plaintiff as intervenor, 180–181

LIABILITY–LIMITING FUNCTION
  Generally, 4 et seq.
Corrective justice, 7 et seq.
Deterrence function, 7

LIABILITY–LIMITING FUNCTION—Cont'd
Historical background, 30 et seq.
Intentional tort cases, 7
Reasons for, 7 et seq.
Strict liability cases, 7

MANNER–OF–OCCURRENCE SCENARIO
Generally, 14, 93 et seq.
Corrective justice, 94
Different-risk scenario, distinguished from, 103 et seq.
Duty-risk test, 98–99
Hindsight test, 96–98
Intervention distinguished, 142–143
Risk-foreseeability test, 95–96

MINORS
Alcoholic Beverages, this index

MULTIPLE FORESEEABLE RISKS
Generally, 108 et seq.
Products liability, 241 et seq.

NATURAL AND CONTINUOUS SEQUENCE TEST
Generally, 51 et seq.

NATURAL EVENTS
Extraordinary natural interventions, 154 et seq.
Non-human interventions, 146–147
Spillage scenario, 146–147

NATURAL FORCES
Intervention by, 15–16

NEGLIGENCE
Delay in shipment of goods, 147 et seq.
Intervention, this index
Spillage scenario, 153–154

NOT–TOO–ATTENUATED TEST
Generally, 56

ORGAN DONATION
Future harm, susceptibility to, 124

PALSGRAF V. LONG ISLAND RAILROAD CO.
Generally, 43 et seq.
Dissenting opinion, 49
Duty-risk test, distinguished from, 80

INDEX

References are to pages.

PALSGRAF V. LONG ISLAND RAILROAD CO.—Cont'd
Kinsman Transit case, comparison with, 73–74
Majority opinion, 46 et seq.
Operative facts, 44
Polemis case, comparison with, 47
Questions of law and fact, 49
Wagon Mound case, comparison with, 69–70

PEDESTRIANS
Flying pedestrian, impact with plaintiff-bystander, 115–116

PERSONS–AT–RISK SCENARIO
Generally, 111 et seq.
Flying pedestrian, impact with plaintiff-bystander, 115–116
Intentional torts, 224–226
Transferred intent, 114
Unknown other person variant, 113 et seq.

POLEMIS CASE
Christianson case, comparison with, 55–56
Demise of, 66 et seq.
Direct consequences rule, 39 et seq.
Loaded gun hypothetical, distinguished from, 110–111
Negligent delay in shipment of goods, 151–152
Palsgraf case, comparison with, 47, 50

POWER LINES
Uninsulated guy wires, 156

PRE-EXISTING WEAKNESS
Generally, 13–14
Unexpectedly Serious Harm Scenario, this index

PRIMA FACIE CASE
Proximate cause as element of, 4

PRIOR RELATIONSHIP CASES
Generally, 186 et seq.

PRODUCTS LIABILITY
Generally, 237 et seq.
Duty-risk test, 243 et seq.
Hindsight test, 239, 242 et seq.
Interventions, 245 et seq.
Manufacturer's warnings, 145
Misuse, 249–250
Multiple risks, 241 et seq.
Negligence theory, use of, 239–240

PRODUCTS LIABILITY—Cont'd
Risk-foreseeability test, 239, 241 et seq.
Termination of responsibility for risk, 204

PROPERTY DAMAGE
Conversion of property, self-injury scenario, 218–219
Good Samaritan, saving valuable property, 123
Unexpectedly serious damage, 91–93

PROXIMATE CAUSE
Duty–Risk Test, this index
Foreseeability, this index
Hindsight Test, this index
Historical background, 29 et seq.
Intervention, this index
Liability–Limiting Function, this index
Risk–Foreseeability Test, this index
Terminology, 3 et seq.
Third Parties, this index

QUESTIONS OF LAW AND FACT
Arbitrary line, 63
Duty-risk test, 24 et seq.
Fairness test, 60 et seq.
Hindsight test, 20
Palsgraf case, 49

RACKETEERING (RICO)
Proximate cause, application of, 12

RECKLESS CONDUCT
Intervention involving, 182 et seq.

REMOTENESS
Generally, 57–59
Criminal interventions and relationships with third persons, 190 et seq.
Innocent human interventions, 160
Key-in-ignition cases, 177
Time or space, 20

RESCUE DOCTRINE
Generally, 118 et seq.
Cardozo view, 119
Duty-risk test, 120, 122, 125
Firefighter's rule, 128 et seq.
Intentional torts, 226–227

INDEX

References are to pages.

RESCUE DOCTRINE—Cont'd
Risk-foreseeability test, 119, 122, 127

RESTATEMENT OF PRODUCTS LIABILITY
Balancing approach, 239

RESTATEMENT OF TORTS
Abnormally dangerous activity, 236
Animal interventions, 232
Hindsight test, 64–66
Intentional infliction of emotional distress, 226
Preliminary draft of new Restatement, 258 et seq.
Risk standard, 22–23
Self-injury scenario, 218

RICO (RACKETEERING) ACT
Proximate cause, application of, 12

RISK
Different–Risk Scenario, this index
Duty–Risk Test, this index
Persons-at-Risk Scenario, this index
Restatement of Torts, risk standard, 22–23
Risk–Foreseeability Test, this index
Risk-or-injury-to-another scenario, 15, 137 et seq.
Termination-of-responsibility-for-risk scenario, 16–17

RISK–FORESEEABILITY TEST
Generally, 21 et seq., 70
Abnormally dangerous activity, 234–235
Accidental self-injury, 131–133
Aggravated negligence, intervention involving, 183
Criminal interventions and relationships with third persons, 190 et seq.
Different-risk scenario, 99–101, 104 et seq.
Emotional harm, 107
Financial harm, 107
Flying pedestrian, impact with plaintiff-bystander, 115
Innocent human interventions, 161
Loaded gun hypothetical, 108 et seq.
Manner of occurrence scenario, 95–96
Multiple foreseeable risk variation, 108 et seq.
Negligent delay in shipment of goods, 148
Negligent interventions, 166–167
Products liability, 239, 241 et seq.
Rescue doctrine, 119, 122, 127
Risk-or-injury-to-another scenario, 138

RISK–FORESEEABILITY TEST—Cont'd
Suicide cases, 136–137
Termination of responsibility for risk, 190 et seq.
Unexpectedly-serious-harm scenario, 87–88
Uninsulated guy wires, 156
Unknown kind of damage, 117

SELF–INJURY
Accidental Self–Injury, this index
Intentional torts and self-injury scenario, 216–219
Suicide, this index

SHIPMENT OF GOODS
Negligent delay, 147 et seq.

SMITH V. LONDON AND SOUTH WESTERN RAILWAY
Analysis of holding, 33 et seq.
De facto foresight approach, 36
Hindsight test, 37

SOCIAL HOSTS
Serving intoxicating beverages to minors, 164

SPILLAGE
Intervening natural events, 153–154

STRICT LIABILITY
Animal owners, 233
Defective products, 237 et seq.
Proximate cause and strict liability, 10 et seq., 228–229

SUBSEQUENT INJURIES
Self-injury, 134–135

SUBSTANTIAL FACTOR TEST
Generally, 56

SUICIDE
    Generally, 135 et seq.
Hindsight test, 136
Intentional torts and self-injury scenario, 216–219
Restatement position, 218
Risk-foreseeability test, 136–137

TAVERN OWNER
Serving liquor to minor, 144–145

TERMINATION OF RESPONSIBILITY
Intervention, this index

TERMINOLOGY
Generally, 3 et seq.

THIRD PARTIES
Criminal act of, 16
Criminal interventions and prior relationships with third persons, 189 et seq.
Innocent act of, 16
Intentionally tortious act of, 16
Intervention, this index
Negligent act of, 16
Rescue Doctrine, this index
Risk or injury to another scenario, 137 et seq.

TRANSFERRED INTENT
Intentional torts, 225
Unknown other persons, 114

TRESPASS TO LAND
Different risk scenario, 222–223

UNBROKEN SEQUENCES
Natural and continuous sequence test, 51 et seq.

UNEXPECTEDLY–SERIOUS–HARM SCENARIO
Generally, 82 et seq.
Corrective justice perspective, 85
Damages law, recovery based on, 85 et seq.
Duty-risk test, 88–90
Full recovery, arguments for and against, 83 et seq.
Hindsight test, 90–91
Intentional torts
    Aggravated harm scenario, 214–216
    Different risks, 220
Property damage, unexpectedly serious, 91–93
Risk-foreseeability test, 87–88

UNITED STATES V. CARROLL TOWING CO.
Risk-foreseeability test, 21–22

UNKNOWN KIND OF DAMAGE
Generally, 116–118
Hindsight test, 117–118
Risk-foreseeability test, 117

UNKNOWN PLAINTIFFS
Flying pedestrian, impact with plaintiff-bystander, 115–116
Mirror image cases, 128 et seq.

UNKNOWN PLAINTIFFS—Cont'd
Rescue Doctrine, this index
Transferred intent, 114
Unforeseeably present plaintiffs, 111 et seq.
Unknown other person variant, 113 et seq.

WAGON MOUND CASE
Generally, 66 et seq.
Factual background, 66 et seq.
Holding, analysis of, 68 et seq.
Palsgraf, distinguished from, 69–70

WILFUL OR WANTON CONDUCT
Intervention involving, 182 et seq.

†